KETO
FOR LIFE

KETO FOR LIFE

RESET YOUR BIOLOGICAL CLOCK IN **21 DAYS** AND OPTIMIZE YOUR DIET FOR LONGEVITY

MARK SISSON

WITH **BRAD KEARNS**

Hardie Grant

BOOKS

This edition published in 2020 by Hardie Grant Books,
an imprint of Hardie Grant Publishing
First published in the United States in 2019 by Harmony Books,
an imprint of Random House,
a division of Penguin Random House LLC, New York

Hardie Grant Books (Melbourne)
Building 1, 658 Church Street
Richmond, Victoria 3121

Hardie Grant Books (London)
5th & 6th Floors
52–54 Southwark Street
London SE1 1UN

hardiegrantbooks.com

Keto for Life
ISBN 978 1 74379 610 8

10 9 8 7 6 5 4 3 2 1

Book design by Jennifer K. Beal Davis
Jacket design by Jessie Bright
Jacket photograph by Jennifer May

Printed in Italy by Elcograf S.p.A.

To Carrie and Mia, Jack and Maria, Kyle and Devyn, Walter in heaven

To devoted health enthusiasts who have the courage to support the primal/paleo/keto/ancestral health movement, who think critically in the face of flawed conventional wisdom, who take personal responsibility for their health, and who spread the word and walk their talk

CONTENTS

INTRODUCTION

Time flies. Here I am today at age 65, talking about longevity—a concept I hardly ever considered during the first four decades of my life. Ironically, in my youthful oblivion, I engaged in an assortment of lifestyle choices that directly opposed longevity and compromised my day-to-day health. My obsession with qualifying for the United States Olympic Trials in the marathon meant running over one hundred miles a week throughout my twenties. I bailed on my medical school fast track and moved from New England to California to paint houses, open a frozen yogurt shop, shovel mass quantities of nutrient-deficient refined carbohydrates down my throat every single day, and run myself into the ground.

When I did ponder my own mortality for fleeting moments, I smiled smugly with the belief that my grueling training regimen was making me invincible to the epidemic disease patterns of modern life that appeared to be caused by gluttony and sloth. This hubris was ridiculously off base, of course. Fortunately, I found out sooner rather than later. I was fit enough to place fifth in the national marathon championships and qualify for the Olympic Trials, and later place fourth in the Hawaii Ironman world triathlon championships, but these accomplishments came at an extreme cost to my health. I was the fittest guy any of my friends knew, adorning magazine covers with my lean, mean physique, but inside I was a disaster.

My crazy workouts, and the nutrient-deficient, high-carb, high-insulin-producing diet that fueled them, resulted in system-wide inflammation, oxidative damage (aka free radical damage), glycation (excess glucose binding with important structural proteins and causing dysfunction throughout the body), hormonal dysfunction, musculoskeletal breakdown, and immune suppression. I caught at least six upper respiratory tract infections each year. I battled chronic fatigue, osteoarthritis in both feet, severe tendonitis in both hips, chronic gastritis, and irritable bowel syndrome. My pipes were so fragile that I was compelled to design running routes around opportune restroom locations. Seriously.

During my glory days on the endurance circuit, the cellular, immune, and metabolic stress I inflicted upon myself every day accelerated the aging process in cells throughout my body. My overstress patterns and inflammatory genetic signaling were similar to the abuse generated by a hard-partying rock star—life in the fast lane of accelerated aging. While I would have scoffed at such a comparison at the time (alas, we both wore lots of Lycra . . .), recent advancements in longevity medicine can validate that my fifteen-year competitive endurance career aged me biologically by twenty or thirty years.

BURNING THE CANDLE AT BOTH ENDS

This commentary is not mere whining from a has-been. Today, we can measure the length of our *telomeres* to obtain a decent estimate of our rate of aging and prospects for longevity. Telomeres are little caps that protect the ends of chromosomes when they divide—like the plastic protector on the end of a shoelace. As your cells divide over your lifetime—at either a healthy rate, or an accelerated rate, based on your lifestyle behaviors—telomeres get worn down like a burning candle. When telomeres become too worn, a cell cannot divide anymore and it dies. Eventually, we succumb to a finite number of cell divisions; this is the essence of the aging process in the body. Hence, your telomere length can predict longevity much like the growth plates on a teenager's X-ray can confirm that he's still growing.

Adverse lifestyle practices can shorten telomeres such that you actualize the metaphor of burning the candle at both ends. Slamming junk food and blasting artificial light after dark will burn down the wicks on your cellular candles—your telomeres—more quickly. On the flip side, new research reveals that healthy lifestyle behaviors, including not just ketogenic eating, fasting, exercise, and sleep, but also activities like meditation, gratitude practices, and a thriving social life, can actually lengthen your telomeres so that your biological age will compare favorably to your chronological age.

While my youthful indiscretions accelerated my aging, I'm convinced that I have repaired much of this damage over the past two decades. Most prominently, I ditched grains and sugars in favor of nutrient-dense primal foods starting in 2002. This, along with abandoning my crazy training schedule some fifteen years prior to my primal dietary transformation, took me from inflamed, immune-suppressed, and hormonally dysregulated, to healthy and vibrant.

In recent years, I've escalated my efforts to promote longevity through the ketogenic eating strategy outlined in *The Keto Reset Diet* (with numerous updates and refinements in this book), in combination with some cutting-edge fitness and movement strategies, and increased attention to the psycho-emotional elements of longevity. I've been on a quest for health since I was a teenager (that's over fifty years now!), and I must admit that the breakthroughs in the past few years have been astounding. Just when you think you know everything you need to know and are doing all that you can do to maximize energy and delay aging, new strategies emerge that can take you even deeper. I'm excited to package everything here into a comprehensive strategy for living long and well. Whether you are new to my message, or have a long devotion to primal-style living, the information and strategies presented here are going to knock your socks off! We are going where no previous book has gone before to pull in the best tips, tricks, and techniques from every corner of healthy, fit living and longevity research, including:

- Sophisticated ketogenic strategies to avail the highest intended benefits of keto eating without the increasingly common mistakes and backslides, reducing inflammation and repairing damage in your body.
- Miniature high-intensity exercise bouts that boost antiaging hormones and turbo-charge fat burning without making you sore and tired like a typical HIIT session.
- Disciplining your use of technology to minimize stress and maximize productivity.
- Cultivating an attitude of gratitude to prevent the (now medically validated) epidemic disease condition called FOMO (fear of missing out).
- Engaging in fasting and Time Restricted Feeding the right way, to boost hormone and immune function without stress hormone spikes.
- Nurturing loving interpersonal relationships by overcoming destructive subconscious programming and opening your heart at all times.

These bullet points represent the cutting edge of longevity potential much more than do the many overhyped biohacks, high-tech gadgetry, and sci-fi interventions du jour. By getting out of your own way and refocusing on the most basic of health practices (*Move! Sleep! Eat real food!*), you can dramatically elevate your current quality of life and set yourself up to remain healthy for the rest of your life. The *Keto for Life* program will expand your scope beyond nailing the mechanics of eating cleanly and cranking out killer workouts. Resetting your biological clock will also require other life-style adjustments to help you achieve mental flexibility to control stress and halt the signs of aging. You will learn to respect the importance of having a smile on your face while you dutifully knock off your goals and objectives, and balancing all your healthy living rituals and accomplishments with sufficient rest and recovery.

I'll be the first to admit that I'm still a work in progress when it comes to chilling out, gracefully managing the day-to-day pressures, risks, and dramas of the crazy high-stress entrepreneurial journey that I've been on for decades, and slowing down to appreciate life's simple pleasures. In fact, when I was first presented with the opportunity to write this book, I nearly turned it down. At the time, I was dusting myself off from what was easily the most stressful year I've ever had in my life. My attempt to manage an extremely fast-growing and diverse business enterprise (great news!) simply wore me out (not great news). Granted, I was still on autopilot, easily nailing the mechanics of healthy eating, exercise, sleeping, and living, but I was often lacking the peace of mind and fresh perspective that the healthy food, killer workouts, and lavish vacations were supposed to provide.

In the summer of 2017, I collapsed while vacationing with extended family in Greece and required medical attention. I was fine after some oxygen and a big dose of orange juice. I attributed the incident to jet travel combined with overly ambitious fasting (fasting is actually how I beat jet lag. It works . . . unless you overdo it!). In the fall of 2017, a routine prostate screening went awry and I contracted a serious infection that hospitalized me for several days. In the summer of 2018, my annual dermatological checkup turned into a nightmare. I had to endure a painful process of burning the top layer of skin off my entire face (as seen on my Instagram post . . . NOT!), and having atypical skin cells surgically removed off both of my legs. As you might imagine, being of fair-haired, fair-skinned Scandinavian descent and spending much of adult life in Malibu, California, often outdoors, is a recipe for skin problems after around six decades of living. So I moved to Miami in 2018 (what was I thinking?). These skin procedures were annoying and painful, but perhaps the worst of it was not being able to go out in the sun, or work up a sweat exercising, for several weeks.

Medical experts assured me that stuff like the aforementioned happens routinely and randomly to healthy people, but these answers were unsatisfying. My wife, Carrie, has a master's degree in spiritual psychology and works extensively in the field with university students and in retreat settings. Her teachings promote the maxim that your thoughts are the source of all your pain. If you had a rough childhood, a string of dead-end jobs or relationships, or assorted other misfortunes that are eating at you right now, it's not what happened to you that's causing you to suffer, it's *what you think about what happened to you*. Hence, you have the power to immediately change your thinking and free yourself from pain.

I mention this here because I believe that despite my healthy body and healthy lifestyle practices, my sorry string of setbacks might be reflective of unhealthy thoughts, namely too much stressing about the business matters of the day. While I've succeeded in building a healthy and diverse primal enterprise, I've also made some atrocious investments costing me a fortune, been *this close* to bankruptcy on more than one occasion in my younger years, and been taken to the cleaners many times in unbalanced and manipulative business dealings. My personal life has also not been without struggles, summit meetings, compromises, and less-than-simple recalibrations.

But I'm still smiling. And it's not a manufactured smile: That's a great way to make whatever stresses you face in life even more stressful, by the way. No, this smile is a result of hard work in every area of my life—every pillar in the book—every single day. Heaven forbid had I encountered the aforementioned stressful events without my excellent diet, exercise, and sleep habits! And when faced with

the task of writing dozens upon dozens of checks to unwind a multimillion-dollar loss on a failed restaurant venture in 2017–18, at a certain point all I could do was laugh. One, because I realized it was just money, and money is a renewable resource. Two, because the same attributes that got me into that mess—hubris, grand ambitions, and unflinching optimism gone wild—facilitated the home run of selling my fledgling Primal Kitchen product line to the Kraft Heinz Company in late 2018.

I'm here to help you implement the disparate skills that will help you live a long and happy life. It's definitely going to require some hard work. I'm talking not only about dietary restrictions and keeping workout commitments but also engaging in deep examination of your self-destructive habits, self-limiting beliefs, and dysfunctional relationships. But it's going to be fun every step of the way, because immediate positive feedback begets more success, more compliance, and more enjoyment of the "work" of leading a healthy, happy, balanced life. Granted, it may be difficult if not impossible to transform your basic nature away from a Type A to a Type B, for example, or completely extinguish proclivities like a sweet tooth or late-night Netflix binges. However, I am here to help you get as close as possible to your ultimate potential within the limitations of your genetic attributes and core daily responsibilities in a hectic modern life.

THE FOUR PILLARS OF *KETO FOR LIFE*

Today, with my Social Security paperwork filed, I am healthier, and in many ways fitter, than I was when I was a narrowly adapted creature suited for running or pedaling long and hard, and not much else. Come to think of it, the same "narrowly adapted" characterization might apply to when I became successful in business, but not very successful at regulating my attendant levels of stress and anxiety. This is one of the reasons that the scope of this book extends beyond superfoods, super workouts, wonder supplements, and bio-hacking strategies to embrace a comprehensive mind, body, and lifestyle approach to longevity. While overhauling your lifelong high-carbohydrate eating patterns can be a challenge, working on the intangible elements of longevity can be just as daunting, maybe more so.

Keto for Life will help unlock your peak performance potential and maintain it throughout your entire life—not only in the high-impact categories of shedding body fat, improving physical fitness, or minimizing disease risk factors in blood tests, but also in the more refined aspects of healthy living, like nurturing interpersonal relationships or balancing stress and rest. Ultimately, my goal is to help you enjoy an extended *healthspan*: not just making it to 90- or 100-plus, but feeling vibrant, energetic, happy, productive, and fulfilled until the end.

As you might imagine, the ketogenic diet is a centerpiece of this approach, but this book branches out into four distinct categories that I call the Four Pillars of *Keto for Life*. You'll understand the scientific rationale and benefits of honoring each of these pillars, and also receive practical, step-by-step guidance to nail the objectives in each pillar. Finally, you'll put everything together during the intensive 21-Day Biological Clock Reset, building momentum and clarity for a lifetime of healthy habits and happiness. Here is where we are headed:

Pillar #1—Metabolic Flexibility: Time to escape carbohydrate dependency and become a fat-burning beast! You'll start by ditching toxic modern foods and progress comfortably through the multistage process detailed in *The Keto Reset Diet* to the highest level of metabolic flexibility through ketogenic eating. Then, you'll discover and adopt some advanced strategies based on the latest anti-aging research that will help to promote longevity and make a huge improvement in your rate of aging. I'll also help you create targeted goals for fat reduction and peak performance that you can sustain for a lifetime. Metabolic flexibility doesn't have to mean rigid adherence to ketogenic macronutrient guidelines forever. Rather, I convey a concept of living in the *keto zone*, where you become adept at burning a variety of fuel sources based on your specific goals, eating preferences, genetic attributes, and ongoing experimentation and refining.

Pillar #2—Movement and Physical Fitness: Surprisingly, the priority here is not crazy sweating in the gym, but rather to make a concerted effort to increase all forms of general everyday movement. Our genes are hardwired to move around all day long. This keeps us physically energized (thanks to turbo-charged fat burning) and cognitively sharp. Fitness and health start with movement. Emerging science is showing that even a devoted workout regimen cannot save you from the destructive health consequences of too much stillness. Once you get into a good groove with daily movement patterns, you can boost your longevity quotient with a strategic blend of low-level cardio workouts and regular brief, intense strength and sprint efforts—in much less time and with less stress than you might think!

Pillar #3—Mental Flexibility: Under this broad definition falls an assortment of powerful mindset and behavior practices that promote resiliency for life in the same manner that metabolic flexibility makes you resilient enough to skip meals and maintain energy and focus. Strategies to develop mental flexibility include reframing self-limiting beliefs, "pivoting" (going with the flow when facing life change), being mindful and appreciative of the present instead of ruminating about the past or the future, having a formal practice for meditation and/or gratitude, nurturing healthy reciprocative social connections (being vigilant to prevent digital connections from crowding out real ones), and pursuing your passions and highest purpose to make a positive contribution to society throughout your life. Put those all together and I call it living awesome!

Pillar #4—Rest and Recovery: Optimizing your sleep practices will be the prominent focus here, but we must also consider a broad-based approach to chilling out amidst the hectic pace and constant stimulation of modern life. Rest and recovery strategies for longevity include disciplining your use of technology, taking frequent breaks from peak cognitive function to refresh depleted brain neurons, and conducting specially designed workouts that promote relaxation and rejuvenation.

21-DAY BIOLOGICAL CLOCK RESET

This is where the book transforms from a pleasant read into a blueprint for action! Each day will contain one challenge item from each pillar, for a total of four daily assignments. While brief in duration, the Reset is a very intense journey where I will ask you for a sincere commitment of time, energy, and focus. In return for your significant effort and commitment, you will experience the payoff of life transformation. You will extinguish some lingering bad habits and implement some empowering new habits—hopefully lasting forever in both cases. We must all acknowledge that modern life has made us soft, lazy, and undisciplined in many ways. If you disagree with me, see if you can fast for 72 hours on demand, put your phone in a drawer for 24 hours starting on a Sunday morning, or plunge into near-freezing water for a few minutes every morning for a year. Even the fittest and most disciplined among us deserve fresh challenges, escalating goals, healthy competition with peers, and a system-wide reboot now and then.

The 21-Day Biological Clock Reset is going to rock your world and deliver noticeable results. You will feel awesome in mind, body, and spirit after completing this engrossing challenge, proving that you are capable of prioritizing your health and increasing your healthspan. You'll eat nourishing foods instead of basing your diet on nutrient-deficient processed carbs and oils, move throughout the day instead of sitting for most of your waking hours, sleep instead of consuming more digital entertainment, and escape the addictive lure of overexercising and treat your body with care like the human athlete that you are. If you want some supporting scientific data about the effectiveness of your Reset, consider some before and after telomere testing at TeloYears.com. Results from nearly five thousand nurses in the high-profile Nurses' Health Study associated adherence to a Mediterranean-style diet (representative of a huge improvement from the Standard American Diet) with longer telomeres. Health leader Ben Greenfield has blogged extensively about increasing his telomere length through focused diet and fitness practices.

Completing the 21-Day Reset will help you implement your favorite, most effective strategies and practices into a long-term daily longevity routine that feels natural, comfortable, and easy to maintain. This will help you reset your biological clock and repair damage that has been accelerating the aging process in your body for years. For example, it's widely recognized that you can correct four of the five markers for metabolic syndrome—blood pressure, triglycerides, HDL, and fasting glucose—in as little as 21 days of dietary modification. You can make huge progress on important fitness longevity markers, such as the mile run, max-effort pushups, grip strength, and squat competency with a few weeks of challenging, but sensible, workouts. Emerging sleep science confirms that turning off your screen and implementing calming, wind-down rituals before bed can boost growth hormone levels, enhance cellular repair, and even help correct dysfunctional fat metabolism—by tomorrow morning! As you'll learn in our detailed discussion of how the perception switches on your cell membranes influence genetic function immediately, just *thinking* about getting healthier and more disciplined with your daily routine can trigger a boost in mood, cognitive function, and immune function that you can leverage into action.

It's time to start getting excited about the very real possibility of becoming a new person in 21 days, and then make it happen! The 21-Day Biological Clock Reset should be performed on an annual basis to reboot your system, flush out damaged cellular material, reprogram self-limiting beliefs into empowering beliefs, and reclaim certain healthy habits that have slipped a bit as a consequence of hectic modern life. I'm continually amazed at how many times I think I have everything dialed in and optimized, and then an annual 21-Day Reset will uncover new practices that bring me to the next level.

Besides, we all need freshness and inspiration to stay the course of healthy living and continually challenge ourselves. For example, I recently connected with retired Olympic runner Ryan Hall, still the American marathon and half marathon record holder. After hanging up his singlet in 2016, Ryan has unleashed his competitive intensity in the weight room. He's packed on 50 pounds of muscle in a few years and can deadlift, squat, and bench a combined weight in excess of 1,000 pounds. The 1,000-pound club is an esteemed milestone among the muscle community, and absolutely extraordinary for a former 130-pound elf who could run like the wind all day. Previously, I always thought of myself as the strongest ex-marathoner out there! I used to race at 140 pounds dripping wet but have added 25 pounds of muscle and hundreds of pounds to my strength standards over the years. Now I have to up my game another notch, and continue to do so no matter how many birthdays have passed. So, Ryan, tighten your lifting belt—I'm coming after you, man!

AN EVOLVED PERSPECTIVE ON LONGEVITY

An explosion of scientific discovery in recent years has given us powerful tools to understand and combat the sad, steady demise in physical and cognitive function (and enjoyment of life!) that we have erroneously come to believe represents the aging process. Compelling scientific evidence is accumulating each day to confirm that the conventional understanding of the aging process is an absolute farce. The aging process should really be defined as: *the accelerated decline in function and healthspan caused by adverse lifestyle practices that conflict with our genetic expectations for health.*

Dr. Art De Vany calls aging "an illusion," and this is validated by a scientific concept known as the DNA damage theory of aging. De Vany, author of *The New Evolution Diet*, is one of the forefathers of the ancestral health movement. He has been a great inspiration to me on my journey, for he was blogging thoughtfully about some of the foundational elements of the primal/paleo/keto diet many years before they achieved wide acceptance. De Vany also walks his talk, maintaining exceptional physical fitness into his eighties with a truly primal exercise regimen featuring brief, ultra-explosive workouts followed by hours of fasting to achieve what he calls "cellular renewal." De Vany elaborates on the illusion of aging: "The only genes that have been discovered to have any bearing on aging are regenerative or defensive pathways. The aging process is a loss of cell function, a loss of cell integrity, a loss of the ability of stem cells to renew tissues. Aging, basically, is damage." Furthering the thought, De Vany asserts that, "there is no such thing as 'healthy aging' because damaged cells are not healthy."

While DNA damage occurs as a consequence of living life (e.g., sore muscles after a workout, or getting a sunburn at the beach), it is the *unrepaired accumulation of routine cellular damage* that we inaccurately perceive to be normal and inevitable consequences of chronology: wrinkled skin, loss of bone density, declining neuron firing efficiency in the brain, proliferation of cancerous cells, and so forth. You now have permission to recategorize these and other markers as "damage" instead of "aging." Of course, the reason we don't routinely live to 150 is that even with clean living and efficient cellular repair processes happening, some DNA damage inevitably lingers and accumulates. This is particularly apparent in the most prominent areas of disease or obvious decline as we get up in years: the eyes, brain, cardiovascular system, and skin—some of the longest lasting (and hence most vulnerable) cells in the body.

In progressive health circles, chronic inflammation—a prolonged and unhealthy activation of your body's inflammatory fight-or-flight response due to the stressors of modern life—is often characterized as the root of all evil. In contrast, genes are hardwired to respond to brief fight-or-flight stressors with an acute inflammatory response. When you hoist a heavy weight or take off sprinting, a powerful cocktail of stress hormones floods your bloodstream—cortisol, epinephrine, norepinephrine, dopamine, and serotonin. You feel alert, alive, and energized, with your brain, muscles, and organs performing far beyond baseline. Same goes for a cold-water plunge. Then, when you complete your sprint workout or exit the cold tub or sauna, your body works hard to return hormone levels, body temperature, and overall energy systems back to homeostasis. Consequently, you adapt and become more resilient against not only the specific stressor you endured but all manner of future stressors. It's the same fight-or-flight response whether you're in a sprint or a traffic jam. These appropriate fight-or-flight stressors that promote an adaptive response are called *hormetic* stressors. In contrast, the many forms of chronic stressors in modern life abuse and eventually exhaust delicate fight-or-flight hormonal mechanisms. When your fight-or-flight mechanisms get cooked, you end up with suppressed immune function and chronic pain and inflammation, and arrive at the familiar modern destination of burnout.

Generally, the distinction between healthy fight-or-flight inflammation and destructive chronic inflammation is the duration and/or frequency of the stressor. When you engage in a pattern of prolonged moderate-to-difficult workouts with insufficient recovery time between them, you promote breakdown, burnout, illness, and injury. Similarly, when you overconsume nutrient-deficient foods like gluten and sugar, you inflict chronic stress upon your body, because we are not well adapted to consuming processed foods. In particular, heavy gluten consumption can damage the delicate microvilli that line your intestinal wall. These are hair-like extensions on intestinal cell membranes that help with absorption, secretion, and other cellular functions. When microvilli become compromised by chronic inflammation, the resultant "leaky gut" condition allows undigested foreign particles to infiltrate the bloodstream (i.e., instead of just food and vitamins).

When shit enters your bloodstream (sorry, but the statement is literally true), your body's defense systems perceive these foreign protein molecules to be a virus. As a consequence, an autoimmune response—the body attacking itself—occurs. Over time, leaky gut and autoimmune disturbances can manifest in conditions like arthritis, allergies, asthma, colitis, joint pain, and even cognitive conditions like ADHD, depression, and anxiety. Your body is chronically stressed because your inflamed intestinal cells are not processing energy efficiently. In fact, because these foreign protein molecules are similar to healthy proteins, your immune, endocrine, and digestive systems integrate them into routine cellular functions, a process known as molecular mimicry.

When you eliminate gluten—a prominent instigator of chronic inflammation—conditions often vanish quickly. Similarly, when exercise stress is minimized by slowing down the pace of your typical cardio workout into the fat-burning zone (so fight-or-flight stimulation is minimal), or shortening your high-intensity strength sessions (so the fight-or-flight hormone spike dissipates quickly), you can boost both your fitness and your general health, instead of falling apart from chronic stress.

Unfortunately, the modern human existence features both too many chronic stressors (bad foods, overly stressful exercise patterns, insufficient sleep, etc.) and not enough optimally brief fight-or-flight experiences. Instead, we indulge in ridiculous conveniences and luxuries, epidemic inactivity, little or no high-intensity exercise (many devoted fitness enthusiasts are content to watch CNN on the elliptical machine every time), and exist in temperature-controlled environments day and night. Our overly comfortable modern life causes atrophy to an assortment of critical fight-or-flight survival mechanisms. We go soft, become less resilient to all forms of stress, sustain more cellular damage from routine daily living, and trash our longevity prospects accordingly.

While we are all compromised by the many unhealthy elements of modern life that inflict damage upon our cells, we can do our best to mitigate modern hazards by engaging in behaviors that promote optimal gene expression. Instead of the accelerated decline that has become the norm, you can instead expect and demand a nice long run of peak function, and gracefully accept the inevitable gradual slowdowns caused by chronology. This book is not about cheating the laws of nature with biohacking lotions, potions, drugs, supplements, and contraptions. As you might imagine, most of this fountain of youth stuff is a waste of energy and money. This program is about repairing your cells at the DNA level, allowing you to realize the dream of feeling younger and more vibrant even as you add chronological years.

This evolved perspective about living a long, purposeful life is captured beautifully by Dr. Deepak Chopra and his *Four Daily Intentions*. Chopra, a longevity expert and mega-bestselling author, reminds himself of these guiding principles each morning in conjunction with a lengthy meditation session:

- *Joyful, energetic body:* No toxic substances allowed in! Ditto for being around toxic people.
- *Loving, compassionate heart:* Give others attention and acceptance as they are; that's what everyone is looking for deep down.
- *Reflective, quiet, alert mind:* This entails being chill and intuitive more than manufacturing eternal peppiness and positivity.
- *Lightness of being:* Stay focused on the present, free from both regrets about the past and worries about the future.

The Four Daily Intentions have little to do with obsessively tracking your macros or pricking your fingers to generate glucose and ketone values. However, when you are able to live by ideals like these, you are very likely going to avoid today's main health disconnects by default. For example, you'll likely have a healthy relationship with food, enjoying celebratory, nutritious meals as one of the great pleasures of life. You'll likely lead active, energetic days, balancing peak cognitive function with sufficient movement, exercise, exposure to nature, and time for quiet reflection. Your lightness of being may steer you clear of toxic relationships and exhausting exercise patterns that seem to be an outlet for the frustrations that accumulate when we live and think in rat-race mode. It also wouldn't hurt to meditate for 2 hours every morning like Chopra!

Granted, you are going to have to nail your baseline diet, exercise, sleep, and stress-management objectives if you want to aspire to loftier goals of enlightenment. Iconic entrepreneur and adventurer Sir Richard Branson calls maintaining this healthy baseline "looking after yourself," and references it as a mandatory gateway to living a life of both high productivity and happiness. When you take decisive action each day to advocate for not just instant gratification but also for longevity-promoting behaviors, you can embrace an evolved perspective about longevity whereby you have not one but three relevant ages for health and longevity: *chronological, biological,* and *psychological,* detailed as follows:

CHRONOLOGICAL AGE

This is how many birthdays you've had—pretty simple! We can't get too cocky and pretend chronological age is irrelevant. Many who are fond of the quip, "Age is just a number," might want to pay more attention to their numbers—their blood markers, results of their fitness assessments, macronutrient intake ratios—you get the point! After all, in athletics, the most honest and revealing of peak performance arenas, the effects of chronological aging are quite apparent. No matter how hard you try to stave off decline, explosiveness starts falling off at age 35 at around 1 percent per year. Peak endurance competency can be sustained all the way up to around age 40 before a similar gradual decline commences. Guys like Hawaii Ironman legend Mark Allen demonstrated this when he retired on top at age 38 after his sixth Hawaii victory, in 1995, in the fastest time of his career.

And while guys and gals in their 40s, 50s, and 60s can perform incredible feats to fill the record books of U.S. Masters age–group swimming, track and field, triathlon, or the CrossFit Games, there is universal acknowledgment among the fittest of elder athletes that recovery time is significantly slower than in their younger years. Alas, the incremental declines in peak performance associated with chronological aging can become virtually irrelevant when placed against a larger backdrop of optimizing your biological and psychological ages. Witness the late fitness legend Jack LaLanne, who had a standing offer of $10,000 to anyone who could hang for the duration of his personal daily workout. It was never claimed, lasting until 1970, when he was 56 years old.

BIOLOGICAL AGE

This represents your current physiological functioning and physical performance capabilities in relation to norms for your chronological age. As you might imagine, biological age is vastly more important to your longevity, and quality of life, than your chronological age. You can compare your sex hormone levels, body fat percentage, blood pressure, hearing acuity, bone density, the level of calcification in your arteries (aka, coronary calcium score), and your time in the 1-mile run against age-specific averages from millions of patients. Accordingly, you can generate an excellent estimate of your current biological age, obviously coming in either younger, the same, or older than your chronological age. For example, one of LaLanne's notorious birthday feats, performed at age 45, was doing 1,000 pushups and 1,000 chinups in 1 hour 22 minutes. This is a world record performance, period. Hence, you could conclude that LaLanne's biological age was that of a male half of LaLanne's age at the typical male human biological peak.

Granted, 45-year-old collagen and elastin carving lines in LaLanne's sunbaked skin might not have compared favorably to a college kid's, but it's important to broaden our perspective about aging from the flawed idea of programmed decline caused by chronology to something that we have tremendous control over when we promote cellular renewal and mitigate cellular damage. When we see Olympic swimming legend Dara Torres and her glistening six-pack win three Olympic silver medals at age 41 at the 2008 Beijing games, it's easy to scoff and say she's a genetic freak. Better to marvel at the fact that Torres was swimming faster times at 41 than in her "peak" years when she was bagging medals at four previous Olympic Games. Magnificent athletic feats offer a dramatic example of biological age superseding chronological age; but you can also quietly excel in longevity by optimizing sleep, eating a nutrient-dense diet (and ditching the toxic stuff), and establishing daily practices for meditation, movement, and gratitude.

Regarding the high-tech longevity supplement and drug regimens that are a big deal today, there are no pharmaceutical miracles yet invented to counteract unhealthy lifestyle habits. Granted, some interventions can offer benefits to those who are already highly devoted to health. On my blog, MarksDailyApple.com, I've written about the hormone replacement regimen I've followed in recent years, as well as my longtime involvement with formulating and selling nutritional and dietary supplements. I consider this stuff icing on the cake, and not even worth considering until you are doing virtually everything right with the healthy living basics. There are no SHORTcuts to LONGevity!

While the telomere tests and other sophisticated biofeedback attempt to give you a basic sense of how your biological age stacks up against your chronological age (as well as the Internet "aging score" questionnaires that are pretty worthless), the ultra low-tech 1-mile run turns out to be an extremely accurate marker of biological age and longevity potential. The 4-lap race of truth is favored by the Cooper Institute in Dallas, Texas—a prominent longevity authority since 1968, when Dr. Kenneth Cooper published his landmark book, *Aerobics*. Large studies from the Cooper Institute and the University of Texas Southwestern Medical

School reveal that your time in the mile run at age 50 correlates strongly with your probability of living to age 85, as well as your risk of heart disease as you age.

Dr. Jarett Berry, a cardiologist at University of Texas Southwestern Medical Center, in Dallas, says about their study data: "If you are fit in midlife, you double your chance of surviving to 85." In contrast, if you are unfit, as represented by an unsatisfactory mile time (among other routine revelations, like getting winded after climbing a flight of stairs), you will take 8 years off your projected lifespan. Data from 66,000 participants in the Cooper Institute and UT Southwestern studies reveal some mile-time standards for you to appreciate. Remember now, this is an all-out effort of 4 laps around a standard running track: Envision scientists in white coats wielding clipboards and stopwatches and cheering you on! Males who can break 8 minutes, and females who can break 9 minutes, are in the top category—extremely likely to make it to 85 and beyond. For the uninitiated, these times represent brisk jogging/moderate running—no walking. Males who can break 10 minutes, and females who can break 12 minutes, are considered to have "good" fitness and longevity prospects. Males worse than 12 minutes, and females slower than 13 minutes (meaning you cannot sustain a brisk walk for even a mile), are considered low-fitness, high-risk.

Dr. Berry elaborates, "Heart disease risk increases markedly for every minute longer it takes you to run a mile." That said, if you are able to complete a 12- or 13-minute mile, that's not too bad; it indicates a semblance of physical fitness to try to improve upon. If you're vastly inferior to that standard, big trouble awaits. Dr. Mehmet Oz, everyone's favorite TV health expert, relates that if you cannot walk a quarter-mile in 6 minutes (that's twice as slow as the Cooper "low fitness" benchmark, and only for a quarter of the distance), your chances of dying in 5 years is *three hundred times greater* than if you are able to walk the distance in 5 minutes or less!

Note that a similar protective effect has been observed in the area of pushup competency. Researchers at Harvard conducted a ten-year study of over one thousand healthy firefighters with an average age of 40. Those who could perform 40 pushups at 40 were 96 percent less likely to develop a cardiovascular problem than those who could not do more than 10 pushups.

When you stack the odds in your favor with lifestyle habits that support pushup competency and a respectable mile time (squat competency and grip strength are also respected longevity markers . . . more later), you can leverage this longevity momentum more powerfully than you might realize at first glance. First, understand that once you reach 65 and the ravages of the accelerated demise we call aging take hold, you are statistically twice as likely to die during each passing year. However, once you make it over the hump of the big 8-0, something extraordinary happens—your runaway odds of demise start to slow down. This insight emerged from a study by an international team of demographers and statisticians, published in 2018 in the journal *Science*, which generated a statistical model of the likelihood of death in every year between 65 and 105.

Obviously, you are still more likely to die each passing year, but the rate slows down. You might envision this concept as a deflection point on an actuarial graph that calculates how much to pop your life insurance each year. Your premium increases every year—fair enough—but rate of increase slows after you hit 80. Get out there and start moving, running, lifting, and sprinting—your life depends on it!

PSYCHOLOGICAL AGE

This represents how old you *feel*. Obviously, this is strongly correlated with your biological age, and it's possible to feel younger than you did ten or twenty years ago if you are healthier and fitter today. Chopra and other spiritual folks offer the scientifically validated argument that psychological age is also vastly more relevant and predictive of your longevity than your chronological age. Indeed, longevity studies identify the predictable attributes like nutritious foods, adequate exercise, low-stress daily rhythms, and healthy social circles. But an important common attribute emerges among the longest-lived on the planet, which Chopra has described beautifully as a "youthful spirit."

People who live to the oldest ages don't feel old, don't complain about being old, and remain fiercely committed to self-sufficiency.

If you want to dismiss this commentary as new-age pep talk, it's time to fully comprehend and appreciate the notion that cultivating a youthful spirit, and the attendant beliefs that support it, can be manifested into reality on a quantum physical level. In Dr. Chopra's landmark 1993 book, *Ageless Body, Timeless Mind*, he corrects our flawed layman's notion that we are physical beings separate from the world around us, operating with a body that ages a bit more every day until expiration. What we perceive as our physical body—head, shoulders, knees, and toes—is literally a swirling mass of atoms that are constantly renewing based on signals received from the environment. Tying into the premise that formed the centerpiece for my 2009 book, *The Primal Blueprint*, we have the power at all times to influence gene expression and cellular function through the thoughts that we think, the foods we eat, the movement we engage in, and so forth.

In *The Biology of Belief*, Dr. Bruce Lipton provides further explanation: "The function of the mind is to create coherence between our beliefs and the reality we experience. Your mind will adjust the body's biology and behavior to fit your beliefs. If the perception in your mind is reflected in the chemistry of your body, and if your nervous system reads and interprets the environment and then controls the blood's chemistry, then you can literally change the fate of your cells by altering your thoughts."

Unfortunately, our minds are often too maxed out with stressing, obsessing, ruminating, and complaining to ponder evolved concepts like influencing cellular function with our thoughts. As Dr. Lipton argues persuasively, your swirling mass of atoms is literally floating through hectic modern life in a daze. By age 35, 95 to 99 percent of your thoughts and actions originate from the habitual programming of the subconscious mind—a combination of memorized behaviors, emotional reactions, beliefs, and perceptions that run in the background like an app on your smartphone. Brain scientists report that we think between 12,000 and 60,000 thoughts per day, that 98 percent of them are identical to yesterday's thoughts, and that 80 percent of your subconscious thoughts are negative!

Most of your subconscious programming happens in childhood, and Lipton explains the already obvious bad news that keeps therapists in business: "The subconscious mind has the tendency to interfere with our conscious desires by programming undesirable thoughts and behaviors, which could lead to a great deal of stress and turmoil in our lives." As dysfunctional childhood programming plays out, we adopt an assortment of narrow, flawed, and self-limiting beliefs. It's common to believe that our genes are fixed heritable traits from our parents, and that they will largely determine our health destiny. For example, if you have a family history of heart disease, obesity, breast cancer, depression, an impatient temperament, flat feet, or whatever else, you may believe that you have been bestowed with these curses by your similarly endowed parents and grandparents, and can't do much to alter your course. These have been proven scientifically to be categorically false assumptions. Your health destiny will be determined by whether you decide to go to sleep or watch another hour of Netflix, whether you decide to go into road rage mode or just smile and wave at an aggressive and discourteous motorist, and whether you decide to nurture healthy social connections or get stuck in toxic relationships.

If you view chronological aging as a glass half empty that continues to drain every year, you will validate these beliefs and temperaments, and experience a steady drain of energy and vitality in conjunction with your chronological aging. Alternatively, you could view your time on earth as a journey of continued exploration and growth—a glass that started empty and continues to fill with wisdom and life experience. We all know se-nior citizens who are cranky and lonely, as well as those who are vibrant and happy. This is not random distribution of genetic good fortune, but rather a product of intention and execution. Dr. Chopra describes this as "expectations determining the outcome." Granted, some people really are blessed with genetic variations (known as single nucleotide polymorphisms, or SNPs) that promote enhanced cellular repair. One study revealed that a group of centenarians aged 100 to 107 had higher levels of two specific DNA repair enzymes than a group of random seniors aged 69 to 75. The less fortunate may have ordinary genes, and more destructive beliefs and traumatic life experiences to overcome in order to embrace new possibilities. However, regardless of the cards you have been dealt, a grand new vision for your life journey is within your reach, starting with the formulation of empowering new beliefs.

HOW TO LOWER BIOLOGICAL AND PSYCHOLOGICAL AGES

Let me ask you right now: How old do you estimate you will live to be? I imagine you'll start with some biological age calculations, such as your current sensations of vitality (or lack thereof), your waistline, recent blood test values, or maybe your pushup or mile-run chops. Regardless of fitness level, most everyone reflexively links chronological age with a steady decline in fitness and vitality. Indeed, this is highly likely to happen, to you and everyone else you know, if you *expect* it to happen. That's why they have separate basketball leagues for people over 50! As you continue to ponder the original question, perhaps you will reference the ballpark average lifespan of 80 in developed nations. FYI, the United States, the richest and most technologically and medically advanced nation in the world, is an abysmal thirty-seventh in life expectancy, at 78.7 years. This is largely due to the two-thirds of the adult population being classified as overweight or obese. Perhaps you are even reflecting upon the current health or lifespan of your parents and grandparents to finally come up with an educated guess?

What if we put aside stats and self-limiting beliefs about familial genetics for a moment and reflect on Chopra's description of your body as "a field of energy, transformation, and intelligence." Then, let's acknowledge the truth that human organs are capable of lasting for 120 years before they wear out as a consequence of routine healthy use. Hence, might you envision 120 as an entirely sensible and realistic longevity goal to pursue? Why not! We know that modern medicine will get you through many unexpected traumas and misfortunes, and that you can blow today's averages out of the water simply by avoiding the most sinister modern hazards of processed foods, sedentary patterns, rat-race mindsets, and tech addiction. Remember, inside you right now is a kind, forgiving heart that's just happy to beat along for the ride, forgives you for all your past misdeeds that have caused it harm, and is willing to continue working hard for up to 120 years with your cooperation!

Please get out a spiral notebook and write down your chronological age, along with honest estimates of your current biological and psychological ages. Then, write down some of the issues that are influencing your estimates, and some potential ways to improve them. Remember, these challenges can be in the form of self-limiting beliefs as well as unhealthy lifestyle practices. Rather than vague proclamations like "I want to be healthier," try to make each comment and proposed resolution as specific and detailed as possible, so that you may convert it into an effective and sustained belief or behavior change. For example:

- I'm forming a new belief that my father's early demise has minimal influence on my destiny, and that I have the potential to live to be 120, or at least 100.
- I ruminate too often about things out of my control, like my kid's career decisions. I will let go of expectations and judgments and offer unconditional love, support, and acceptance.
- My consumption of refined sugars and industrial seed oils is compromising my health, and likely exacerbating my arthritis. I will do a total elimination for 21 days and expect improvement in my symptoms.
- I spend too much time inactive. I will walk the dog every morning and every evening for at least 10 minutes to support my daily movement obligation—and be a great pet owner!

We know all about the hard work involved in dietary restriction, a major fitness commitment, or honoring a consistent bedtime, so the idea that you can also make profound longevity gains simply by changing your thoughts should be appealing. Try it out, starting right now: new thoughts, new belief systems, new actions, new outcomes!

GRABBING THE LOW-HANGING FRUIT

What's happened on my journey and that of other thought leaders in the primal/paleo/ancestral/keto world is that we have performed a deep dive into the science of optimal diet, fitness, sleep, and peak cognitive and physical performance, and emerged with a mind-blowing realization: First, an overly complex or strenuous approach has a high risk of attrition. Second, you can make fantastic progress with a simple, low-budget, no-frills approach.

Dr. Peter Attia is one of the world's leading experts on longevity, ketogenic eating, and fat-adapted athletic performance. He has performed extreme endurance feats on land and at sea, from marathon cycling events to swimming 21 miles across the Pacific Ocean from Catalina Island to Los Angeles. Attia maintained strict nutritional ketosis for 3 years straight from 2011 to 2014, painstakingly tracking macronutrient intake at each meal, daily blood ketone levels, and athletic performance metrics. He had the earliest version of a continuous glucose monitor surgically implanted into his abdomen to generate real-time blood glucose values on his smartphone. All this in the name of science and advancement of what today has become the keto craze! When asked recently on my coauthor Brad Kearns's *Get Over Yourself* podcast to dispense his sophisticated dietary insights to eager listeners, he said, "Perhaps only eat stuff that your great-grandmother could have eaten."

Attia was not being flippant. Rather, informed by deep scientific analysis, he assures us that we can get to 80 percent of our health and longevity potential simply by picking off the low-hanging fruit. Ditch processed modern foods, move around more during the day, do some regular brief, high-intensity exercise, get enough sleep, and work on being more mindful and less harried in daily life, and you are well on your way to becoming a centenarian (surprisingly, there are over 500,000 alive today, with 3.7 million predicted globally by 2050). Attia indicates that he is "obsessed" with that final 20 percent of dietary and lifestyle practices that can help you reach your longevity potential. Attia asserts that healthspan boils down to preserving three attributes for as long as possible: brain function, physical function, and your spirit (sense of purpose and social support network).

In this book you are going to absolutely nail that 80 percent low-hanging fruit objective, then turn your attention to cutting-edge longevity strategies that will help you reach your highest potential. Remember, this is a journey toward longevity, not a boot camp certificate. This means you are going to have fun the whole time, enjoy delicious meals, conduct challenging but not exhausting workouts, leverage technology to your advantage instead of becoming an addict, and elevate rest and recovery into the highest priority of healthy living. Before we get into the practical step-by-step elements of each pillar, it's important to understand why adherence to the principles laid out in these pillars is so crucial for lasting health.

THE ART AND SCIENCE OF THE FOUR PILLARS

I've been obsessed with nutrition, human biology, and athletic performance since I was a teenager, and made it my life's work. Over the past decade, I've worked hard to counter flawed and dated conventional wisdom by promoting a primal approach, where you can achieve optimal gene expression by modeling the lifestyle behaviors of our hunter-gatherer ancestors. I and other leaders in the ancestral health movement have fought a royal battle against the entrenched forces of big agriculture, big pharmaceutical, manipulative corporate advertising, and the consequent rigid belief systems that have been programmed into even the most devoted health enthusiasts. It's been incredibly gratifying to see the ancestral health movement explode in popularity. More people are taking personal responsibility for their health, awakening to the idea that the accelerated decline we call aging is not inevitable. A decade after I published *The Primal Blueprint*, words like keto and paleo are widely recognized, and I no longer get blasted on the Internet or shouted down when talking at a physician's luncheon like I did back in the early days—accused of spreading an irresponsible and even dangerous message.

And while diet and fitness are big-ticket items, they are only ingredients in the complete recipe for longevity. My blind spots have been mental flexibility (I admit to being a stresshead at times and have blogged frequently about the matter at MarksDailyApple.com) and making absolutely sure to emphasize rest and recovery in everyday life. I do my best to share an enlightened message, especially to the Type A, "more is better" crowd. But let's face it: It's difficult if not impossible to undo all of your hardwiring and subconscious programming. After all, I'm from a hardscrabble fishing village in Maine, dripping with Puritan work ethic. I pushed myself to exhaustion competing in the most grueling athletic endeavors in the world, and my entrepreneurial journey has been forged out of pure grit and competitive intensity. Even though I know better, rest and recovery often get the short shrift. Perhaps you can relate? Consequently, it is imperative to implement systems and strategies that allow you to stumble into success. If you set a beeper alarm on your heart rate monitor, or a reminder alarm to go to sleep at 10 p.m., you are acknowledging your inclinations to squeeze a little too much into a workout, or a day, and giving yourself powerful reminders to stick to the script.

The goal of *Keto for Life* is to combine four incredibly disparate pillars into a recipe for health, happiness, and longevity. The use of the word pillar to describe the sections is appropriate, because the definition of pillar is "essential support for something." Indeed, each of the four pillars complement the others to the extent that it makes no sense to consider or attempt them in isolation. We know from sleep science that you become insulin resistant in a matter of days of compromised sleep. We know from the compensation theory that the benefits of your ambitious daily workout will be hugely compromised if you lead an otherwise sedentary lifestyle. Regarding mental flexibility, if you live in FOMO instead of gratitude, or are immersed in toxic relationship dynamics instead of mutually rewarding and reciprocative relation-

ships, you might as well be eating grass-fed cardboard instead of premium quality food.

This section presents the scientific rationale behind each of the Four Pillars and how they complement each other in general. This education will enable you to have a complete understanding, trust, and buy-in for the entire process. This fosters *intrinsic* motivation—doing something to achieve self-satisfaction. This is much more predictive of success and long-term adherence than when you are driven primarily by *extrinsic* motivators, such as desperately trying to lose 10 pounds in the 6 weeks before your bridesmaid gig.

Dr. Lindsay Taylor is a senior writer and researcher at Primal Blueprint Publishing and my recipe contributor/coauthor on four keto books. She earned a PhD in social and personality psychology, and she explains that "When a goal feels personally meaningful, and when the rewards bolster your sense of who you are or who you want to become, you will likely find it easier to engage in goal-directed behavior, avoid the temptation to stray from the path, and be resilient in the face of setbacks." That said, please don't misunderstand intrinsic versus extrinsic as an either-or choice. Extrinsic motivators can indeed be useful, but best results come when they are combined with a strong foundation of intrinsic motivation. Let's learn the how's and why's behind the *Keto for Life* program, then plunge into the pillars and the 21-Day Biological Clock Reset with full energy, enthusiasm, and intrinsic motivation.

METABOLIC FLEXIBILITY

Metabolic flexibility is not only the gateway but also the mandatory first step to a healthier body and a longer life. If you can't achieve it, you will be doomed to an accelerated demise featuring pain and suffering. If you don't believe me, look around today in America, the richest and most technologically advanced society in the history of the world, and you will also see the fattest, least fit population in the history of mankind. Metabolic flexibility describes the ability to burn a variety of stored or ingested fuel sources, gracefully delivering to your body the exact energy it needs at all times, whether or not you eat regular meals. Metabolic flexibility entails breaking free from the disastrous modern epidemic of carbohydrate dependency and becoming what I affectionately call a *fat-burning beast*. With fat (from either natural, nutritious dietary fats, or from storage areas on the body) as your preferred fuel choice, you are no longer reliant upon regularly timed high-carbohydrate snacks and meals as your main source of energy. Instead, as millions of keto followers enthusiastically report, you experience more stable mood and appetite, significantly improved cognition, faster recovery from exercise and other forms of life stress, and more resiliency against both minor illness and the tragic diet-related disease patterns—especially conditions of cognitive decline that are being increasingly tied to high-carbohydrate, high-insulin-producing diets.

When you are reliant upon regular doses of dietary carbohydrates as your primary source of energy—the reality for almost every human on the planet today—you promote the disastrous health condition of *systemic inflammation*. This undesirable system-wide and chronic form of inflammation is believed by most experts to represent the root cause of almost every form of disease and dysfunction in the body. This includes the leading killers of modern humans—heart disease, cognitive disease, and cancer.

Systemic inflammation is a result of your body being ill-equipped to handle the wildly excessive carbohydrate load of the Standard American Diet (SAD), as well as other modern stressors like excess exercise or insufficient sleep. If you spike blood sugar and flood the bloodstream with insulin as a routine daily pattern, you overstress/chronically inflame the extremely delicate hormonal processes designed to keep your mood, energy, and cognition stable at all times. A high-glucose/high-insulin eating pattern also causes mitochondria to atrophy and/or become dysfunctional, leaving you more vulnerable to oxidative damage from free radicals.

Slamming carbs morning, noon, and night also triggers an undesirable chemical reaction known as *glycation*, whereby excess glucose molecules floating around the bloodstream will bind to important structural proteins throughout the body and inflict long-term damage. The body's longest lasting cells—brain, cardiovascular system, eyes, kidney, and skin—are the most vulnerable to glycation. This is why diabetics (who have difficulty regulating blood glucose) frequently have vision and kidney problems, and why wrinkles are reflective of aging. Hardened arteries and the senile plaques and neurofibrillary tangles of Alzheimer's disease are also reflective of cellular damage caused by glycation.

It follows that with improved mood, energy, and cognitive function, you are better able to adhere to the exercise, sleep, and stress management objectives that are essential to health, but we are often too lazy, tired, fried, and discouraged to adhere to them. Metabolic flexibility unlocks the true secret to losing excess body fat and keeping it off, without the suffering and sacrifice that comes with calorie-restriction diets. Metabolic flexibility is perhaps best achieved through a ketogenic eating pattern, but there are many ways to get there. Whenever you restrict or deplete your cells of energy, as with fasting or conducting a strenuous workout, you are promoting metabolic flexibility; your body has to find other ways to sustain energy besides yet another high-carbohydrate meal coming down the hatch. This means vegans and vegetarians can achieve metabolic flexibility, enthusiasts of the newly popular carnivore diet can get there, as can anyone eating wholesome foods and avoiding the offensive refined carbs and industrial seed oils that inhibit fat metabolism—provided they are highly active and don't overeat.

Metabolic flexibility is a hardwired genetic attribute that our ancestors honed through 2.5 million years of the withering selection pressures of starvation and predator danger. Generally speaking, primal humans had to work hard for every bite of food they ate and were never assured of where or when their next meal would be. This forced our ancestors to become good at burning stored fat and glycogen (the storage form of carbohydrate) and making ketones in the liver when dietary carb intake was insufficient to meet the needs of the extremely high-energy-demand human brain. Remember, since the brain can't burn fat or protein, it's mostly reliant upon glucose or the appropriate glucose substitute of ketones (Note: The brain can also burn lactate under certain circumstances such as vigorous exercise.)

You may have never heard of keto until your recent exposure to a random viral YouTube video, but it was arguably the single most critical metabolic attribute for human survival throughout our evolutionary history. Without ketones, our ancestors would have gone on failed hunting or gathering missions, collapsed due to hypoglycemia, and not been able to survive day after day of hard work with no certainty of a meal. Instead, our ancestors not only survived, they thrived, due to their metabolic flexibility.

Today, we have completely trashed this magnificent gift from our ancestors—the human genetic attribute of metabolic flexibility and fat- and keto-adaptation—by burying it under giant piles of *beige glop*. That's my pet name for the refined grains that form the foundation of the Standard American Diet—bread, pasta, rice, corn, cereal, etc. SADly, this great American cultural centerpiece has been exported to most other developed nations across the globe. Consuming too many carbohydrates, too many total calories, and eating too frequently has atrophied our metabolic muscles, sending us on an express train to metabolic syndrome, the catch-all term to convey an assortment of disease symptoms caused by chronically excessive insulin production. We spend billions on long-term care for people with metabolic syndrome, especially type 2 diabetes, largely ignoring the fact that four of the five markers that define metabolic syndrome (elevated fasting glucose, high blood pressure, low HDL, and high triglycerides) can be righted in as little as 21 days of carbohydrate restriction for most people. The fifth marker, excess waistline measurement, will often take longer to correct, but steady progress is assured when you escape SAD patterns.

Unfortunately, modern humans exist in a state of metabolic *inflexibility*, entirely reliant upon regularly scheduled high-carbohydrate meals (and between-meal snacks that boost blood sugar) for energy. Dieticians, food marketers, and the medical establishment tell us this is normal and healthy. We are urged to get our first dose of carbs at breakfast, "the most important meal of the day," and to carefully orchestrate meals to get plenty of carbs and not too much of the dietary fat we have been programmed to believe is harmful. As we chow down on breakfast, lunch, dinner, dessert, and frequent snacks every day for decades, ample supplies of body fat remain locked away in storage—inaccessible due to chronically elevated

insulin levels. Ketone production is suppressed due to a constant caloric surplus, evidenced by full glycogen storage tanks and high blood levels of glucose and insulin.

When carb-dependent modern humans skip a meal, instead of transitioning elegantly into accelerated fat burning and ketone manufacturing, as our genes are primed for, they get *hangry*—that's street talk for hungry and angry. Your afternoon blues of sagging energy, mood, and cognitive function are perceived as a matter of life or death—as they really were during primal times. Consequently, fight-or-flight hormonal mechanisms are triggered, particularly *gluconeogenesis*—the conversion of lean muscle tissue into glucose to keep the brain supplied with energy. Interestingly, our brains require around 150 grams of glucose each day. A carb-dependent brain will burn virtually 100 percent glucose, while a highly keto-adapted brain can obtain two-thirds of energy from ketones and one-third from glucose. Not coincidentally, the 50-gram minimum baseline glucose requirement for the keto-adapted brain correlates with the often-referenced keto limit on daily carb intake of 50 grams per day.

Fight-or-flight gluconeogenesis is the reason why, during prolonged periods of extreme stress, you can feel alert and wired all day even if you don't eat. What's happening is you are delivering a steady drip of glucose to the brain in order to continue to function well without food. The problem with gluconeogenesis and related fight-or-flight hormonal mechanisms is that they're designed for emergency use only. Fight or flight is designed to put healthy, homoeostatic functions on the back burner to deal with brief life-or-death threats—to run from a predator and the like. Unfortunately, in hectic modern life, we egregiously abuse the fight-or-flight response with all manner of prolonged stressors (traffic jams, arguments with loved ones, or too many grueling early-morning spin classes) to the extent that these emergency hormonal functions wear out and we become exhausted.

If you restrict carbs and/or total calories before you have built some measure of metabolic flexibility, you'll stimulate fight-or-flight mechanisms—making your own sugar to manage the hunger, mood, and energy level swings that come with crash dieting. For a few weeks, the stress hormone buzz might even give you more energy and alertness. Maybe you'll even drop some weight—a little from fat reduction, but mostly from less water retention and cellular inflammation. However, when your buzz wears off and you feel fried and exhausted, your body will reflexively respond to this traumatic experience by overeating (especially quick-energy carbs) and under-exercising to restore energy and hormonal balance.

THE LONGEVITY BENEFITS OF KETOSIS

Unlike fight-or-flight gluconeogenesis, ketone production in the liver is not an emergency mechanism, but an elegant metabolic function that can be sustained for a lifetime if necessary or desired. Remember, our ancestors might have been starving for months on end, but still demanding extreme energy expenditure and cognitive alertness to (hopefully) ultimately succeed in finding food. What's more, some of our ancestors at the highest latitudes survived and thrived for tens of thousands of years with virtually no dietary carbohydrates and turbocharged ketone production.

Ketones are an internally manufactured source of caloric energy for the brain, heart, and muscles. They are produced in the liver as a by-product of fat metabolism when—owing to extreme restriction of dietary carbohydrates—insulin, blood sugar, and liver glycogen levels are very low. Ketones burn like glucose in the brain (as well as the heart and skeletal muscles to a lesser extent), enabling you to function at high capacity when dietary calories and/or carbohydrates are scarce. What's more, ketones burn significantly more cleanly and efficiently than glucose, earning a deserved reputation as a superfuel. When you ingest a refined sugar or grain food, it is converted into glucose and immediately burned for energy in the bloodstream without requiring the use of oxygen. Consequently, inflammation and free radicals are generated, giving glucose the characterization of a cheap and dirty fuel. In contrast, burning ketones and fat requires oxygen, so *mitochondria*—the oxygen-utilizing power plants located inside most of your cells—offer a protective benefit against inflammation and oxidative stress. Realize that even complex carbohydrates are rapidly broken down into glucose in the bloodstream, so carbs are a much lower octane fuel than fat or ketones.

To compare carb dependency with metabolic flexibility, it may be helpful to envision two different campfires. Glucose burns like the twigs and wadded up newspaper. You get an instant big flame, with lots of smoke (i.e., free radicals), and you have to constantly add more kindling to sustain the fire. This would be like the carb addict needing regular high-carb meals and snacks to maintain energy and cognitive function. A fat and ketone campfire features big logs, glowing with warmth, burning for hours without spewing smoke or requiring much attention. This is the fat-burner enjoying peak physical and cognitive function even when skipping meals or significantly restricting carbs.

Burning clean fuel is especially important in the brain, because these cells are highly sensitive to inflammation and oxidative stress. Today's alarming increase in cognitive decline conditions is being increasingly tied to high-carb, high-sugar diets. With impaired glucose metabolism as a hallmark of Alzheimer's and related conditions, scientists now use a catchy nickname (coined by noted researcher Dr. Suzanne de la Monte of Brown University) to describe these brain conditions: "Type 3 diabetes." Ouch. Indeed, as the work of de la Monte details, Alzheimer's is literally diabetes occurring in brain cells, and the condition "has molecular and biochemical features that overlap with both type 1 and type 2 diabetes."

On the flip side, ketones give such a profound boost to brain function that the ketogenic diet has been used with great effectiveness for over a century to treat drug-resistant seizures. Ketone burning raises the threshold at which mitochondria become deranged by a lack of oxygen, which is the trigger for a seizure. Relatedly, many keto enthusiasts report a benefit of increased mental clarity, possibly attributed to improved blood circulation and oxygen delivery in the brain, when you transition away from burning pure glucose to burning mostly ketones.

When you achieve metabolic flexibility, you will experience, perhaps for the first time in your life, stable energy, mood, and cognitive function without having to rely on regular meals. You will be burning cleaner energy sources than glucose, thereby sparing yourself from the oxidative stress that represents the essence of aging. Also, you will hone the incredibly powerful health and longevity skill of fasting. Actually, if you want a candidate for the single most life-changing insight from this book and the entire keto movement, how's this? *Every aspect of hormonal, immune, and metabolic function works more efficiently when you are fasting: repairing damaged cells, firing brain neurons, controlling inflammation, and burning off stored body fat.* Or as Art De Vany likes to say, "We are perhaps most human when we don't eat."

Furthering that insight, De Vany argues that one of the most profound longevity markers among centenarians across the globe is low insulin levels: "Insulin is the aging hormone: when nutrition is abundant, the body thinks it's time to reproduce." This is great when we are in adolescence and trying to grow to full maturity, or during those periods of life when we are trying to reproduce. Alas, De Vany explains that the gene switches that prime us for reproduction are in conflict with longevity: "Turning on genes geared toward reproduction turns off genes that are geared toward stress resistance, repair, and maintenance." Once you exit your reproductive years, you can start to pay more attention to longevity and minimizing insulin. However, growing youth or people in their fertility window who carry excess body fat or other markers of metabolic dysfunction have overshot their target for reproductive fitness. They will also benefit from reducing insulin and turning on genes for stress resistance, repair, and maintenance.

I haven't even mentioned how keto benefits fat reduction yet, because it's best to view this as a natural by-product of your keto journey, rather than the main focus. In fact, I'd prefer that you de-emphasize fat-reduction goals until you complete your first 6-week keto stint. If you are trying to transition to keto as well as create a caloric deficit to stimulate fat reduction at the same time, this might be overwhelming. Remember, when dietary transformation becomes too stressful, your body can always kick into fight-or-flight mode and mess up your long-term progress.

Once you have built the metabolic machinery to excel at fasting, burning fat, and making ketones, you can get your next meal from your plate, or from your butt and thighs—your choice. Call this metabolic flexibility or call it *hormone optimization*, but this is the true secret to losing excess body fat and keeping it off. In contrast, the traditional approach of burning exercise calories like crazy, then fighting off hunger to achieve a temporary caloric deficit only leads to hormone dysfunction. In short, your depleting workouts will prompt sugar cravings, which you will either resist (triggering fight-or-flight response and gluconeogenesis) or eventually cave in to. When this happens, your hopes and dreams for longevity are compromised, as your body faces the immediate crisis of carbohydrate dependency. Here, you will activate genes that help you survive (e.g., flooding the bloodstream with insulin), but that directly oppose longevity goals.

When you eliminate nutrient-deficient grains and sugars, and reduce dietary carbohydrates from over half of your daily calories to a small fraction of 5, 10, or perhaps 20 percent at most, your longevity prospects skyrocket for two reasons: First, you are able to get the vast majority of your calories from extremely nutrient-dense foods. In contrast to the SAD filler foods that give you the macronutrients to burn for energy and little else, ancestral foods give you both macronutrients and the micronutrients (vitamins, minerals, antioxidants, phytonutrients, etc.) you need to optimize cellular and hormonal function. Second, you are able to spend more time in a fasted state, which is when you optimize cell repair, immune function, and mitochondrial biogenesis. These renewal and repair mechanisms are the antidote to the accelerated cell division, oxidative stress, and glycation that are the essence of accelerated aging.

The recent explosion in the popularity of the ketogenic diet arises from the well-established ancestral health/low-carb dietary movement. However, keto is more stringent with carbohydrate restriction in order to prompt the delicate process of ketone production in the liver. When you achieve this delicate but fragile metabolic state (a single medium- to high-carb meal can knock you out of ketosis for an extended period of time, requiring fasting or a string of keto-aligned meals to return to a state of nutritional ketosis), you can achieve superior weight loss, disease protection, cognition, and athletic performance in comparison to a standard low-carb diet.

An optimal *Keto for Life* eating pattern entails looking beyond macronutrient calculations and striving to include the most nutrient-dense foods possible at every meal. I'll never tell you to eat stuff you hate in the name of longevity, as this concept is actually antithetical to longevity. However, the Longevity Superfoods and Longevity Supplements sections in Pillar #1: Metabolic Flexibility, as well as the recipes section at the end of the book, will give you plenty of options to pick and choose your favorites and cover all of your bases. This is especially true when it comes to supplements. If you hate liver, don't get sufficient sun exposure, or need additional support for aching joints or connective tissue injuries, you can supplement strategically in support of a healthy dietary foundation.

MOVEMENT AND PHYSICAL FITNESS

Movement and physical fitness are two distinct concepts; together, along with preserving sharp cognition, they represent the essence of aging gracefully. In contrast, when you lose cognition and mobility, your life expectancy and quality of life plummet as you are relegated to a walker, wheelchair, and eventually bed. Medications can keep you alive for much longer than ever before, but you may be tragically diminished in mind, body, or both. I'm not the least bit interested in that kind of longevity—how about you?

While regular everyday movement will pick off a bunch of low-hanging fruit, aggressive intervention is necessary with physical fitness in order to resist the damage and demise of aging and live an active, energetic, playful life. If sports aren't your thing, and the gym's not your thing, and you don't consider yourself an athlete of any kind, don't worry. You can still become a shining example of a physically fit human without buying into the often overhyped, extreme, and unhealthy modern fitness scene.

For now, let's learn about the incredible brain boosting, fat-burning, longevity-promoting benefits of a primal-style exercise program, how to avoid the drawbacks of an overly stressful "chronic exercise" approach, and how easy and time-efficient it can be to become not just fit and trim, but superfit and ripped!

MOVING TOWARD LONGEVITY

The cheeky axiom, "sitting is the new smoking" has garnered great attention in recent years, as mounting science links sedentary living patterns with all manner of disease, dysfunction, and decline. Nielsen Media Research reports that the average American adult watches video for 6 hours per day. The Kaiser Family Foundation says the average American teen is engaged with a screen for 9 hours a day. Statistics referenced by James Levine, MD, PhD, a Mayo Clinic researcher, international expert on obesity, and author of *Get Up! Why Your Chair Is Killing You and What You Can Do About It*, suggests that the average Westerner working in an office environment sits for some 13 hours per day (at work and at leisure), sleeps for 8, and moves for only 3.

Granted, it's hard for any such stats to shock us these days, and we all hear that little voice admonishing us to be active instead of lazy. Unfortunately, even when we harbor good intentions, we've become conditioned to pursue shortcuts, quick fixes, and instant gratification over simple and sensible lifestyle changes. Crazy as it seems, the idea of taking an evening stroll with the dog becomes less appealing, and harder to motivate for, than going for the big score with an extreme 6-week fitness regimen or crazy calorie-restriction diet.

Today, we must reverse engineer our way back to genetically optimal behavior patterns by artificially creating winning circumstances that compel us to use our bodies (and our minds) as evolution intended. One Mayo Clinic study revealed that a leisurely (1 mph) 15-minute walk after a meal lowered by half the 2-hour-long blood sugar spike that occurs after a typical meal. Mayo Clinic's Dr. Levine cites research that performing an activity as simple as standing up at your desk instead of sitting increases caloric expenditure by 10 percent, while taking frequent movement breaks during the day can add up to an additional 1,000 calories burned or more.

With more and more science emerging to support the concept that little things really do count, the Physical Activity Guidelines Advisory Committee at the US Department of Health and Human Services updated their exercise recommendations for Americans in 2018 to encourage even short bouts of exercise. Previously, the 2008 guidelines conveyed a minimum duration of 10 minutes was needed to count as an "official" exercise session. This is not a winning recommendation when research suggests lack of time to be the biggest hurdle to achieving exercise goals! Regarding the updated guidelines, Dr. Haitham Ahmed of the Cleveland Clinic says, "Even just going up the stairs instead of using the elevator or going on short walks throughout the day will increase your step count [toward the frequently recommended 10,000 steps per day; equivalent to 4 to 5 miles of walking] and also add cumulative aerobic exercise. This has tremendous benefits over the long term."

Regular exercise has a direct correlation with improved brain function and prevention of cognitive decline in part because it boosts the production of an important protein called *brain-derived neurotrophic factor* (BDNF). BDNF has been shown to help improve neuron firing and build new neurons, increase blood circulation and oxygen delivery, help prevent cognitive decline, alleviate symptoms of depression and anxiety, and improve plasticity—making your brain more resilient against stress. Harvard psychiatrist John J. Ratey, MD, calls BDNF "Miracle-Gro for the brain." Granted, long-duration aerobic workouts will intensify these benefits beyond what you get walking the dog around the block, but making a concerted effort to increase all forms of general everyday movement will absolutely make you smarter and more resilient against cognitive decline. What's more, BDNF is also boosted by positive social interactions and sun exposure (via increased vitamin D production), so here's sufficient reason to get going with a weekend hiking club!

If you aren't inclined to jump out of bed at the alarm and into a predawn Spinning class, know that a simple morning stroll will boost mood-elevating hormones like dopamine, serotonin, and norepinephrine, teeing you up for a happy, productive day. Furthermore, getting out and exposing yourself to direct sunlight first thing in the morning will entrain your circadian rhythm so you can fall asleep smoothly that evening.

When you make frequent daily movement a lifelong habit, the hippocampus and other areas of your brain grow thicker, indicating better memory formation and consolidation, and more resilience against cognitive decline. A 2017 UCLA study comparing MRI scans revealed that active older folks (over 60, and walking more than 3 kilometers per day) have faster brain processing speed, better working memory for quick decisions, and better memory consolidation than inactive folks. In his book *The* Real *Happy Pill: Power Up Your Brain by Moving Your Body*, Swedish researcher Dr. Anders Hansen reports that just taking a daily walk can reduce your risk of dementia by 40 percent. If you fail to achieve a bare minimum of walking and modest muscular activity each day, you are most definitely headed for pain, suffering, and demise. In the UCLA study, those falling short of the 4,000 steps per day had thinner brains, slower, less-efficient functioning, and greater risk of accelerated decline.

You may be familiar with the bestselling book and lifestyle movement known as *The Blue Zones*. It's a global longevity study, presented by health journalist Dan Buettner in concert with *National Geographic*. The Blue Zones project has spanned the globe to discover five distinct pockets of extreme longevity: the long-celebrated and scrutinized Japanese island of Okinawa (lots of energy-rich seafood, socializing, and minimal modern-day stressors); Loma Linda, CA (home of clean living and socially connected Seventh-day Adventists who are choosing out of the surrounding American cultural mores of junk food, consumerism, and hyperconnectivity); the Italian island of Sardinia (where their ancient ways of homegrown food and active low-stress lifestyles still prevail); and Costa Rica's Nicoya Peninsula and the Greek island of Ikaria (two isolated populations who are doing things right without much Internet, nor HMO coverage).

Of course, genetics are a piece to the longevity puzzle, but one of the big takeaways from Blue Zones research is how the longest-lived humans exist in environments that compel them to be active. The Blue Zones "Power 9" list is a "cross-cultural distillation of best practices...a shorthand for the Blue Zones approach." Number one on the list is "Move Naturally," which *The Blue Zones* author Dan Buettner describes as "living in environments that constantly nudge them into moving." Blue Zones folks have gardens, walk to errands or social occasions, and either eschew or have no access to many modern mechanical conveniences.

If you wonder what's the harm of an honest day's work in your office, followed by a commute home, followed by hours of digital entertainment to hit that 13-hour daily average, it boils down to this: Humans have been hardwired over 2.5 million years of evolution to be active as a life-or-death survival necessity. When you sit or lounge for extended periods during your wakeful hours, you turn off genes that promote health, vitality, and longevity, and turn on genes that promote systemic inflammation, insulin resistance, diminished cognitive function, and musculoskeletal weaknesses and imbalances.

Katy Bowman, MS, bestselling author of *Move Your DNA* and a biomechanist (studying human movement) by training, promotes the concept of "Movement Nutrition;" it's not just the brain, but every cell in our bodies that require frequent and varied movement to express health. When you sit for long periods of time, your gluteals, hamstrings, and hip flexors—the muscular foundation for all manner of daily activity and athletic performance—get seriously messed up. Prolonged sitting causes hamstrings and hip flexors to shorten and tighten. Katy explains that assuming a single position like sitting or lounging for extended periods will also mess you up at the cellular level. "Muscles, joints, and arteries will adapt to this repetitive positioning by changing their cellular makeup and becoming literally 'stiff,' with reduced ranges of motion and an actual hardening of the arterial walls in those areas."

Hard-core athletes with logbooks chock full of impressive energy expenditures might scoff at any of these dire warnings, thinking their ambitious workouts leave them immune to the diseases and dysfunctions of inactivity. Bowman warns otherwise:

> Even serious athletes can damage arteries in areas of the body that get stuck in a fixed position for too long. Furthermore, when you engage in narrowly-focused workout patterns that shunt blood into the same areas over and over, you potentially compromise your overall cellular and cardiovascular health due to lack of variation. You also invite the well-chronicled risks of overstressing the heart with inflammation and scarring.

Inactivity also leads to metabolic and hormone imbalances that compromise glucose metabolism, elevate triglyceride levels, promote excess body fat storage, and elevate blood pressure. In short, inactivity promotes disease and dysfunction independent of diet. Even if you are making a devoted effort to get fat-adapted, the genetic and hormonal disturbances driven by inactivity can wash much of your progress away. You have to cut processed carbs in order to reduce insulin and start burning fat, but you have to move around all day long in order to keep burning fat.

Of particular concern is how inactivity disturbs the all-important *leptin signaling* between the digestive system and the brain. Leptin is a key hormone that regulates appetite, satiety, fat metabolism, and reproductive functions. Dr. Ron Rosedale, author of *The Rosedale Diet*, asserts that leptin has equal or greater importance than insulin in regulating appetite and body fat storage. For example, leptin exerts a strong influence on other appetite hormones such as ghrelin (promotes hunger) and CCK (promotes satiety and speed of digestion). Leptin also influences the production and distribution of sex hormones, and is involved in the processes that promote bone density. Leptin signaling must be optimal for these processes to work as intended and prime the human for reproduction. When leptin signaling is compromised, typically from a high-carbohydrate/high-insulin-producing diet, it can cause increased hunger, increased body fat storage, irregular sex hormone function, and loss of bone density.

As with the slippery slope of accumulating a little spare tire and it getting bigger and bigger, when prolonged periods of stillness become a habit, you experience chemical changes in your brain that promote inactivity. This can be quantified by a lower measurement of *non-exercise activity thermogenesis* (NEAT). Conversely, when you implement excellent movement habits, your brain becomes wired toward more activity, higher NEAT readings, and better appetite stability. Besides good sleep being the catalyst for success in all other longevity pursuits, it's hard to find a more impactful example of complementary lifestyle success behaviors than eating well and moving well.

STRENGTH TRAINING FOR LONGEVITY

Movement is your first objective before we even discuss fitness, but if you want to maximize your longevity potential and deliver an 8- or 9-minute mile time at age 50, it's going to take some extra effort to develop both aerobic (endurance) and anaerobic (strength and power) fitness. In addition to living an active life, building and maintaining broad athletic competency will boost the critical health attribute of *organ reserve*. This is the functional capacity of your organs when asked to perform beyond baseline, as happens when you are challenged by illness, injury, surgery, or the inevitable atrophy associated with chronological aging.

Because all of your organs and body systems work synergistically, you are constantly exposed and vulnerable to your weakest link. For example, an unfit person suffering an accident, acute illness, or difficult surgery may come to demise from an occasion that would be gracefully weathered by a stronger person. Witness how healthy females over

80 who break their hip are three times more likely to die within a year, or how 12 percent of Medicare patients admitted to the hospital for pneumonia die within 30 days—typically due to the inability of their weakened lungs to help clear the germ-laden mucus effectively through coughing.

As with the Cooper Institute's mile-run longevity marker, many studies reveal a direct correlation between strength and longevity, as measured by competency in basic exercises like squats, deadlifts, pushups, and grip strength. The reason you see that contraption with the squeeze handle attached to a readout meter inside every doctor's office is because grip strength is easy to measure in a clinical setting and has been proven to be an extremely reliable indicator of your general rate of aging. Insufficient grip strength has been found to be a superior predictor of mortality risk than blood pressure! It's an independent risk factor for type 2 diabetes, a proxy for other functional limitations such as poor walking speed, and even a depression risk factor. In the 25-year Honolulu Heart Program study of 6,000 participants between ages 45 and 68, it was discovered that grip strength, even in midlife, could accurately predict mortality 25 years later.

The US National Institutes of Health conducted a longitudinal study from 1997 to 2011 of 3,000 Americans living in Memphis, Tennessee, and Pittsburgh, Pennsylvania, who were in their 70s at the study's inception. At the start of the study, known as the Health, Aging, and Body Composition Study (Health ABC), all participants were able to walk one-quarter mile and climb a flight of stairs without difficulty. Those who lost these abilities over time had a greater incidence of inflammation, cancer, diabetes, heart disease, and death—even factoring out morbidity factors like race, socioeconomic status, and depression score. The study also factored out muscle size to calculate relative strength, enabling comparison between a smaller but sturdy female and a much larger, but perhaps weaker, male.

A 1999 study in Brazil of 2,000 subjects between 51 and 80 was able to predict mortality risk with great accuracy based on a subject's competency performing a basic squat. Those who were incompetent were five times more likely to die in the next 6 years, while those who had some difficulty squatting were twice as likely to die. A British study of identical twins revealed a profound link between leg strength and cognitive health. Lead researcher Dr. Claire Steves said, "It's compelling to see such differences in cognition and brain structure in identical twins, who had different leg power 10 years before." Dr. Michael Roizen, coauthor with Dr. Oz of the popular *You: The Owner's Manual* health book series and leader of the Cleveland Clinic Wellness Institute, says you can preserve bone mass in the spine and lower extremities by simply jumping up and down 20 times, every morning and every night.

Beyond these "get stronger, live longer" physical benefits, loads of studies have shown regular strength training facilitates better evening sleep; improved glucose metabolism and insulin sensitivity; lower blood pressure; improved bone density; improvements in back pain, osteoarthritis, and fibromyalgia; and increased protection against heart attack and stroke. For those with chronic fatigue who can manage to get started slowly and build some momentum toward regular strength sessions, pumping iron has been shown to improve fatigue symptoms better than drugs or cognitive behavior therapy.

Strength training has also been shown to deliver extensive cognitive and mental health benefits. A 2010 article in the *American Journal of Lifestyle Medicine* titled "Mental Health Benefits of Strength Training in Adults" examined dozens of studies and reported that strength training helps improve depression's symptoms, boosts self-esteem, promotes a profound improvement in memory and memory-related tasks, and serves as "a meaningful intervention for people suffering from anxiety." From University of New Mexico researchers Amenda Ramirez and Len Kravitz, PhD, this analysis of the study: "Improved cognition from exercise is likely to be from multi-factorial adaptations involving new nerve cell generation in the brain, an increase in neurotransmitters and new brain blood vessels for more efficient oxygen delivery and waste product removal."

Putting the scientifically validated long-term benefits aside for a moment, realize that a single high-intensity session prompts a spike in adaptive hormones that gives you an immediate sense of euphoria. A good strength training session makes you feel alive, alert, and physically satisfied. The adaptive hormonal response to strength training works like this: When you perform an intense workout, microtears occur in the proteins that control the muscle contractions. The muscle that has received the exercise stimulus sends a message to the brain that it needs some extra protein to heal the tears and rebuild itself even stronger in order to withstand a similar future assault. Consequently, growth hormone and testosterone flow through the bloodstream to supervise the rebuilding process. Growth hormone, responsible for growing young bodies to adult size, promotes vitality at any age by regenerating muscle mass, bone, cartilage, hair, nails, and skin. Growth hormone stimulates deeper sleep, and even helps you shed excess body fat. Testosterone influences energy, motivation, cognitive focus, and libido, and also plays a central role in recovery, fat metabolism, and the maintenance of a lean, fit body. This is the case for both men and women, even though men operate with twenty times more testosterone than women.

These benefits make strength training, as well as sprinting, particularly important to do when you are 35 and up, because blood levels of these and other adaptive hormones decline steadily with age. Senior citizens take note: It's never too late to tap into the benefits of strength training. Older adults devoted to a progressive (increasing degree of difficulty over time) strength training regimen were able to put up some impressive numbers. They can boost plasma sex hormone levels to match that of much younger unfit subjects. At Dr.

Marcas Bamman's Center for Exercise Medicine at the University of Alabama, Birmingham, strength trainers in their 60s and 70s were able to develop muscles of size and strength at or above an average 40-year-old.

On the other hand, if you neglect strength training, your decline accelerates at an alarming rate. Dr. Bamman states that skipping strength training causes you to lose 30 to 40 percent of your muscle fibers by the time you're 80. What's more, the muscle fibers that do stick around will shrink and atrophy. Your hormone values will tank in accordance with your decline in strength. So will your bone density, mitochondrial function, cognitive function, and ability to withstand all forms of life stress. Perhaps most harrowing is your increased risk of injury. Stuff you may take for granted now, such as scrambling down a hillside trail, chasing grandkids around the play structure at the park, or balancing on a ladder to clean out your rain gutter (bad idea even for strong people; hire a professional instead!) become opportunities for serious injuries. In Pillar #2, you will learn about the safest, most basic and hassle-free way to introduce strength training with the Primal Essential Movements.

PLAY FOR LONGEVITY

The idea of play as a longevity strategy has been almost entirely overlooked in our high-productivity society, but it is one of the most urgent genetic disconnects to correct today. Dr. Stuart Brown, psychiatrist, author of *Play: How It Shapes the Brain, Opens the Imagination, and Invigorates the Soul*, and founder of the National Institute for Play in San Diego, calls play a "profound biological process." He explains that play, across the span of a lifetime, promotes the development and maintenance of a "cognitively fluid mind." Possessing a cognitively fluid mind—being able to go with the flow, think outside the box, process what-if scenarios, and react quickly and effectively to changes in our environment—is believed by anthropologists to represent one of the most profound breakthroughs in the history of human evolution. This increased sophistication in brain function, probably emerging around 60,000 years ago, meant that humans' brains could link knowledge from different domains. The way humans understood and approached the world became both more flexible and more expansive. This enabled more creative use of technology, better transfer of knowledge between generations, and a resultant spike in longevity.

As it did for our ancestors, a playful life means a longer, more enjoyable life. Play allows you to break free from the linear, goal-oriented, tightly wound mindset that is demanded in today's fast-paced, hyperconnected economy. It's an antidote to the obsessive calorie burning, regimentation, and self-quantification that characterizes the fitness scene. Play encourages spontaneity, creativity, free expression, and an enhanced appreciation for being out in sunlight, fresh air, and open space, stimulating your mind and moving your body. Play also enhances intimate relationships by injecting humor, lightheartedness, vulnerability, imagination, and ultimately a deeper sense of connection than you might experience when sharing routine daily events. Reading between the lines, play serves as an overlay to enhance the benefits of numerous other endeavors in the pillars. For example, nurturing loving relationships require "work," but they also require play for best results.

Learning disability specialist Dr. Lorraine Peniston enumerates many research-proven psychological benefits of play, including: increased sense of freedom, independence, creativity, adaptability, resiliency, and autonomy; enhanced self-worth, self-reliance, and self-confidence; better ability to socialize with others, including greater tolerance and understanding; a better sense of humor; and a more positive outlook on life. Conversely, Dr. Brown's research reveals that adults who are deficient in play demonstrate a narrowing of social, emotional, and cognitive intelligence. Without play, we become creatively stifled, less resilient to all forms of stress, and experience a narrowing of many elements of life that represent the essence of aging: fewer friends, fewer pastimes, less physical activity, less travel, less passion, less happiness, and accelerated aging.

MENTAL FLEXIBILITY

Mental flexibility is a concept that is of equal importance to metabolic flexibility when it comes to longevity. Mental flexibility makes you resilient for life in the same manner that metabolic flexibility makes you resilient enough to skip meals and remain energetic. Your thoughts can profoundly affect your brain and body chemistry at every moment, and cultivating a longevity mindset can become a self-fulfilling prophecy. Unfortunately, the more common manifestation of the mind-body connection is to form flawed and rigid beliefs that the genes you inherited from your parents determine your health destiny. We talk incessantly about family histories of heart disease and cancer predicting a similar fate for us, and make assorted rationalizations and excuses to validate these narrow, self-defeatist mindsets.

This line of thinking is known as *genetic determinism*, whereby genes are erroneously believed to be self-actualizing. As Bruce Lipton explains in *The Biology of Belief*, the concept of genetic determinism has been completely refuted by recent discoveries in the field of epigenetics—the study of how environment influences gene expression. In the reality we create with mental flexibility, virtually every genetic and hormonal function that influences health and longevity is a product of environmental signals combined with your perception of those signals.

Environmental signals can be food coming down the pipe, a workout stimulus such as lifting a weight, exposure to cold or hot temperatures, or the formation of a thought. All of our cells have extremely thin membranes with receptors that extend from the inside to the outside of the membrane. These receptors process signals from the environment, signals that are mediated by switches in the membranes, which Lipton calls *perception switches*. Our perception switches send signals to kick-start the process of transcription and translation as per the central dogma of molecular biology: DNA information in the cell's nucleus flows to the RNA, which interacts with ribosome—the protein-making machinery in your cells—to assemble the specific amino acids into the protein molecules required to make a liver cell, muscle cell, other highly specialized cells, as well as hormones, neurotransmitters, and enzymes.

If the perception switches in your cell membranes detect that you are having a lousy day, the victim of a traffic jam and a mean boss, then they will consult the blueprint's instructions for making stress hormones and tears of anguish, and gene transcription factors will manifest your tearful reality. If your perception switches detect that you are taking the opportunity of a traffic jam to engage in deep, diaphragmatic breathing and listen to a great audiobook, good vibes will literally permeate your being. You will instead produce mood-elevating neurotransmitters like serotonin and dopamine, along with a smile and a lightness in your step when you finally arrive at your destination.

When our perception switches trigger the protective response because of a traffic jam, mean boss, argument with a loved one, or fearful thought about your future, it literally has life-or-death repercussions. In *The Primal Prescription*, coauthor Dr. Doug McGuff references research published in the *Annals of Family Medicine* in 2013 about women who received false positive results on mammograms and had to sit in fear for a while until the accurate diagnosis came through. These women experienced the same level of psychosocial harm as those with cancer and it lasted for a full 6 months after they were cleared. Furthermore, negative health repercussions traced to the ordeal continued for 3 years. They don't call it a cancer scare for nothing! Whatever the circumstances that generate our negative thoughts, we might as well have a tiger chasing us for the level of destruction it causes to our "renewal" potential.

Similarly, when we harbor those all-too-common beliefs about genetic determinism, our perception switches will try hard to manifest thoughts into reality. Try this: The next time you utter, or receive, a harmless little quip along the lines of, "I feel old," or, "back in the day," or, "I can't do that anymore," take a deep breath and reflect for a moment. As the comment floats into the ether, might it influence your future habitual behavior? If you haven't done any pull-ups, nor run an 8-minute mile in a while, you might speculate that you can't do that anymore. You will be spot on! Granted, you can't get into 8-minute-mile shape just by thinking about it, but you can certainly adopt the belief that renewal is possible at any age, then go out and create the environmental signals to make it happen.

CULTIVATING A YOUTHFUL SPIRIT

Understanding how perception switches direct genetic and hormonal function is easy when you are talking about lifting weights to build stronger muscles, or how drinking a soda prompts inflammation and oxidative stress. Getting the mind right is where even the most devoted health enthusiasts often develop a blind spot. Dr. Deepak Chopra, in *Ageless Body, Timeless Mind* and many of his other works, cites extensive research that the cultivation and maintenance of a youthful spirit is perhaps the most profound longevity marker seen among disparate pockets of centenarians across the globe. *The Blue Zones* data reveals the same thing: healthy centenarians simply don't feel that old.

In 2018, Brad had the good fortune during a road trip across New York to get a haircut from the late Guinness World Record–holding oldest practicing barber, Mr. Anthony Mancinelli, of Newburgh, New York. (Mancinelli passed in September 2019 at age 108). He cut hair for ninety-seven years from age eleven until just before his death. He worked the usual 40 hours a week, drove himself to work every day, and lived alone without assistance. On his off time, he would shop, prepare meals, do chores, and relax self-sufficiently. Brad found Mancinelli to be sharp as a tack, engaging in playful banter while working (you just need to speak a little louder than normal), and could have easily pass for 80, maybe 85 at the most. While Mancinelli reveled in the attention and had ready-made sound bites for interviewers ("I maintain my weight by eating skinny pasta"), his matter-of-fact answers revealed the true power of his youthful spirit. Why, of course he drives himself to work ("How else would I get here?"); of course he works 40 hours a week like everyone else.

Mancinelli discounted the influence of genetics, relating how his five brothers and sisters are long gone. He discounts medical care, too: "Why should I see a doctor? I feel fine." He took no regular medications, singlehandedly taking a chunk off of the shocking average of 18 prescriptions per year that Americans over 80 consume. Brad was most touched by what he saw as he was leaving the joint, after the podcast recording, photo ops, and goodbyes were complete: Mancinelli grabbed a broom and started sweeping up Brad's hair, working his way over to the neighboring stylist's station to clean up after her haircut as well. Just another day at the shop.

Consider the optimism data from the highly regarded Nurses' Health Study, one of the largest and longest-duration epidemiological studies in health science. The study has tracked the lifestyle habits of over 120,000 nurses since 1976. One component of the study was a sophisticated questionnaire given to nurses in 2004 to calculate their "optimism score." Then, all-cause mortality was tracked between 2006 and 2012, revealing that "optimism was broadly and robustly associated with a lower risk of mortality." An interesting observation appears in the study results: "It has been demonstrated in randomized trials that optimism can be learned. If associations between optimism and broader health outcomes are established, it may lead to novel interventions that improve public health and longevity." Granted, studies with twins suggest that optimism is estimated to be around 25 percent heritable (from the Life Orientation Test examining twins reared both together and apart), but that means a pessimist started with a glass only one-quarter empty, not half empty!

If you can formulate an optimistic mindset toward longevity, you will pick off the lowest hanging fruit in the entire book. A longitudinal study from Yale tracked a group of 50-plus folks from a small town in Ohio for 23 years, comparing their health outcomes to their level of "self-perceptions of aging." Their scores came from answers to questions like, "As you get older, you are less useful," and the like. The results were nothing short of astonishing. Controlling for key factors like socioeconomic status, gender, loneliness, and functional health, those with a positive self-perception about aging lived an average of *7.5 years longer* than those with a negative self-perception about aging! That's right around the same return on investment as quitting smoking, as oft-cited stats suggest that quitting before age 35 will add 10 years, while quitting between ages 35 and 65 will add 5 years to life expectancy. As Medium.com writer Michael Simmons remarked in his article about the Yale study: ". . . changing our beliefs about aging might be the cheapest, simplest, and safest health intervention ever created."

These ideas have been validated by the groundbreaking work of the late Dr. Robert Butler, a longevity physician, gerontologist, psychiatrist, Pulitzer Prize winner, and founding director of the National Institute on Aging. Butler pioneered the study of *healthy* elderly folks, advancing the breakthrough conclusion that aging was certainly a risk factor for disease, but not the cause. Rather, most conditions associated with aging, particularly cognitive decline, are caused by disease, socioeconomic adversity, and health-compromising personality attributes and beliefs. You have a surprising amount of control over the rate at which you age!

If you are in your peak decades of energy output and earning power, you might be too young and too busy kicking butt to worry about cultivating a youthful spirit. However, if you aren't honoring the objectives in the other pillars, you may gradually realize that your youthful spirit has become diminished by cellular damage and the ensuing formation of damaging beliefs. Virtually everyone in modern society except extreme health-freak outliers is playing out this story in both mind and body. Think about the diminishing physical fitness prerequisites for your weekend warrior outings over the years, from the tackle football mud bowls in your 20s, to half-court pickup basketball in your 30s, to softball tournaments in your 40s, and then golf in a cart after that.

When you reach major life transitions like retirement or children leaving home, maintaining a youthful spirit becomes increasingly important—particularly amidst the pervasive ageism and peer influences that can discourage your good intentions. After all, attaching your identity solely to your economic contribution or greatest accomplishments (and judging others similarly)—is the essence of mental rigidity. For example, during my running days when my social and athletic lives were intertwined, I'd be introduced at parties as "Mark, the 2:18 marathoner." Not, "Mark, the guy whose favorite color is blue, loves the movie *Caddyshack*, and comes to California by way of a small fishing village in Maine," or anything of the sort. And I must admit, I enjoyed the distinction. But when you're constantly humming the greatest hits of your past, you aren't able to move forward.

It is an urgent priority to remain in growth and renewal mode no matter what, with both your thoughts and your actions. This stuff is not easy to execute, especially if you harbor some lingering skepticism from a lifetime of rigid programming. However, if you can focus on nailing the other three pillars, the benefits of eating nourishing foods, exercising, and getting enough sleep will help you to manifest a youthful spirit.

REST AND RECOVERY

I hope you are starting to realize the importance of working hard to optimize your diet and become fat- and keto-adapted, achieve the requisite amount of daily movement, stay physically fit with a sensible blend of aerobic and high-intensity workouts, and cultivate a youthful spirit. Oh yeah, and don't forget about enjoying life, with parties, travel adventures, engrossing hobbies, and nonstop digital entertainment offerings at your fingertips. Forget anything? Oh yes, balancing our hectic, hyper-stimulated modern existence with adequate rest, recovery, and downtime. You see, the aforementioned endeavors all promote healthy, awesome living, and they can counterbalance one another nicely (e.g., vigorous workout after a stressful day at the office), but they each represent a different form of stress to your mind and/or body.

The conventional use of the term "stress" is in a negative context, where it might be more accurately described as "overstress." In the context of striving for stress-rest balance in life, we must acknowledge that stressors can be negative and upsetting, or they can be positive and enjoyable. On the Holmes-Rahe scale of the most stressful life events, you'll see death of a loved one, divorce, and imprisonment up at the top, but also marriage, retirement, and even winning the lottery high up in the rankings. These high-stimulation events elicit the same fight-or-flight hormonal mechanisms as the negative stuff. Consequently, a comprehensive approach to longevity means you have to balance all of your health-promoting activities with sufficient downtime, as well as manage traumatic life events as best you can.

While this all sounds incredibly obvious, even devoted health enthusiasts seem to disrespect the importance of rest, recovery, and downtime. We view our vigorous workouts as a great stress release from the pressures of the workplace or looking after little ones all day. On one level, burning up nervous energy is a healthy coping mechanism, but we must acknowledge that both the hectic day at work and the awesome trail run you did afterward weigh down the same side of the scale of justice measuring stress-rest balance in your life. If you are unable to keep your scale in a general state of balance, big trouble ensues. It might be next week when you catch a cold. For an athlete, it might be next month when a knee or shoulder gives out. For the harried soccer mom, frequent flying hotshot executive, or CrossFit or triathlon freak, long-term overstress patterns can lead to chronic disease and dysfunction.

The connection between Type A overstress patterns and the assorted system-wide breakdowns that occur as a consequence are typically less obvious than partying too hard on spring break and coming home with a cold. These days, as any functional medicine practitioner can tell you, many burnout-type conditions escape conventional medical diagnosis and treatment: chronic fatigue syndrome, fibromyalgia, autoimmunity, thyroid dysfunction, leaky gut syndrome, SIBO (small intestinal bacteria overgrowth, aka yeast overgrowth), Lyme disease, and adrenal dysfunction among them. My email inbox is full of horror stories of high-energy, extremely successful people who have fallen apart, often suddenly and without warning, and face painful and prolonged reckoning and recalibration.

THE CONSTRAINED MODEL OF ENERGY EXPENDITURE

When we go and go, in pursuit of more and more, then collapse into bed and repeat the process the next day, we are essentially taking recovery for granted. Ditto for when we consider an hour-long gym workout to be a stress release from a hectic workday. There is a deeper dimension to rest and recovery as follows: Recovering from the physical and mental stress of a high-achieving life *requires energy in and of itself*! Restocking depleted muscle glycogen, refreshing the sodium-potassium pumps that allow your brain neurons to fire effectively, or returning inflammatory and homeostatic mechanisms into balance after a tough workout or a busy day are all energy-consuming processes. Even during the ultimate form of rest that is overnight sleep, all kinds of hormonal, cognitive, immune, and metabolic mechanisms are taking place that require energy.

To fully appreciate this truth, you might envision a pie chart representing the amount of energy you have available to expend in a given week. Pie cutter in hand, you will allocate generous slices to your lengthy commute and challenging job, household chores, childcare duties, community service efforts, or workout routine. However, you are also obligated to carve out a big slice for rest, recovery, and downtime. Two profound revelations should hit you right now: First, that you are actually obligated to cough up a precious slice of pie to rest, recovery, and downtime. Historically, we have thought of restoration in a separate dimension from the energy pie—like a whipped cream topping making your pie more delicious (i.e., giving you more energy)—instead of an actual slice.

The second revelation is that your energy expenditure is contained inside the borders of your pie. You see, no matter how hard you try to wake up earlier, burn additional calories in predawn workouts, or express your workaholic tendencies to get more done across the board, your body will engage in assorted mechanisms to economize and constrain to a certain daily maximum.

These counterintuitive concepts are validated by a landmark study of the Hadza, modern-day hunter-gatherers in Tanzania. The study was led by Herman Pontzer, PhD, an evolutionary anthropologist at Hunter College in New York City, and published in the *American Journal of Human Biology* in 2017. Researchers traveled to the African savannah and wired up participants with heart rate monitors and GPS units to track caloric expenditure during their days of virtual nonstop moderate physical activity: Hadza men walk 7 miles per day tracking game; women walk 3, picking berries and tubers at a feverish pace. The results were shocking: A subway-riding, office-working modern slacker burns a similar number of calories (controlling for age, gender, and body size) as our hard-working, primitive-living counterparts! Pontzer and his team concluded: "The similarity in [total energy expenditure (TEE)] among Hadza hunter-gatherers and Westerners suggests that even dramatic differences in lifestyle may have a negligible effect on TEE."

This idea is known as the "constrained model of energy expenditure," and counters the popular misconception that we operate in an "additive model of energy expenditure." With this flawed thinking that has long been entrenched in conventional wisdom, you erroneously believe that your 45-minute Spinning class burns extra daily calories that day, helping you lose excess body fat. It's difficult to accept that this simple and logical thought process is inaccurate, but this is what science and practical experience shows again and again. Perhaps you can reference days or time periods where you delivered an unusual amount of physical or cognitive effort, followed by a counterbalancing day or time period of energy preservation as a consequence? I reflect back to my triathlon days and admit I wasn't good for much of anything else on a day of a hilly 100-mile bike ride.

SLEEP: PERHAPS THE BIGGEST GENETIC DISCONNECT OF THEM ALL

For billions of years, the consistent rising and setting of the sun each day has driven the evolution and survival of nearly every life form on earth. This circadian rhythm governs our sleeping and eating patterns as well as the precise timing of important hormone secretions, brain wave patterns, and cellular repair and regeneration based on a 24-hour cycle.

Unfortunately, the delicate circadian-influenced hormonal processes have been decimated primarily by the introduction of artificial light and digital stimulation after dark, as well as other modern disruptors such as irregular bed and wake times, sleep medication, alcohol, junk food (particularly excess carbohydrates in the hours before bedtime), jet travel across time zones, graveyard and swing shift work, and alarm clocks. These extreme offenses to the human organism's billions of years of synchronicity with the sun have occurred only since the advent of the light bulb around 140 years ago. Modern humans are the only species ever to engage in deliberate sleep deprivation in the history of the planet, and things have escalated dramatically in the new millennium, with the ubiquitous use of portable screens for the first time ever. This genetic disconnect is battling neck and neck with the consumption of refined carbohydrates and seed oils for the distinction of the most health-destructive modern behavior. In fact, science confirms that you will die of sleep deprivation much sooner than you will die of starvation!

Today, healthy hormonal function and optimal restoration is no longer about sunset and sunrise, but rather when we decide to make it dark. Harvard School of Public Health researchers found that 40 percent of Americans get less than 5 hours of sleep, and 75 percent suffer from some form of sleep disorder. Even a lifestyle with slightly less than optimal sleep will adversely influence mood, concentration, memory retention, and productivity, and can lead to hypertension, increased stress hormone levels, irregular heartbeat, compromised immune function, sexual dysfunction, premature aging, certain cancers, and heart disease.

Dr. Matthew Walker, professor of neuroscience and psychology at UC Berkeley, and author of *Why We Sleep*, spouts a litany of disturbing stats about sleep deprivation. A week of sleeping 6 hours instead of the general recommendation of 7 to 8 distorts the function of 700 genes. A night of 4 hours sleep renders you legally drunk with respect to your cognitive abilities. Males who sleep 5 to 6 hours per night have testosterone levels of males 10 years their senior, and so on. Sleep deprivation is also associated with diminished emotional control ("the amygdala seems to be able to run amok," says Walker), rational thinking, problem solving, decision making, and working, declarative, and procedural memory.

A 2013 NIH sleep study with mice revealed that the distance between brain cells increases during sleep in comparison to being awake. The expanding space between brain cells enables a plumbing operation known as the *glymphatic system* to rapidly flush metabolic waste products that accumulate during a routine day of brain use. When you skimp on sleep, you are more likely to accumulate toxins that are directly associated with neurodegenerative disorders. While we've long known that memories are organized and embedded during sleep, recent studies of this nature help us realize that sleep also activates important detoxification processes. Skimp on sleep and you will experience compromised neurotransmitter firing and inflammation in the brain—the driving factor behind diseases of cognitive decline.

Sleep deprivation can also sabotage your devoted eating and exercise efforts to drop excess body fat. Dr. Rhonda Patrick mentions numerous studies on her podcasts and YouTube videos about how even short stints of sleep deprivation can cause impaired glucose tolerance and insulin resistance. One prominent study had brave University of Chicago student volunteers sleep 4 hours a night for 6 days. Their weeklong party binge (let's hope they somehow had some fun in the lab at night!) triggered adverse and wide-ranging health consequences: higher cortisol levels, higher blood pressure, drastically diminished immune function, and acute insulin resistance. Other studies revealed that just a single night of 4 hours of sleep causes acute insulin resistance, and dieting while sleep deprived results in 70 percent of any weight lost coming from lean mass, not fat.

If you feel overwhelmed at how many disparate objectives you have to tackle in order to enjoy an impressive healthspan and compressed morbidity, remember how taking baby steps in any pillar will make even seemingly unrelated lifestyle practices much easier. For example, most junk food binges happen late at night, so going to sleep on time helps prevent dietary transgressions. Athletes call this the cross-training effect—where a sprint workout helps your endurance performance, or a cardio workout helps your basketball game. If you are the highly motivated, goal-oriented type, perhaps your most valuable implementation of this concept is to emphasize that fourth pillar of Rest and Recovery. This will ensure you enjoy maximum benefits from your devoted efforts in Pillars 1, 2, and 3.

PILLAR #1: METABOLIC FLEXIBILITY

opefully, you are starting the *Keto for Life* journey with a decent level of metabolic flexibility thanks to some level of exposure and participation in the primal/paleo/keto/low-carb lifestyle movement that has come to prominence over the past decade. If not, we will certainly cover the low-hanging fruit (but not too much fruit—that's our first keto inside joke . . .) to reach 80 percent of longevity potential, and make sure you successfully escape from carbohydrate dependency. However, in order to stay focused on the longevity strategies, you are going to move quickly through the basic strategies so you can do a deep dive into that additional 20 percent of potential that a sophisticated approach to keto offers.

If you are currently in the crisis that is carbohydrate dependency, with adverse blood values like high glucose or high triglycerides, or are battling a chronic health condition, you must correct these issues before you strive for more ambitious longevity-related goals. The methodical approach to ditching carbohydrate dependency and becoming fat- and keto-adapted detailed in *The Keto Reset Diet* is a great homework assignment for you. Overall, the path to metabolic flexibility is straightforward, but it will take some focus and discipline to unwind decades of carb-dependency patterns and related social customs to transform into a fat- and ketone-burning beast. It's time to forget what you may have absorbed from flawed conventional wisdom over your lifetime and acknowledge that humans were not designed to eat regular meals, nor become habituated to constant snacking or wolfing down energy-boosting substances like sugar and caffeine (sorry, Starbucks). Rather, we evolved into lean, efficient metabolic machines, capable of generating the exact amount and type of fuel necessary to sustain peak cognitive and physical function at all times, whether we eat or not.

No matter your starting point right now, you can make steady progress one day at a time toward a healthier, happier, more energetic life. Reawakening your genetic potential for metabolic flexibility is as simple as ditching the big three most offensive foods from your diet—refined sugars, grains, and industrial seed oils—and allowing fat-burning mechanisms to reawaken. Granted, changing bad habits requires heightened awareness, discipline, and repetition. With diet, transformation is even more difficult because of the addictive properties of wheat, sugar, and high-carbohydrate eating patterns in general. However, becoming metabolically flexible is going to be easier than you think, because you will also escape from the psychological suffering and self-esteem hits caused by an energy-sapping, fat-storing, brain-fogging dietary pattern that is creating a big fat roadblock on the path to your dream body and dream life. Instead, you become sharper, happier, more productive, more patient, and less stressed. You will hardly ever feel hungry, due to the optimization of appetite and metabolic hormones. You will live the awesome life of a fat-burning beast!

Conveying a simple approach is important because we are wading into a subject that is rife with controversy, hype, misinformation, mischaracterizations, and heated debate among respected experts. The diet wars are enough to make even the most well-intentioned and focused health enthusiast wary and discouraged.

I want to correct course here by asserting that your path must be defined by personal preference instead of dogma. Of course, you'll want to honor some virtually indisputable big-picture guidelines for healthy eating. Bestselling author Michael Pollan sums it up beautifully in seven words: *Eat food, not too much, mostly plants.* Note that when Pollan says, "eat food," he is making a critical distinction between wholesome foods (i.e., natural plants that have been minimally altered from their natural state, as well as sustainably raised meat, fish, fowl, and eggs) and what he calls, "edible food-like substances"—the heavily processed sugars, sweetened beverages, grains, industrial seed oils, and feedlot animals that unfortunately comprise the majority of calories in the Standard American Diet (SAD). Loren Cordain, PhD, author of *The Paleo Diet* and one of the forefathers of the paleo movement, reports that 71 percent of the calories in the Standard American Diet come from modern processed foods that were nonexistent in paleolithic times.

Once you clean out the junk food and replace it with colorful, nutritious, wholesome foods, you can custom-design a sustainable and enjoyable eating strategy that you can honor for the rest of your life. Following is a quick overview of the strategic progression from carb dependency to attaining the highest level of metabolic flexibility through a sustained period of ketogenic eating, as detailed in *The Keto Reset Diet*. If you are already eating a keto-friendly diet, you will likely breeze through this commentary, but a little tune-up and review can't hurt. I'm amazed at the number of Keto Reset enthusiasts we engage with in our online community group and educational program who write in to express their frustration with weight-loss stalls, who then get the suggestion to more carefully track their food intake, macronutrient profiles, and exercise and sleep patterns, and write back in amazement that they were slacking more than they realized.

The material in this Pillar is organized into steps that escalate in their level of sophistication. You must take care of business out of the gate by getting fat- and keto-adapted before worrying about the advanced longevity foods, supplements, and strategies in the latter steps. What's more, you absolutely must start the 21-Day Biological Clock Reset with a high level of metabolic flexibility. This is evidenced by your ability to skip meals and maintain peak energy and cognitive function, and report a near-total elimination of bread, cookies, French fries, and other "evil big three" fare. We can't waste precious time on the basics if we are going for dramatic lifestyle transformation in a short time period during the Reset.

ESCAPE CARB DEPENDENCY, GET FAT- AND KETO-ADAPTED

The on-ramp of the highway to keto is escaping carbohydrate dependency with a total elimination of the big three toxic modern foods: refined sugars, grains, and industrial seed oils. You will replace these foods with your choice of nutrient-dense, keto-friendly plant and animal foods—the ancestral line-up of meat, fish, fowl, eggs, vegetables, fruits, nuts, and seeds, as well as certain nutritious modern foods such as high-fat dairy and high-cacao-percentage dark chocolate. This means we can still work together whether you're inclined to be vegetarian/vegan, or whether you like butter in your coffee and bacon in your omelets and salads—provided you ditch the nutrient-deficient, insulin-stimulating modern processed foods.

Due to the addictive properties of sugar, and the appetite-stimulating properties of modern-day wheat, it's best to make a cold-turkey commitment to completely eliminating the big three for 21 days. This will allow you to detox from whatever level of carbohydrate dependency or leaky gut syndrome you may have currently, and transition over to a nutrient-dense, insulin-balanced diet. What follows are some suggested foods to eliminate in each category. These agents have a way of sneaking into your diet because they are so commonplace, so apply the spirit of these lists and extend outside the boundaries as necessary. When in doubt, pass!

FOODS TO ELIMINATE

Sugar: Candy, candy bars, cake, baked sweets and treats, cookies, donuts, ice cream, milk chocolate, pie, sweeteners (agave, artificial sweeteners, brown sugar, cane sugar, evaporated cane juice, high fructose corn syrup, honey, molasses, powdered sugar, raw sugar, table sugar), popsicles, and other frozen desserts.

Sweetened beverages: Designer coffees (mochas, blended iced-coffee drinks); energy drinks (Red Bull, Rock Star, Monster); bottled, fresh-squeezed, and refrigerated juices (açai, apple, grape, orange, pomegranate, Naked Juice and Odwalla concoctions, Nantucket Nectar, Ocean Spray, V8); sweetened almond, rice, soy, and other nondairy milks; powdered drink mixes (chai-flavored, coffee-flavored, hot chocolate, lemonade, iced tea); soft drinks and diet soft drinks; sports performance drinks (Gatorade, Powerade, Vitamin Water); sweetened cocktails (daiquiri, eggnog, margarita); sweetened teas (Snapple, Arizona).

Grains: Cereal, corn, pasta, rice, and wheat; bread and flour products (baguettes, crackers, croissants, Danishes, donuts, graham crackers, muffins, pizza, pretzels, rolls, saltine crackers, swirls, tortillas, Triscuits, Wheat Thins); breakfast foods (Cream of Wheat, dried cereal, French toast, granola, grits, oatmeal, pancakes, waffles); chips (corn, potato, tortilla); cooking grains (amaranth, barley, bulgur, couscous, millet, rye); and puffed snacks (Cheetos, Goldfish, Pirate's Booty, popcorn, rice cakes).

Industrial seed oils: Bottled high polyunsaturated oils (canola, cottonseed, corn, soybean, safflower, sunflower, etc.); buttery spreads and sprays (Smart Balance, Promise); margarine and vegetable shortening; salad dressings and other condiments; processed foods in a bakery, box, wrapper, or frozen section; deep-fried fast food; most cooked restaurant meals (request meals cooked in butter, not oil).

Processed foods: Low- or nonfat dairy products, high-carbohydrate energy bars and grain-based snacks (granola bars, energy bars), frozen meals.

Low-quality foods from ancestral list: Prepackaged meat products, smoked/cured/nitrate-treated meats (bologna, ham, hot dogs, gas station jerky, pepperoni, salami, sausage); meat from concentrated animal feeding operations (CAFOs); conventional eggs (find pastured or at least organic); conventional produce transported from distant origins and out of season; and nuts, seeds, and their derivative butters that have been processed with offensive oils or sugary coatings.

When you are out with the old staples from the grain-based, high-carbohydrate, insulin-stimulating SAD diet, you can usher in your favorites from the following ancestral list and get into a pattern of eating nutritious, satisfying meals. Keep things simple at first and build momentum by picking a few favorites, such as a breakfast omelet and a lunch salad, and repeating them each day. This will eliminate decision fatigue and protect you from temptation when you allow yourself too many choices, such as occasional indulgences that have a way of becoming more frequent. Review the many great options in the Sample Keto Meals section (page 81) and the Longevity Superfoods section (below).

When you clean up your act and get insulin production under control, and dramatically increase the nutrient density of your diet, you will notice some life-changing benefits after a short time. Instead of relying upon your next carbohydrate dose to sustain energy and productivity, you will notice stable mood, appetite, and cognitive function between meals, and even if you delay or skip a meal. You will notice faster recovery from workouts, and feel less fried, inflamed, and agitated after a routine hectic day.

Note: If you are coming from significant metabolic damage from a lifetime of high-carb eating and yo-yo dieting, it may take several weeks for your fat-burning genes to kick in. If you struggle in efforts to break carbohydrate dependency, just indulge in the healthy, nutrient-dense ancestral foods as needed to keep you feeling satisfied and never struggling. Having a delicious omelet every morning for breakfast, a colorful salad for lunch, a handful of macadamia nuts or some celery sticks slathered in almond butter for an afternoon snack, and a delicious steak or salmon dinner with vegetables slathered in butter, with a few squares of dark chocolate for dessert doesn't sound too torturous, does it? Granted, transitioning from carb dependency to metabolic flexibility is not a time to be concerned with caloric restriction and fat reduction. First you have to turbo-charge your fat-burning engines and build excellent metabolic flexibility before you consider a fat-reduction strategy.

LONGEVITY SUPERFOODS

While the word "superfood" is a bit overhyped at times, let's discuss some truly exceptional, nutrient-dense, keto-friendly foods that promote health, particularly gut health, as well as longevity. We'll cover the obvious superstars like fresh fruits and vegetables, pastured eggs, organ meats, and oily, cold-water fish, and also uncover some unsung heroes that are deserving of a concerted effort to integrate into your diet.

FRESH PRODUCE

Brightly colored vegetables and fruits supply high levels of antioxidants, flavonoids, carotenoids, and myriad other important phytonutrients that serve as a powerful first line of defense against oxidative damage from aging, stress, and inflammation. These agents contain cancer-fighting properties, support immune function, aid in healthy digestion, and help protect against the oxidative stress that represents the essence of accelerated aging. Micronutrient-rich plants are especially protective for brain cells, retinal cells, and cardiovascular cells. These are some of the longest-lasting cells in the body, and are consequently more susceptible to oxidative damage. Berry consumption in particular has been shown to increase neuroplasticity—the ability of your brain to continually learn, grow, consolidate new memories and learning, and withstand age-related cognitive decline.

Strive to consume locally grown produce whenever possible, as this will alleviate objections about sustainability and inferior nutrition with produce transported from distant origins. A local farmer may not have official organic certification, but any interventions will be far less objectionable than mass-produced fruits and vegetables. Insist on local or certified organic produce for anything with a soft, edible skin (e.g., berries, leafy greens). If produce has a protective, inedible covering (e.g., melons, avocados), there is little or no risk of pesticide exposure, so organic is of less concern.

For a quick primer, red plants (beets, red bell peppers, radishes, red cabbage, pomegranates, cherries, watermelons) have been shown to help reduce the risk of prostate cancer as well as some tumors. Green fruits and vegetables (avocados, limes, bell peppers, zucchini) are high in antioxidants and phytonutrients, delivering potent anti-aging benefits and helping vision in particular. Avocados are a true superfood, delivering the many fruit-like antioxidant benefits, along with high levels of monounsaturated fats that boost memory and learning and enhance the absorption of other vitamins and minerals. The tyrosine in avocados helps boost the feel-good neurotransmitter dopamine.

Yellow and orange fruits and vegetables (oranges, papayas, carrots, butternut squash) offer high antioxidant and anti-inflammatory properties. Cruciferous ("cross"-shaped, with a branch and leaves) vegetables—including broccoli, Brussels sprouts, kale, arugula, turnips, bok choy, horseradish, and cauliflower—have demonstrated specific anticancer, antiaging, and antimicrobial properties. Nuts and seeds provide high levels of beneficial unsaturated fatty acids, fiber, phytonutrients, antioxidants (e.g., vitamin E and selenium), and a host of essential nutrients (e.g., manganese, magnesium, zinc, iron, chromium, phosphorous, and folate).

When it comes to fruit consumption, honor the ancestral spirit by consuming fruit only during the natural ripening season. Especially in the wintertime, avoid eating fruits that have been transported from distant origins. Realize that our modern cultivation and transport methods have resulted in grossly excessive year-round fruit intake. Especially in the context of a grain-based, high-carbohydrate Standard American Diet, fruit consumption can exacerbate the problem of excess insulin production and lifelong fat storage. In fact, fruit is considered the most *lipogenic* (fat-forming) carbohydrate source, because fructose (the predominant carbohydrate source in fruit) must be processed in the liver before it can be used for energy in the bloodstream. The liver is also where excess carbs are converted into fat, so your devoted efforts to eat zero-point foods will likely have you watching your weight increase!

Remember, our ancestral experience was to binge on fruit during narrow ripening periods in the summer or fall. Yes, we have a genetically programmed sweet tooth as a survival mechanism. Enjoying the fruit harvest would spike insulin, and trigger extra fat storage to survive the winter ahead—all good! Today, we artificially lengthen our days year-round with indoor light and have constant access to fruit, much of which has been overcultivated to be sweeter and larger than wild fruit. These dynamics trick our bodies into thinking we are in summer fat-storage mode at all times— not good!

Berries earn special distinction in the fruit family because they have the highest antioxidant values and lowest glycemic values. Pitted fruits (apricots, peaches, cherries; avocados count here, too), lemons, and limes are highly ranked also. Dried fruits and high-glycemic tropical fruits (dates, mangoes, papayas, pineapples, plums) are on the opposite end of the spectrum (high-glycemic, low-antioxidant) such that you might

just consider them "sugar." When you are in a strict ketogenic phase, fruit is pretty much off the table, unless you enjoy an occasional handful of truly high-quality, locally grown fresh berries.

"NOSE-TO-TAIL" ANIMAL FOODS

Sourcing grass-fed or pasture-raised animals and honoring the "nose-to-tail" consumption strategy has ascended into the mandatory category for today's devoted ancestral health enthusiast. We've heard enough disturbing stories about the negative greenhouse and ecological consequences of feedlot operations, the dispensing of hormones, pesticides, and antibiotics to these animals, and the harsh treatment at slaughter that fill the tissues of these animals with stress hormones. By contrast, sustainably raised animals have minimal environmental objections (some experts contend that free-roaming animals contribute a carbon net positive to their environment) and have a vastly superior nutritional and fatty acid profile. Widely cited reports state that pastured animals offer two to six times more omega-3 and monounsaturated fats than feedlot animals do.

We are also compelled to reclaim the ancestral and cultural tradition of consuming animal products in a nose-to-tail manner, instead of the typical narrow focus on lean, high-protein muscle meats. In particular, strive to consume "bone-in" cuts of meat and organ meats. The nose-to-tail concept that was the centerpiece of our ancestral diet has been widely disrespected in modern American cuisine. Part of this is due to irresponsible propaganda convincing us to avoid animal fats, while another part might be blamed on the fast-food culture and the consequent loss of generational cooking traditions. Today, we can look to authentic French or Latin cuisine to gain inspiration for reclaiming forgotten nose-to-tail traditions.

Consuming bone-in meats and bone broth (quality store-bought products or homemade) delivers a host of additional nutrients not found in muscle meats, including the all-important collagen (details in the supplements section, page 75), as well as *glycosaminoglycans*, a compound that helps repair and make new connective tissue. Bone-in meats and bone broth also deliver more calcium, magnesium, phosphorous, sodium, and other important micronutrients in comparison to muscle meats, due to the proximity of nutrient-rich bone and connective tissue material. Since meat on the bone delivers more fat than a typical preparation from lean muscle meat, and toxins concentrate in fat cells, it's especially important to source grass-fed when you choose bone-in cuts.

Make sure your bone broth is authentically derived from joint material. Your product should be gelatinous when refrigerated, indicating a rich supply of the aforementioned special agents. This contrasts with the inexpensive containers labeled chicken, vegetable, or beef broth (better described as "stock") that remain as liquids even when refrigerated. Make bone broth at home by slow-cooking leftover bones from your latest feast for 48 hours. This will release the beneficial compounds locked into the bone marrow. Bone broth will give you even more potent and concentrated doses of collagen and glycosaminoglycans, and many other vitamins and minerals, because you are extracting every last bit of nutrition from the original meal.

In addition to the connective tissue benefits, bone broth has been shown to help combat leaky gut (glutamine helps intestinal cells produce beneficial mucus to strengthen gut lining), alleviate cold symptoms (the amino acid cysteine helps clear mucus, opens respiratory pathways), facilitate good sleep (due to the amino acid glycine), and deliver an anti-inflammatory effect. Due to its gut-healing properties, bone broth has become a featured element of the Gut and Psychology Syndrome (GAPS) healing protocol. GAPS has been shown to be highly effective in managing depression, anxiety, ADHD, and autism spectrum conditions, likely owing to the fact that the mood-elevating neurotransmitters dopamine and serotonin are produced mainly in the intestinal tract.

You can make your own bone broth using a chicken or turkey carcass, or bones from your steak. Joint material is the best, and it's also inexpensive at the butcher! Dump your bones into a slow cooker or Instant Pot, along with assorted vegetables, exotic spices and flavorings (tomato paste is popular), some apple cider vinegar to help with the extraction of cartilage and marrow from the bones, and extra water or stock to cover the bones. Cook in the slow cooker on Low for 48 hours, or on High pressure in an Instant Pot for just 3 hours. Strain the liquid into a container and discard the bones. You'll know you succeeded when you refrigerate your product and it turns gelatinous. Try this ultranutritious morning drink from *The Paleo Primer* coauthors and Fitter Food.com health coaches Keris Marsden and Matt Whitmore: Heat a couple cups of bone broth in a pan, then stir in 2 to 3 egg yolks!

There are more and more quality bone broth products in the fridge or freezer at quality grocers, but you must read labels carefully to avoid the watered-down products. Sharon Brown, holistic nutritionist and founder of a bone broth company called Bonafide Provisions, says to look for organic products with "bones" on the ingredient list and a long cooking time specified on the label. Be prepared to spend significantly more for a quality bone broth product than an inferior one.

Organ meats have more nutrient density than virtually any other food on the planet, rich in B vitamins, iron, zinc, magnesium, selenium, hard-to-obtain choline, and fat-soluble vitamins (A, D, E, and K). Evolutionary biologists assert that it was the ability to cook and consume the concentrated nutrition found in organ meats and nose-to-tail animal foods in general that helped the human brain grow much larger and more complex in only a few thousand generations. This was the key factor— the key to branching up and away from our mostly vegetarian ape cousins.

Organ meats are a centerpiece of world cuisine, particularly the French cuisine that is lauded by foodies as both nutritionally superior and more gourmet than a certain sovereignty known for burgers, fries, and apple pie. (Check out *The Bordeaux Kitchen* by Tania Teschke for an immersion into French food, wine, and culture, and great recipes.) It's time to branch out into the wonderful world of offal that's anything but awful. Liver is the most popular organ meat, and the concentration of nutrients earns it the nickname "nature's multivitamin." Other popular consumable organs are heart, kidney, brain (rich in omega-3s, just like our brains!), sweetbread (from the thymus or pancreas), and tripe (stomach lining). If you're a kitchen novice unsure how to cook organs, or don't immediately swoon over the taste of liver, you can start by pureeing some liver and/or kidney into your hamburger patties and frying up the infused burgers as usual. Try frying up some tongue or heart if you want a milder flavor. The popular Mexican soup menudo uses the very chewy tripe, along with beef feet and tendons, to obtain its distinctive flavor.

If you are a devoted keto enthusiast but not quite on your A-game with organ meats or collagen-rich bone-in cuts, it's time to raise the bar. Dr. Cate Shanahan, whose *Deep Nutrition* tome is credited as a major catalyst for the ancestral health movement, goes so far as to label offal as one of the "Four Pillars of World Cuisine": Fresh foods (fruits, vegetables, nuts, seeds, etc.), fermented foods, meat on the bone, and organ meats. I have met many hard-core ancestral health enthusiasts over the years who report falling embarrassingly short in three of those four food groups!

EGGS

Eggs have been a centerpiece of the human diet for a couple million years, and one of the most nutrient-dense foods on the planet. Most of the spectacular nutritional benefits are contained in the yolk, with abundant B vitamins, choline, and folate. Forget the outdated cholesterol scares or ridiculous egg white recipe alternatives. All the major longitudinal studies refute egg scares, including a Harvard Medical School study of 115,000 subjects that showed no correlation between egg consumption and disease.

Pastured eggs are vastly superior to mass produced eggs, because these chickens consume a nutrient-rich omnivorous diet of bugs, lizards, and worms, and produce eggs with up to ten times more omega-3s than conventional eggs. One look at the distinctive orange-tinted yolk (from beta-carotene) of a pastured egg compared to the dull, opaque appearance of a conventional egg tells the story, and you will also appreciate the incredible flavor intensity of a pastured egg. Where pastured eggs used to be a difficult-to-find treasure from local hobbyists or farmers' markets, brands like Vital Farms are finally achieving national distribution. Of course, you will pay significantly more per dozen for a pastured egg, but this is still perhaps the single most affordable and impactful dietary upgrade you can make—a no-brainer! As you become a connoisseur of finer eggs, try branching out into other types of eggs, such as duck, emu, goose, ostrich, pheasant, or quail. These less pop-ular options will be free from the objections that come with mass-produced chicken eggs.

FISH

Fish and marine life have been a centerpiece of the human diet and the driving success factor for our ability to leave our origins in East Africa and colonize the entire globe over the past 60,000 years. Fish offer high levels of the omega-3 fatty acids DHA and EPA that are not present in most other foods. They are an excellent source of complete protein; high in vitamins B, D, and E; and rich in selenium, zinc, iron, magnesium, phosphorous, and many other antioxidants and micronutrients. Fish deliver potent cardiovascular and anti-inflammatory benefits as well or better than any other food group on earth.

It's important to choose wisely to alleviate concerns about heavy metal toxicity in certain fish, sustainability concerns with commercial fishing practices, and potential health objections of consuming industrialized farmed fish. In general, oily-fleshed cold-water fish offer the most health benefits, fewest objections about sustainability or pollutants, and are also the most affordable.

Make the SMASH hits a centerpiece of your diet: Sardines, Mackerel, Anchovies, Salmon (wild-caught), and Herring! These cold-water fish are omega-3, antiaging, anti-inflammatory power-houses. Beyond the high omega-3 levels, they are among the most nutritious foods on the planet, with a robust profile of important vitamins, minerals, and antioxidants. Choose from these convenient, affordable fish for a great salad centerpiece or as snack and travel foods. Regular fish consumption has been found to protect against heart disease, cognitive decline, many cancers, and inflammatory and autoimmune conditions.

Beyond the SMASH category, the shellfish family of clams, crab, lobster, mussels, oysters, shrimp, and scallops shine as great choices due to their incredible nutrient density. The extra zinc, magnesium, and B12 in these foods give them a reputation as testosterone boosters. In general, strive to consume fish from remote, pollution-free waters. Certain farmed fish are approved because they are raised in sanitary conditions and have similar nutritional profiles to their wild counterparts. These include mussels, scallops, oysters, catfish, tilapia, domestic trout.

Here are some categories of fish you should mostly avoid:

- Asian imports: Includes both farmed and wild-caught, due to concerns about polluted waters, lax chemical regulations, and long transit time.
- Farmed fish: Farmed Atlantic salmon is objectionable because it is so heavily produced; likely fed dioxins, pesticides, antibiotics, industrial seed oils, and color dye; and living in cramped, dirty conditions. Unfortunately, farmed Atlantic salmon represents some 90 percent of restaurant and store offerings. Choose only salmon specified as wild-caught. *Note*: Atlantic is the species of fish, not the lo-

cation. Wild-caught salmon come mainly from Pacific waters or inland rivers, with species like chinook, chum, coho, pink, and sockeye.

- Processed fish: Stay away from packaged/boxed products that have been breaded and/or contain numerous hard-to-pronounce ingredients on the label.
- Sustainability concerns: Avoid endangered fish or fish caught with intrusive techniques.
- Top of the food chain: Swordfish, shark, marlin, king mackerel, large tuna, and other heavy hitters have the most toxicity concerns.

Visit MontereyBayAquarium.org or the Marine Stewardship Council (msc.org) for details on approved fish and fish to avoid.

SUSHI

As a centerpiece of the longevity-lauded traditional Japanese diet, fresh fish eaten in raw form gives you a significant nutrition boost over cooked fish. While some concern is warranted about exposure to contaminants, finding a reputable sushi restaurant minimizes your risk. Choose wild-caught fish from pollution-free waters, and stay away from the high-mercury-risk fish at the top of the food chain (swordfish, marlin, shark).

The white rice that accompanies sushi can become a healthy choice when it's consumed at room temperature or cooler. When white rice is eaten "cooked and cooled," its molecular makeup changes from a high-glycemic carbohydrate, and becomes a *resistant starch*, also known as prebiotic fiber. Resistant starch passes through the digestive tract and takes up residency in your colon as good bacteria. Fermented foods like miso, natto, and soy sauce, and assorted vegetable offerings such as seaweed salad, also contribute to the top score for a sushi meal. Even the thin sheets of nori (flattened dried seaweed) are packed with nutrition, including the hard-to-obtain iodine, which supports healthy hormone function. Outside of the offerings at your favorite sushi restaurant, look for salmon roe or salmon caviar in finer grocery stores or on the Internet. Wild-caught salmon roe is in the running for the prize of "if you could eat only one food the rest of your life, what should it be?"

FERMENTED AND SPROUTED FOODS

Fermented (aka cultured) foods are the probiotic superstars, helping you maintain the healthy intestinal microbiome that is so crucial to digestive, immune, cognitive, and hormonal functions throughout the body. For example, an estimated 90 percent of the mood-elevating neurotransmitter serotonin is produced in the intestinal tract. Fermentation is an ancient food-processing and preservation technique whereby live microorganisms like yeast and bacteria convert carbohydrates into alcohol or acids. For example, grapes ferment into alcohol, and milk ferments into cheese or yogurt. The process enables harmful agents to be eliminated from certain foods and/or allows foods to remain edible and unspoiled for a long period of time. For these reasons, fermented and sprouted foods have been a centerpiece of the human diet for eons. Unfortunately, with the relatively recent advent of refrigeration and industrialized food processing, we can easily bypass this important nutritional category entirely.

Fermented, cultured, or sprouted foods contain high levels of live "probiotic" organisms that take up residence in your digestive tract when consumed. These "good" bacteria help protect you against undesirable pathogens (aka "bad" bacteria) that can hijack your digestive tract and promote both acute illness and long-term disease. There are many great options for fermented foods, so find a few or more favorites and integrate them into your diet: apple cider vinegar, cheese, kefir, kombucha drinks, miso, natto, olives, pickles, salami (uncured), sauerkraut, tempeh, wine, and yogurt (full-fat).

If you are going to eat anything that is a seed (including grains, legumes, nuts, and seeds), strive to find sprouted varieties of these products to enhance the nutritional value and deactivate potentially harmful antinutrients such as gluten and other lectin proteins that are difficult to digest for humans. Sprouting is the process of germinating the seed by soaking it in water, much like what happens in nature when seeds are watered, which causes the embryo of the seed to "sprout" out of its encasement. Sprouting converts starch into fiber, amino acids, and vitamins, and neutralizes so-called enzyme inhibitors. These agents protect the seed from environmental stress before it has the chance to sprout, but are difficult for many if not most of us to digest. Sprouting is essentially predigesting food to make it more nutritious and easier to absorb without complications.

As you improve your intake of probiotic-rich foods, realize that probiotics also need nourishment in the form of *prebiotics* (aka "resistant starch") in order to survive and thrive. Prebiotics are indigestible agents present in certain foods or supplements that nourish the healthy bacteria already living in your digestive tract. Instead of being processed like regular food calories, resistant starch travels through the small intestine unscathed and into the colon. There, friendly bacteria called *bifidobacteria* metabolize these special starches into a short-chain fatty acid called butyrate, which is the prime energy source for your colonic cells. Butyrate communicates with your immune system, helping to regulate inflammatory processes.

Resistant starch consumption has also been shown to reduce fasting blood sugar and boost insulin sensitivity (promoting lower body fat and increased lean mass); improve the integrity of your gut lining (protecting against autoimmune and inflammatory conditions associated with leaky gut); and help improve thyroid function, sleep quality, and mood stability. Prebiotics are present in an assortment of fruits and vegetables, but the best sources are green bananas, cooked and cooled white rice and russet potatoes, or raw potato starch (added as a supplement to smoothies or soups). When the rice and potatoes are eaten in cooked and cooled form, their molecular composition changes to make them indigestible (resistant)—no calories, no insulin response, just nourishment for your gut bacteria. Once you heat them up, they transform into high-glycemic carbohydrates! Ditto for what happens to a green banana as it ripens.

DARK CHOCOLATE

High-cacao-percentage dark chocolate is a longtime favorite among primal/paleo/keto enthusiasts as a delicious and nutritious substitute for sugary snacks and desserts. Strive to consume bars with 80% cacao or higher, understanding that the higher cacao percentage, the lower the sugar content. Dark chocolate is rich in antioxidants, phytonutrients, and flavonoids. Raw cacao beans are among the highest-scoring antioxidant foods ever tested—higher than blueberries!

Dark chocolate's unique compounds have been found to improve blood flow to the brain, elevate mood, and protect against cognitive decline. One such compound is *phenylethylamine*, a powerful opioid peptide that increases alertness and produces a feeling of well-being and contentment similar to the feeling of falling in love. Another, *epicatechin*, stimulates the production of nitric oxide (NO), helping your arteries become more relaxed and supple. The longest-lived human in history, Jeanne Calment of France, who lived to the age of 122 (1875 to 1997), reportedly consumed a kilo (2.2 pounds) of chocolate per week! Examine your bar labels to favor "bean-to-bar" products, with cacao beans as the lead ingredient, to ensure maximum purity and certainty of origin. Look for the "Fair Trade" designation to ensure farmers were fairly treated and compensated. Expect to pay $3 and up *per ounce* of quality chocolate, recognizing that discount products are very likely the product of child labor and/or inequitable farmer compensation.

NUTS, SEEDS, AND THEIR DERIVATIVE BUTTERS

Nuts and seeds are concentrated "life force" foods, packed with protein, fatty acids, enzymes, antioxidants, and abundant vitamins and minerals. For people in transition from carbohydrate dependency, they are a convenient and satisfying snack option. Numerous respected studies (Iowa Women's Health Study of 40,000 women, Harvard School of Public Health's Nurses' Health Study of 127,000 women, and Physicians' Health Study of 22,000 men are among the most prominent) suggest that regular consumption of nuts significantly reduces the risk of heart disease, diabetes, and other health problems. Strive to find nuts that have been minimally processed, such as raw nuts or dry-roasted nuts. Take care to avoid the many nut products that come in cans, jars, or jugs that often contain refined polyunsaturated industrial seed oils. Don't worry about sourcing organic products, because their hard outer shells protect nuts and seeds from pesticide concerns. Heed the concerns from ancestral health enthusiasts about overdoing nut consumption.

COCONUT PRODUCTS

Coconut is an excellent source of a special type of fat—medium-chain triglyceride, or MCT—that is difficult to find even in a healthy diet. MCT is known to offer protection from heart disease, cancer, diabetes, and many other degenerative illnesses; to improve fat metabolism; to protect against liver damage from alcohol and other toxins; and to deliver anti-inflammatory and immune-supporting benefits. MCT is also known to turbo-charge internal ketone production in the liver, which makes bottled MCT oil a popular supplement for coffee or smoothies among keto enthusiasts.

Integrating coconut products (oil, milk, cream, butter, flakes, and flour) into your diet provides a variety of health benefits and can conveniently replace SAD foods such as milk, wheat flour, and polyunsaturated cooking oils. Due to its high saturated fat content, coconut oil is resistant to oxidation and free radical formation, even when heated to high temperatures during cooking. Coconut butter is hard to find in the store but is one of the great delicacies of life. Incredibly rich and satiating, it can be a fantastic alternative to sugary treats for those transitioning out of a grain-based, high-carbohydrate diet.

HERBS AND SPICES

Herbal extracts have been used for thousands of years in Eastern medicine and continue to enjoy widespread popularity today for their powerful immune- and health-supporting properties. Spices, on the other hand, are typically dried seeds, fruits, and plant parts. Spices are used to enhance flavor, add color, or help prevent bacterial growth on food. There is compelling evidence that herbs and spices offer an assortment of cardiovascular, immune system, and metabolic benefits, including improved cognition and cancer prevention. Some of the highest antioxidant values (from ORAC—oxygen radical absorbance capacity—scores) among all foods can be found in herbs and spices. Two of the best known are turmeric—the anti-inflammatory superstar—and cinnamon, which has antibacterial, anti-inflammatory, antioxidant, and blood glucose regulation benefits.

FINE TUNING METABOLIC FLEXIBILITY

After your initial effort to ditch the big three offenders and emphasize ancestral foods, you will engage in a fine-tuning period marked by fasting in the morning until WHEN—When Hunger Ensues Naturally. If you can comfortably last until 12 noon (from your last meal finishing around 8 p.m. the previous evening), experiencing peak cognitive and physical function and no suffering, you are demonstrating a respectable level of metabolic flexibility such that you are ready to commence a formal nutritional ketosis effort. In *The Keto Reset Diet* book, I even present a midterm exam (passing score, 75 percent!), where you rate your success with assorted metabolic flexibility attributes:

ditching the big three offensive foods, getting adequate daily movement, optimizing sleep, and more.

Essentially, what you are striving for during the fine-tuning period is a graceful ability to not just survive from 8 p.m. to 12 noon the following day without any calories, but actually thrive. This could include conducting a good morning workout, or a busy morning carpooling kids and cranking away at the office, and having stable energy, appetite, mood, and cognitive function. Anyone can last till noon without eating on a wager, but if you force yourself to fast without sufficient metabolic flexibility, you will often experience some fallout: carbohydrate binges in the evening or a crash and burn experience after 3 weeks of inauthentic fasting. When fasting comfortably for 16 hours becomes routine (not necessarily every single day, but easily achieved for several days in a row), that's when you know you are ready for keto. Speaking of fasting, let's define the term literally as consuming zero calories—just drinking water, black coffee, or tea. The practice of dumping hundreds of fat calories into a morning coffee is essentially your break-fast—even if it's not an actual meal.

Speaking of fats and keto, the practice of deliberately stuffing your face with extra fats in an effort to promote ketosis has unfortunately become a popular strategy. This is a ridiculous bastardization of the ancestral legacy behind ketosis, which we evolved as a survival mechanism to keep the human brain functioning optimally even when we were starving. Similarly, witness the popularity of something called "dirty keto," where you are allowed to consume assorted nutrient-deficient foods and snacks as long as they align with the high-fat, moderate-protein, low-carb keto guidelines. One example I noticed on the Internet entailed taking diet orange soda, adding ice and heavy cream, and whipping up into a slushy creamsicle-style drink. Just like our ancestors did . . . not!

The most appropriate time for a purposeful consumption of additional fat calories, such as a high-fat coffee or a snack of macadamia nuts, is when you are in the early stages of escaping carb dependency and want to prevent a backslide. Also, for those who come to keto with a history of metabolic damage or hormone dysfunction, some experts will recommend strategic consumption of additional fats to avoid triggering fight or flight by fasting.

Alas, if you are metabolically healthy and trying to lose excess body fat, you are still compelled to create a deficit between the calories you consume and the calories you burn. Keto makes it easier because it regulates your appetite at the hormonal level, and allows for the easy access and burning of stored body fat. Ketogenic eating also has profound appetite and hormonal regulation properties such that you can fast with more frequency and for longer duration without the fight-or-flight stimulation that might occur when you are not metabolically flexible. A true keto expert is someone who can survive and thrive on an optimally minimal number of calories and optimally minimal amount of insulin production over a lifetime.

SIX-WEEK KETO JOURNEY

The final stage of the Keto Reset journey is to embark upon a focused stint of ketogenic eating for a minimum commitment of 6 weeks. Here are the necessary elements of a proper foray into nutritional ketosis:

Carbs: Carbohydrate intake must be strictly limited to 50 grams of gross carbs per day or below. This entails zero grains and sugars, little or no fruit or starchy tubers (sweet potatoes), abundant consumption of above-ground vegetables, and incidental carbs from nuts and seeds, dark chocolate, and high-fat dairy products. Since a typical ancestral-style eater who eliminates grains and sugars might consume 150 grams of nutritious carbs in a day, keto entails a narrowing of your options into mostly vegetables. *Note*: The 50-gram limit assumes you are moderately to highly active, otherwise your limit is 20 grams. Also, you don't have to count leafy greens or avocados toward your gross carb total.

Protein: Strive for an average daily protein consumption of 0.7 grams per pound (or 1.54 grams per kilo) of lean body mass. This is pretty easy to attain with a typical ancestral eating pattern featuring a variety of clean-sourced, nose-to-tail animal products. You don't need to go looking for extra protein via supplements or by avoiding egg yolks or high-fat cuts of meat.

Fat: Natural, nutritious fats become your main source of dietary calories and satiety: meat, fish, fowl, and eggs; high-fat plants such as avocado, olive, and coconut; nuts, seeds, and nut butters; high-fat dairy products like cheese and full-fat yogurt or milk; and high-cacao-percentage dark chocolate.

Fasting: A devotion to fasting and eating in a compressed time window (such as 12 p.m. to 6 p.m.) should be the centerpiece of your keto effort. Best results with keto come through restriction of both carbs and total calories. Don't buy into the hype about keto as a bacon and butter fat-fest. Eat only as much food as you need to feel satisfied at all times and protect against the carb binges that arise from too much deprivation and suffering.

Exercise/movement/sleep/stress management: You must complement your macronutrient efforts with a comprehensive lifestyle approach that promotes successful fat burning and helps you escape from carb dependency. Lack of daily movement compromises fat burning and promotes insulin resistance and sugar cravings. Chronic workouts compromise fat burning, spike stress hormones, and prompt sugar cravings. Even a tiny bit of missed sleep can screw up fat metabolism and push you back in the direction of carbohydrate dependency. Ditto for when life gets hectic and stressful, promoting fight-or-flight dominance and carbohydrate dependency.

Let's call this 6-week keto journey a bucket-list item for everyone, because completing it will deliver benefits that will last for a lifetime. It's essential for you to commit to a 6-week keto timeline out of the gate. This will ensure that you have the patience to ride out any bumps in the road and also enjoy the maximum benefits of your keto effort over the long run. Unfortunately, many keto enthusiasts bail out before 6 weeks, especially on their first attempt. Typically, this is due to a flawed approach, such as not having a sufficient fat-burning baseline, not consuming enough sodium and other key minerals and electrolytes, or doing excessive exercise.

Even if keto eating strategies and complementary lifestyle behaviors are dialed in, you may experience some difficulty in the first few weeks of keto. You may have heard of the disturbing side effect of ketone breath. This occurs when your liver is prompted to make ketones but you are not yet able to burn them efficiently. Instead, the precious, energy-rich molecules are excreted through breath and urine; that's why darkening ketone urine strips is a misguided goal: It indicates you are wasting ketones! Ketone breath is described charitably as fruity, or more bluntly as something akin to nail polish remover or paint thinner. The latter is literally accurate because the metabolic by-product of the two types of ketones your body makes (called beta-hydroxybutyrate and acetoacetate) is acetone—the same stuff that goes into the commercial solvent products.

Breakthroughs often occur when you persevere past the 3-week mark. Your fat-burning engines kick into high gear, your ketone production and utilization is optimized (eliminating the bad breath), and the afternoon blues and lingering sugar cravings fade away. For fitness enthusiasts, what happens after a few weeks of diligent keto eating is that the muscles and brain stop competing for precious energy sources in the absence of glucose. The muscles get better at burning fatty acids, allowing the ketones made in the liver to be preferentially used by the brain. Accordingly, both workout performance and afternoon blues improve substantially. This is why it's a good idea to scale back your overall workout energy expenditure in the first few weeks of keto. All this is to say, resolve to stick it out for 6 weeks no matter what, and things will get better with each passing week. Remember, if you are struggling with cravings or energy lulls, feel free to satisfy yourself with satiating high-fat meals and snacks.

After completing the Keto Reset journey in its entirety, you will have reprogrammed your genes back to the *Homo sapiens* default factory setting of fat- and keto-adapted. If you happen to binge on cake and ice cream at a kid's birthday party, or indulge in treats over and over during a weeklong cruise, you should be able to gracefully weather the insulin storms and easily recalibrate back to fat burning. All you have to do is string together a series of keto-aligned meals or fasting stints and you will be back in the keto groove.

Granted, you can only pull off these smooth and easy recalibrations once you have done the hard work to prepare properly for, as well as complete, a 6-week keto exercise. When you lower insulin by fasting and/or limiting carb intake, you will start burning fat and making ketones as needed. Even if the worst-case scenario occurs and you purposely backslide into pizza and ice cream binges for months on end, all you have to do is repeat the process of ditching refined sugars, grains and seed oils for a few weeks, fasting until noon until you feel very comfortable, and then a 6-week stint of keto. You can feel confident that your fat-burning genes will awaken again and again, because they have been honed and hardwired through 2.5 million years of evolution.

In contrast, a carb-dependent dieter who wants to right the ship after excessive indulging during a cruise can expect temporary success only. Portion control and vigorous exercise might take off several pounds of inflammation and water retention weight, and even a few pounds of body fat, but the depleting effects of these crash diets will play out over the long run. As long as glucose is the default energy source and fat is inaccessible, you'll activate the fight-or-flight response to make up for any dietary glucose deficits, and you'll eventually overeat and gain the weight back in an effort to recover from depletion and fight-or-flight exhaustion. By using the sample meals at the end of this section as a guideline, you'll be able to stay the course without any problems.

LONGEVITY SUPPLEMENTS

Capsules, powders, potions, and lotions promising longevity have been a robust industry for over a century. We are all suckers for the fountain of youth storyline, as it ain't easy to sit back and absorb the steady decline in our energy and vitality that happens as the calendar pages turn. With the powerful influence of product marketing, we can easily become convinced that we need to swallow a few pills or blend up a magical smoothie to replace something that's missing.

It's important to evolve beyond any sort of desperation mindset and realize that there are definitely no magic potions, that the more amazing a product claim is, the more likely it's unsubstantiated and highly suspect. Take comfort that you can get almost everything you need to succeed from healthy eating and lifestyle habits. That said, among the many concessions longevity enthusiasts can make to the realities of modern life is considering a targeted supplementation program to address modern offenses to our genetic expectations for health. The following supplement categories (we'll cover ketone supplements in a separate section; see page 80) are worth considering to leverage the benefits of a wholesome, nutrient-dense diet.

COLLAGEN PROTEIN

Dr. Cate Shanahan asserts that connective tissue strength is directly correlated with longevity. This makes sense, because brittle joints and connective tissue compromise your ability to do vigorous exercise or even maintain an active lifestyle. A significant portion of your connective tissue health potential is genetic, but you can make significant improvements by consuming more collagen-rich foods and, with the recent introduction of collagen peptides in supplement form, supplement with collagen, too.

I have been enamored with collagen peptides (tiny molecules of collagen that can be ingested) for over three years now, because I've experienced a phenomenal improvement in my long-suffering connective tissue injuries from an ambitious supplement protocol. For decades, my Achilles heel has been my Achilles heel, scarred and shredded from my marathon training miles. After high-intensity sprint workouts or Ultimate Frisbee matches, I could count on waking up the next morning with stiffness and tightness in the Achilles area that would last for two or three days. My devotion to strength training, stretching, and mobility exercises allowed me to play hard instead of get injured, but it was a constant battle. Perhaps you can relate with specific problem areas traced back to old injuries? I don't know many folks my age who don't have balky knees or shoulders!

When research started to emerge that supplemental collagen could benefit connective tissue problems, I embarked upon my study of one. With devoted daily use, I experienced nearly immediate improvement in next-day soreness and tightness in my Achilles. The effect was almost too good to believe. From what I know about athletic training and performance, it's hard to magically rejuvenate broken-down joints and connective tissue. I've even turned down a few opportunities for injections of plasma, placenta, prolotherapy, stem cells, or other expensive exotics because I just wasn't convinced about the safety or the efficacy.

Could a couple scoops of daily collagen protein powder really make a difference in a decades-old degenerative condition? The answer is yes. Collagen has a *heliotropic* effect in the body. This means it finds its way to the areas where it is most needed. My brittle and frayed Achilles tendon was clearly ravenous for collagen material when I started supplementing. Take a dose right before exercise because the pump you get during the workout will help the collagen enter target tissues.

Keep in mind that gelatinous foods are a good source of collagen, and I obtain a decent amount of collagen from bone broth, meats on the bone, and other dietary sources. However, even the healthiest eaters can easily fall short of consuming enough for maintenance of healthy skin and connective tissue, not to mention rebuilding broken-down areas. This is especially true since even hard-core meat eaters tend to focus on muscle meats and skimp on organ meats or cuts with connective tissue included.

Besides helping to regenerate connective tissue and skin, collagen helps strengthen the all-important lining of your intestinal tract—a highly touted "heal and seal" effect that has helped bone broth and collagen supplementation skyrocket in popularity. The glycine in collagen promotes good sleep and reduces anxiety by acting as an inhibitory neurotransmitter (in contrast to other neurotransmitters considered excitatory). Collagen gets special distinction as a longevity supplement, because our natural production of collagen, the most abundant protein in the human body, declines at a steady rate of around 1.5 percent per year after age 30.

MELATONIN

Melatonin is commonly used as a sleep aid, but some progressive health enthusiasts are using this supplement, sometimes aggressively, for defensive and repair purposes. After dark, the pineal gland starts pumping out high levels of melatonin in the bloodstream. Melatonin binds to receptors in various areas of the body to make you feel increasingly sluggish and drowsy. This is a process known as dim light melatonin onset (DLMO). In concert with a melatonin spike, levels of the inhibitory neurotransmitter GABA rise to reduce nerve activity, and dopamine levels drop in the retina to make your eyes feel heavy. Soon, you transition gracefully into a restful night of sleep.

Upon the arrival of light in the morning, your genes are programmed to minimize melatonin production in favor of spiking serotonin and cortisol. If you are struggling to fall asleep on cue, the first thing to do is minimize your exposure to artificial light and digital stimulation after dark. If you still have trouble, experimenting with a melatonin supplement may provide benefit. Travelers trying to reset their circadian rhythms to a new time zone also favor melatonin.

Beyond playing a major role in your circadian rhythm, melatonin plays numerous other important roles in the body. It regulates the function of some 500 genes, and has potent antioxidant and anti-inflammatory properties, particularly in the brain. Research suggests that melatonin helps protect against macular degeneration, alleviate stomach problems like heartburn and GERD, and boost growth-hormone levels in young males. Dr. Art De Vany says melatonin is the only supplement he takes, and specifies that he uses the agent not for sleep, but to deliver a "surge of defensive hormone" intended to boost protective pathways, optimize autophagy in the brain, and deliver antioxidant, anti-inflammatory, and cellular repair benefits.

De Vany uses aggressive doses of 5 to 10 milligrams, while author, biohacker, and cold thermogenesis advocate Ray Cronise reports taking as much as 30 milligrams every night. By comparison, a typical over-the-counter sleep aid product might dispense 1 to 2 milligrams per capsule. Evidence is strong that melatonin supplementation will not interfere with the circadian-triggered natural production that occurs in the pineal gland. Furthermore, some research suggests that doses as low as 0.3 milligrams will deliver benefits. One of melatonin's main benefits is to help lower body temperature, a great facilitator of sleep. The only unpleasant side effect might be feeling groggy and sluggish in the morning, but this can clear quickly when you initiate sun exposure and movement.

OMEGA-3 FISH OIL

If you are hitting the sardines, wild-caught salmon, and pastured eggs frequently, accompanied by large piles of kale and spinach, you probably don't need to worry too much about supplementation. Unfortunately, even some of the offerings in the healthier categories can be nutrient deficient due to modern mass-production methods. Farmed salmon and mass-produced eggs have vastly lower levels of omega-3s and other nutrients than a sustainably raised animal.

Omega-3 fish oil supplements are an extremely popular category, and there are mountains of research validating the anti-inflammatory benefits of fish oil. Peripheral benefits of omega-3 supplementation include lowering cancer and heart disease risk, lowering triglycerides, lowering blood pressure, improving joint mobility, and enhancing mood, cognitive function, and even libido. Mounting research suggests that boosting omega-3 intake can help with assorted cognitive conditions such as depression, ADHD, and autism. Be sure to find the highest quality supplement with no additives or fillers, refrigerate to preserve potency, and use quickly. Experts such as Dr. Andrew Weil recommend taking 2 to 3 grams daily (2,000 to 3,000 mg).

ORGAN MEAT SUPPLEMENTS

Some of us are understandably gun-shy about cooking and eating organ meats. Dessicated liver is widely available and can serve as a decent proxy until you get more competent with integrating real liver and other offal into your diet. Ancestral Supplements.com bottles up all kinds of exotic organ products from New Zealand grass-fed animals for convenient delivery in capsule form.

PROBIOTICS AND PREBIOTICS

The best sources of probiotics are varied, nutrient-dense, enzymatically alive foods, like the aforementioned fermented foods (kombucha, yogurt, sauerkraut, etc.). Supplementing with a high-potency probiotic may be an excellent strategy when you need an extra immune boost or have experienced digestive distress from international travel, antibiotic use, foodborne illness, or any other signs of suboptimal health. Conversely, many folks like to take a small daily dose, like one capsule or liquid spoonful, every day as general gut-nourishing strategy. There is an assortment of high-quality probiotic offerings in health and natural foods supermarkets, and you may benefit from diversity in product choices, just as you benefit from diversity in your gut microbiome.

Prebiotics, aka resistant starch (as discussed with the cooked and cooled white rice served with sushi; see page 67), has gained attention recently as an important dietary element and supplement option. Besides populating your gut with good bacteria, prebiotics have anti-inflammatory benefits, enhance nutrient absorption, help purge bad bacteria, and help balance hunger and satiety hormones. The best supplement form is raw potato starch. You can start by scooping a teaspoon into your smoothie and gradually work up to a tablespoon or more. Experts recommend we consume around 30 grams of resistant starch each day. There are moderate amounts of resistant starch in an assortment of plants, grains, and legumes, but many ancestral enthusiasts who eliminate grains and legumes might be falling short accordingly. The best real food sources are the aforementioned cooked and cooled white rice (white potatoes work well in this context also) and green bananas. Buy unripe bananas, then peel and freeze them for a smoothie base.

VITAMIN D

Vitamin D could be the single most justifiable nutritional supplement to include in your regimen. Maintaining an optimal vitamin D level is critical to healthy hormonal function, cancer prevention, and longevity, but vitamin D deficiency has become epidemic in modern life. This is because the majority of vitamin D synthesis comes from sun exposure, not diet. We lead indoor-dominant lifestyles and also are discouraged from sun exposure due to an often overblown and misrepresented fear of skin cancer. Healthy vitamin D production entails exposing large skin surface areas to direct sunlight during the times of day and year of peak solar intensity in your location. Sun exposure offers many other hormonal and psychological benefits, including helping to regulate your circadian rhythm and optimize mood-elevating serotonin production.

A routine sunbathing session in bathing suit in the midday summer sun can deliver some 10,000 IU of vitamin D in only 20 minutes. Maintaining a slight tan all over your body suggests healthy vitamin D production. Once you tan, vitamin D production stops as your skin strives to protect against burning. Vitamin D is fat soluble, so you store summer production for use in the wintertime, when the sun's rays are not intense enough for vitamin D production or tanning.

In addition to our challenges in obtaining healthy sun exposure, conventional medicine accepts a vastly lower "normal" level than vitamin D advocates believe is essential. You may get a thumbs-up from your doctor with blood levels above 30 ng/ml, but researchers like Dr. Michael Holick, author of *The Vitamin D Solution*, and endurance coach Dr. Phil Maffetone, recommend maintaining levels double that to optimize cancer prevention and sex hormone production. It's extremely difficult for many of us to maintain a slight tan across the large skin surface areas, and even the most nutritious diet does not contribute substantially to your vitamin D needs. For example, a generous serving of oily, cold-water fish, the most vitamin D–rich foods available, might contribute only 1,000 IU, while a grain-based high-carbohydrate diet might deliver only 300 IU per day.

Supplementing with vitamin D, especially in the wintertime, can get you out of the danger zone and into a comfort zone quickly, and ensure that you maintain healthy levels until you can manage some good sunbathing. For comparison, most capsules of vitamin D3 (the preferred supplement form) contain 1,000 to 2,000 IU. Supplementation is further warranted as you age, because vitamin D synthesis from the sun becomes severely compromised. This is due to a decline in renal function, calcium absorption, and cholesterol concentration in skin cells (necessary for vitamin D synthesis). Things start to get extreme once you hit age 65, when vitamin D synthesis routinely decreases by 50 percent. The best approach is to test your levels, look beyond mainstream medicine to appreciate the message from vitamin D advocates, and consider an appropriate supplement regimen with frequent retesting.

KETONE SUPPLEMENTS

The ability to consume the cleanest burning fuel source known to mankind with a couple scoops of powder mixed in water has incredible potential to treat disease conditions like seizures and cognitive decline, and to improve athletic performance and recovery with appropriate targeted use. Consequently, ketone supplements have become very popular in recent years. For athletes, consuming a clean-burning fuel source before, during, and after workouts can minimize oxidative stress and inflammation. This is particularly true during high-intensity, high-glycolytic workouts where you are producing a ton of free radicals while generating the necessary energy to hoist heavy weights or blast some sprints. Even in the hours following a tough workout, sipping a ketone drink can mute the inflammatory processes and speed recovery. Supplemental ketones can deliver even more important and life-changing benefits to those battling diseases of cognitive decline, cancer, and seizures. Recent science makes a compelling case for remaining in strict ketosis to combat disease, and supplements can shore up any dietary imperfections to keep blood levels elevated at all times.

Unfortunately, it seems like ketones are most prominently marketed as a weight-loss tool, often in a manner that is distorted and overblown. When you consume a ketone supplement, you immediately shut off any internal ketone production and even fat metabolism. Your body must first burn through the calories in the supplement before dipping into fat storage or firing up liver ketone production. Hence, making a direct association with consuming calories to lose body fat is illogical and misleading. That said, I can see the benefit of ketone supplements to help with the transition from carb dependency to becoming fat- and keto-adapted. If you are at risk of succumbing to sugar cravings during the afternoon blues, a ketone supplement can deliver a quick energy and cognitive boost that will hopefully prevent binges and backslides. Some science suggests that ketone supplementation can give a turbo-boost to internal ketone production and help suppress appetite, provided the supplements are used in conjunction with a keto-friendly diet.

Keep in mind we are talking about ketone salts here, which comprise most every commercial product you have seen. These formulations bind the ketone beta-hydroxybutyrate with sodium, magnesium, and potassium. Ketone esters are a different form of supplement that became commercially available more recently. Esters are much more potent than salts, and thus a good strategy for advanced disease management or athletic performance. Esters prompt a huge immediate boost in blood ketones, but when you burn through them, it's possible to experience a profound sugar crash. Remember, ketones are burned preferentially upon ingestion, so your blood glucose level will drop accordingly. Furthermore, esters are quite expensive, generally taste terrible, and can cause significant gastrointestinal distress, so they are best used for advanced goals.

If you are in transition from carb dependency, consider ketone supplementation any time you need an energy boost or an appetite-suppression effect. If you have ambitious athletic goals, try consuming 1 to 2 scoops of ketone salts in conjunction with challenging workouts that generate oxidative stress—either high-intensity sprints or weights, or prolonged endurance efforts. Consume a ketone drink before, during, and after these sessions and see if you feel better than usual the following morning with soreness and post-exercise fatigue. Brad and I can both attest strongly to the effect of ketones reducing next-day muscle soreness, and the science supports any hype you may have heard from enthusiastic athletes.

If you or a loved one is fighting cancer or cognitive decline, ketone supplementation is worth strongly considering. Alison Gannett (alison gannett.com), speaker, self-sufficient farmer, and champion skier, has become a prominent figure in the keto community with her remarkable story of self-healing from a malignant brain tumor through a strict ketogenic diet. It is known that cancerous cells feed off glucose at a greater rate than healthy cells, so starving your cells of glucose through ketogenic eating and aggressive supplementation has become a popular adjunct to traditional invasive cancer treatments. Similarly, with dysfunctional glucose metabolism a hallmark of cognitive decline (remember, Type 3 diabetes!), aggressive ketone supplementation can potentially improve cognitive performance and arrest the rate of decline over time.

MCT OIL

Consuming a high-potency medium-chain triglyceride (MCT) oil supplement has been shown to be an excellent catalyst for liver ketone production. These products come in liquid or powdered form and are popular for mixing into coffee or smoothies. Find products that emphasize the caprylic acid (C8) component of MCT oil, such as MiCkey T Eight MCT, Perfect Keto, or Bulletproof products.

SAMPLE KETO MEALS

After careful evaluation of user experiences from thousands of keto enthusiasts on the Keto Reset Facebook group and KetoReset.com online mastery course, some distinct patterns have emerged for both what works and what doesn't. It appears that a simple approach to meal planning is a formula for success out of the gate. By limiting your choices, you avoid the decision fatigue and diminishing willpower that comes when you allow yourself too many options and have to resist temptation all day long. Instead, pick a handful of your favorite meals and repeat them. This ensures that you will hit your keto macros without sweating new daily calculations and also minimize the risk of falling off-track, getting discouraged, and falling further.

BREAKFAST

- Fasting with water, tea, or coffee
- High-fat coffee or other beverage
- Bigass omelet with pastured eggs, vegetables, cheese, avocado, bacon, salsa
- Morning Longevity Smoothie: a macronutrient-balanced smoothie made with a liquid base of full-fat coconut milk, almond milk, kefir, or yogurt; leafy green vegetables; one scoop of whey protein or collagen protein (especially if you're an athlete with increased protein needs); 1 to 2 tablespoons MCT oil; and green banana for resistant starch
- Hard-boiled egg bowl with walnuts, sun-dried tomatoes, avocado, and avocado oil–based mayonnaise
- Full-fat yogurt with nuts, cinnamon, and cacao nibs
- Bone broth with egg yolks

LUNCH

- Fasting after one of the abovementioned delicious breakfast options
- Bigass salad with assorted vegetables, nuts and seeds, healthy protein source, and healthy oil dressing. Search YouTube for "Mark Sisson BASS" (Bigass Steak Salad)
- Salad made with sauerkraut, kimchi, or tempeh

DINNER

- Any of the dishes from Keto Entrées (page 210), Longevity Superfood Organ Meats (page 232), or International Keto Favorites (page 245)
- Grass-fed beef, bone-in cuts
- Organ meats, especially beef or chicken liver
- Whole chicken or turkey
- Wild caught fish or SMASH fish
- Vegetables: steamed, baked, or pan-fried, slathered with healthy fats (butter, lard, coconut oil, avocado oil)
- Sushi offerings (sashimi-style, or with cold white rice)

SNACKS/TREATS

- Dark chocolate (85 to 90% cacao)
- Hard-boiled pastured eggs
- Macadamia nuts or other nuts/seed
- Nuts and seed butter, spread on dark chocolate or vegetables
- Sardines (try pan-fried with sun-dried tomatoes, chopped nuts, and avocado oil–based mayo)
- Smoked salmon
- Uncured salami and cheese slices
- Vegetables with almond or other nut butter

LIVING FOREVER IN THE KETO ZONE

Whatever age you are at right now, it's not too late to start correcting your course and avoiding the accelerated decline caused by carb dependency and unhealthy lifestyle habits. I receive frequent emails from senior citizens who have recently been exposed to keto (often by caring family members) and who report such stellar results that they are able to get off prescription medications and dramatically increase physical activity. Taking an abrupt fork off of the road to demise at an advanced age can be a lifesaver, literally.

Since living awesome is my primary goal in life, I refuse to sweat the details or make my keto experience stressful or regimented in any way. For this reason, I recommend a long-term approach of living in the *keto zone*. This conveys two important big-picture elements: First, keto guidelines are adhered to most of the time, but there can be spontaneous, intuitive departures outside of keto, inspired by things like vacations or periods of extra-ambitious workouts. Even then, carb intake will align with a general primal/paleo/low-carb pattern. This description differs from people who make purposeful departures from keto to binge on junk-food carbs in the name of "cyclic keto" or "refeed" strategies.

Second, living in the keto zone is about more than just food choices. A keto-zone lifestyle honors the Four Pillars of *Keto for Life* such that you are actually able to enjoy the big-ticket benefits of keto: effortless maintenance of ideal body compo-sition, reduced inflammation, enhanced immune function, mitochondrial function, brain function, cellular repair and cancer protection, enhanced athletic performance for both endurance and explosive efforts, and of course, a significant anti-aging benefit.

Here's what my keto-zone approach looks like: I almost always eat in a compressed time window of approximately 1 p.m. to 7 p.m. This means an 18-hour fast each day, with the attendant immune and cellular repair benefits that are afforded when you operate in a fasted state. Well, my morning coffee does have a splash of cream and a pinch of sugar, but I'm still calling it a compressed eating window. *Shhh*, don't tell the fasting police! Most days, I break my fast with my beloved bigass salad, featuring a centerpiece of healthy protein (steak, chicken, fish), some nuts and seeds, a tremendous assortment of colorful vegetables, and heaping amounts of healthy olive oil or avocado oil–based dressing. The fat content of the dressing, nuts and seeds, and meat/fish source makes this a keto-aligned meal. If you are vegetarian and eliminate the meat, it can still be keto-friendly if you add sufficient nuts or vegetable protein like tempeh.

In the evenings, I'll enjoy a delicious meal—usually dining out. Regardless of the type of restaurant, I emphasize animal protein and veggies, and often carefully custom-design my order to be keto-friendly (I'm definitely high maintenance, but hey, I tip well . . .). People ask me if and when I "cheat," and I recoil at the question. My eating strategy is to enjoy every single bite of food that I put into my mouth, and never feel deprived or restricted. I also never miss my old days of blueberry pancakes and pepperoni pizza, because I have authentically de-habituated away from these foods. Upon reflection, I realize that all they ever provided was a few moments of gustatory pleasure and an emotional trigger to a fond memory (such as a gluttonous brunch after knocking out a Sunday morning 20-miler with my running buddies back in the day). In exchange, having these foods in my diet destroyed my intestinal and immune function.

I'd estimate my carb intake lands almost always in a tight range of 25 to 75 grams per day. My outlier days might include a 24-hour fast, a travel day with just one meal and perhaps 10 grams of carbs (such as a room-service steak and broccoli after a day of jet travel), or occasional peaks of perhaps 150 to 200 grams when I'm in vacation mode. Indeed, if I'm in Greece or Italy and I'm presented with some homemade grape leaves or risotto, I'm inclined to indulge. I might even sample some gelato or cheesecake if it's top-notch. Granted, this feast might happen on the heels of a 24-hour fast! In any case, I'm never counting (unless I'm compelled to do a macro report for a book or blog post, and I usually whine to my staff about how tedious it is), and I'm certainly never stressing about how my enjoyment of life might compromise my blood ketone test results.

When I'm traveling, the overriding theme is fasting. Besides not always having access to the highest quality food, jet travel is highly stressful and health compromising: de-energized air, concentrated germs, high EMF exposure in the cabin, circadian rhythm disruption from crossing time zones, and being crammed into a confined space for hours. Fasting helps me counter these negative effects by facilitating a boost in immune and cellular repair function.

DESIGNING YOUR IDEAL KETO-ZONE APPROACH

It's clear from hundreds of thousands of user experiences that a "go with the flow" approach to something as strict as keto may not work well for certain individuals, especially new enthusiasts or those who have struggled with unhealthy emotional attachments to eating in the past. The most undisputed advice I can give you out of the gate is to test, evaluate, retest, evaluate, and refine a long-term strategy to determine what works best relative to fasting, digestive circadian rhythm, compressed eating windows, and macronutrient intake levels. If you are trying to reduce excess body fat, get metabolically healthy first, then consider a focused stint of keto (for which you are well prepared) to get things handled once and for all. Let's see if we can get a little more focused with a brief overview of some distinct keto-zone strategies so that you can try them on for size:

Intuitive keto zone: Predominantly keto-aligned, but macronutrient intake can fluctuate outside of keto limits in an intuitive and often spontaneous manner. Emphasis is on fasting and eating in a compressed time window. Free of refined grains, sugars, and industrial seed oils, but at times including more colorful, nutritious carbs than keto guidelines allow. This is an ideal template for longevity, because it's low stress—sustainable without needing major discipline or tracking.

Strict keto: Pretty self-explanatory, with carbs below 50 grams per day, protein at 0.7 grams per pound of body lean mass, and fat (both ingested and stored, mind you!) the predominant source of dietary calories. Strict keto can be a wonderful solution for many people recovering from metabolic damage or with a tendency to drift away from commitment and into temptation. Check out the clever and hilarious book by Brad and Brian McAndrew, targeting dudes who may be too busy and too good looking (their words, not mine!) for a regimented approach, but still want to access all of keto's benefits: *Keto Cooking for Cool Dudes.*

Targeted/athletic keto: Carb intake fluctuates at times up to the more liberal primal limit of 150 grams per day. This is a distinct strategy to fuel for and recover from serious workouts. This strategy is most appropriate for those with excellent body composition and metabolic flexibility. Extra calories and extra carbs (and perhaps protein as well) are consumed either in a regimented manner (e.g., before or after workouts) or an intuitive manner.

WHAT NOT TO DO!

Cyclic keto: Regimented refeeds and "cheat days" have potentially detrimental effects, both physical and psychological. Studies from keto pioneers Dr. Jeff Volek and Dr. Stephen Phinney suggest that a single high-carbohydrate meal can knock a novice out of ketosis for up to a week. (FYI, after a carb indulgence, I've noticed I can return to nutritional ketosis blood values—0.5 mmol/L or higher—after a single 18-hour fast.) Deliberate carb cycling can also spike appetite hormones, destabilize fat metabolism, promote insulin resistance, and lead to muscle catabolism, as the body gets confused about which fuel substrates to prioritize. Carb cycling can also foster an unhealthy relationship with food, where you suppress intuition and foster a binge mentality where you go crazy on hot fudge sundae weekends just because you can.

Dirty keto: Don't get me started. No matter how many calories you burn with impressive workouts, there is never any rationale or justification for consuming nutrient-deficient processed food, especially under the guise of following keto. Focus on making the best possible choice in every category of food you eat: grass-fed beef, wild-caught salmon, pasture-raised eggs, and organic produce (insist on organic when you consume the skin instead of peeling it). For anything that's been wrapped or packaged, read labels carefully to make sure there are no harmful additives. Many seemingly healthy "energy" snacks, meats, nuts, jerkys, and condiments are laden with sugar, preservatives, and toxic industrial oils. Make a habit of asking waiters to have the kitchen cook your meal in butter instead of vegetable oil.

Incomplete keto: Many keto enthusiasts "try" keto and bomb out after 3 weeks, concluding that keto is too difficult or not right for them. Instead, pick a low-stress time of life, start when you are fully prepared, and resolve to complete a minimum 6-week stint of nutritional ketosis. Be vigilant against the common pitfalls by dialing in your minerals and electrolytes, toning down your exercise energy output (and life stress levels) for the first few weeks, and snacking on high-fat foods as needed.

Keto in a can (or bottle, or wrapper): If you are enticed into a regimented keto program centered around a ketone supplement product, be wary. While many ketone supplement providers dispense sound information and product use guidelines, sometimes the focus can drift into product sales instead of a simple, sensible, sustainable, and affordable long-term dietary transformation based on real foods. Folks, keto is not SlimFast, it's reawakening your human genetic hard-wiring to elegantly manufacture and burn internal fuel sources.

Peer pressure keto: Proceed at your own pace, enjoy the journey, and don't compare your results to others. Realize that transforming your physique is a by-product of the more important health, dis-

ease protection, and longevity benefits of keto. I get tons of emails from people complaining about lack of "results" (i.e., rapid fat reduction) with keto. In the next breath, they admit that they feel great, have stable appetite, energy, mood, and cognitive focus. I call those results! And yes, once you have built a respectable level of metabolic flexibility, you can absolutely expect to achieve targeted fat reduction goals with precision and efficiency.

Quick keto: If you are preparing for bikini season and see an offering like, "Seven-Day Keto Blast," run screaming in the opposite direction. A keto crash course might be better named a Seven-Day Stress Hormone Bath—you'll make the sugar you need from fight-or-flight mechanisms instead of magically shifting over to ketones. It's best to view keto as a patiently acquired skill that you can use as a tool to hone metabolic flexibility for the rest of your life.

Suffering keto: You may have heard of the term "keto flu," often described as an inevitable consequence of the ketogenic diet, and something to endure with awesome willpower if you are a worthwhile human being. I hereby and forever more call bullshit on the keto flu. The keto flu is an indication that you have a flawed approach, whether from poor preparation, overly stressful exercise patterns during a significant dietary transformation, deficient sodium intake, pre-existing leaky gut, thyroid dysfunction, or adrenal burnout conditions, or perhaps even a keto that's a little dirty instead of nutrient dense.

If your keto efforts make you feel cranky, edgy, stressed, and fatigued, spend some extra time in basic mode of ditching offensive modern foods and emphasizing nutritious foods, and don't stress about your carb intake levels. If you are eating in an ancestral-aligned pattern, your carbohydrate intake won't be more than 150 grams a day, and you can try cutting back further into keto levels when you are ready. The awesome sensations of never feeling hungry and enjoying stable energy and mood without food cannot be faked; metabolic flexibility is a skill that requires hard work. Nowhere does it say that suffering is a necessary stepping stone to metabolic flexibility.

Underprepared keto: If you don't yet feel absolutely comfortable and productive for 16 hours without food (e.g., 8 p.m. to 12 noon), you're not ready for keto. Spend more time in Reset mode to hone your skills. Realize that both wheat and sugar have physically addictive properties—they trigger a dopamine burst and stimulate opioid receptors in the brain. As you likely realize, this makes you want more and more when you start indulging, and makes it difficult for you to completely rewire away from carbohydrate dependency. I hear from many struggling keto aspirants who reveal they were "pretty good" about ditching grains and sugars out of the gate. This simply doesn't cut it when we are talking about rewiring decades of carbohydrate addiction; it's essential to commit to zero tolerance so that ensuing steps will be easier.

✦ ✦ ✦

The great thing about a keto-zone approach is that keto enthusiasts can coexist peacefully whether we're fasting until noon, or powering down six-egg omelets as a morning custom. Again, back to the 80 percent concept: If your movement, exercise, sleep, and mindset are healthy, and you are consuming colorful, nutrient-dense foods and eliminating processed junk, your carb count—often touted as the end-all by overcaffeinated, overly simplistic promoters—actually becomes something of minimal significance. Of course, there is no justification to ever consume nutrient-deficient refined carbs and oils, even for athletes who burn them off. Beyond that, if you are inclined to enjoy a sweet potato now and then, we can still be friends and you can still keep your Keto Club Card—especially if you make fasting a regular practice.

The day that you ditch the foods that cause inflammation, oxidative stress, and glycation and start emphasizing the longevity superfoods and super supplements, you start rewinding your biological clock. The good news about making dietary changes is that you get immediate validation that you are on the right track, because you experience a stable mood, appetite, and energy level right away. Running some before and after blood tests is also a fantastic strategy, especially if you have any hesitation about any elements of the ancestral and keto message that are still disputed by conventional wisdom, such as the idea of ditching grains and eating more fat.

PILLAR #2: MOVEMENT AND PHYSICAL FITNESS

As someone who has frequented the gym for decades, both as a personal trainer back in the day and an enthusiast for my entire adult life, it's concerning to see the prevalence of narrowly focused fitness enthusiasts. I see many females in particular who are champs on the cardio machines but are seemingly intimidated by anything resembling a weight or a contraption you have to operate with muscle power. Conversely, I see plenty of thick bros hoisting giant racks and stacks of steel, but look like they might have difficulty running a couple laps around a track without stopping, let alone attain the gold-standard 8-minute mile. Many in the endurance athletic world follow grueling and sophisticated programs that make them excellent in a tiny area of competency, but woefully inadequate in the broad fitness attributes that promote longevity. Still others don't have any steady workout routine at all.

Even more disturbing than a narrow approach to fitness is a chronic approach—doing too much of a good thing to the extent that it compromises health. When I first published a lengthy article titled, "A Case Against Cardio," on MarksDailyApple.com in 2006, it took awhile for the endurance community to accept the message. The endurance ethos has long been that mileage is king, competitive fitness equates to exceptional health, and you have a free pass to slam junk food due to your impressive caloric output. Today, emerging science, along with a disturbing number of case studies of longtime athletes blowing out their hearts, immune, and endocrine systems, has validated the previously unimaginable concept that the lean, mean fitness machine running through your neighborhood is in many respects less healthy, and has a greater disease risk, than the sensibly active folks walking their dogs and working in their gardens. What's more, chronic exercise actually compromises metabolic flexibility. That's right, the energy-depleting and fight-or-flight–abusing effects of chronic workouts compromise round-the-clock fat burning and dysregulate appetite and satiety hormones such that you are prone to carb binges and fat storage.

Hence, this pillar offers a simple, sustainable, intuitive approach to developing functional, broad-based fitness competency for life through these four objectives:

- *Low-level movement:* Blend all forms of everyday movement with a few hours per week of structured cardiovascular workouts at a comfortable, fat-burning "aerobic" pace.
- *Brief, high-intensity strength workouts:* Whether with weights, gym machines, or just bodyweight resistance, you must regularly put your muscles under resistance load and conduct brief, high-intensity, short-duration workouts. A couple of strength sessions per week lasting 10 to 30 minutes is plenty.
- *Sprinting:* The ultimate antiaging workout! Perform a handful of explosive all-out efforts (lasting just 10 to 20 seconds, with extensive rest between) in running, or a lower-impact activity if necessary. One sprint session every 7 to 10 days is sufficient.
- *Play:* Utilize your physical fitness base to have some unstructured outdoor physical fun. Play is a fundamental human need, a necessary stress release from confinement and predictability of high-tech modern life, and an opportunity to nurture that all-important longevity attribute of youthful spirit.

This is all you really need to get fit and healthy and ace all of your longevity checkpoints! No mandatory gym membership, no need to toe any starting lines or set the alarm for predawn suffer-fests in Spin class. You can get superfit in your own home or with a few trips to the park each week. If you are into CrossFit, lively group exercise classes, or outdoor competition in endurance or obstacle course racing, hey that's great. Your main objective in this area might be to tone down the all-too-common overly stressful approach that can destroy your health, dysregulate your hormones, and compromise your longevity prospects. In Pillar #2, you'll get tons of suggestions and practical guidance to implement each of these objectives.

INCREASE GENERAL EVERYDAY MOVEMENT

Even if you don't have the time or inclination to become a lean, mean fitness machine, you can still arrive at the 80-percent benchmark that we're calling low-hanging fruit with JFW: Just F*&%ing Walk! Today, many fitness experts assert that simply moving around more (especially avoiding the prolonged periods of stillness that are so common in the digital age) has become the most important objective to become fit for life—more than following a structured workout routine. Certainly there are wide-ranging benefits to being fit for group cycling, CrossFit, a 10k race, or summiting a mountain peak, but let's not even go there until you establish a fantastic base of consistent and varied everyday movement.

Besides JFW, the "move more" objective comprises formal movement practices like yoga, Pilates, and tai chi; anytime/anywhere calisthenics and bodyweight resistance exercises (e.g., rattling off some deep squats or plank time while binge-watching a Netflix series); or a morning stretching/flexibility/mobility sequence (search YouTube for "Brad Kearns Morning Routine" for inspiration). Even self-myofascial release (foam rolling) can count toward your movement objective. Integrating this stuff into your daily routine is easy and fun, and delivers an instant payoff of reinvigorating mind and body after periods of stillness. You also don't have to hassle the often-challenging logistics of carving out time to get to the gym for formal workouts.

MOVEMENT FOR FAT REDUCTION

Believe it or not, routine daily movement may help you drop excess body fat more effectively than a devotion to lively group cardio classes, CrossFit sessions, or high-volume endurance training programs. This is because regular movement keeps you in an energized, fat-burning state, with stable mood and appetite. In contrast, vigorous workouts—especially ones that are a bit too stressful, last too long, or are done too frequently with insufficient rest between them, can easily leave you feeling depleted and hungry. A scientifically validated concept called the *compensation theory* reveals that calories burned during workouts will stimulate a requisite increase in appetite, along with generally increased laziness and diminished self-discipline throughout the day. Your workout regimen may deliver assorted health and fitness benefits, but it's a break-even when it comes to fat-reduction goals. If you've ever done a lively 40-minute Spinning class (burns around 600 calories) and then celebrated at Jamba Juice with a medium banana berry smoothie and a small KIND fruit and nut energy bar afterward (delivers around 600 calories, including over 100 grams of carbs), you have actualized the compensation theory.

Compensations also occur subconsciously. Buoyed by the self-satisfaction of completing your ambitious early-morning workout, you may trend toward laziness and overeating the rest of the day. Maybe you'll opt for the elevator instead of the stairs, phoning a colleague down the hall instead of scooting over for a quick visit, or wolfing down an entire bag of trail mix instead of a planned handful. You may unwittingly spend lazy evenings in front of the TV instead of taking the dog to the park as you might without the lingering mental and physical malaise from the workout. The more strenuously or chronically you train, the more ravenous you may be, and the lazier you may act when not working out. These are genetically programmed survival mechanisms against the perceived life-or-death threat of energy depletion.

There are plenty of folks burning calories maniacally and trying hard to control caloric intake to no avail, and you can see the compensation theory in action on the starting lines of extreme events like ultramarathon runs and Ironman triathlons. It's commonplace for serious athletes who train 10 or 20 hours a week to still carry 10 or 20 pounds of excess body fat. One disturbing study revealed that 30 percent of the participants in the Sanlam Cape Town (South Africa) Marathon were classified as overweight or obese. This is about the same percentage of the world's population in general, meaning the physical appearance of the participants in a 26.2-mile marathon race is indistinguishable from that of the spectators along the route. Ouch!

There's gotta be a better way, and there is. It's time to reject the psychologically harmful programming that says you have to suffer through a grueling workout regimen to look good. Chronic exercise will make you tired, sick, and fat. Unless you train like crazy and starve yourself, at which point you can become a lean, mean, inflamed machine—until you cut back your training a bit and throw on a quick 10 pounds. Instead, you can embrace the concept that 80 percent of your body composition success comes from how you eat, particularly the amount of insulin you produce on a daily basis. The other 20 percent is reliant upon optimal sleep habits, effective stress management, and a sensible exercise routine.

While this "80 percent from diet" is not a scientific assertion, it's become a maxim of the ancestral health approach that has been realized by millions of case studies (visit some at the MarksDailyApple.com "Success Stories" section). Embracing this concept will help you redirect your focus to making healthy food choices (ditching sugars, grains, and refined oils for starters, and making steady progress to fat- and keto-adaptation), increasing general everyday movement (up-regulating fat-burning genes and stabilizing appetite and satiety hormones, without the appetite spikes caused by overly stressful workouts), and conducting a sensible blend of comfortably paced cardio and brief, high-intensity sessions.

Cardio in the fat-burning zone will contribute to your weight-loss goals instead of make you depleted and hungry. A sensible pattern of brief, high-intensity sessions that aren't exhausting or depleting, and always balanced with sufficient recovery, will help you drop those final few pounds to attain and maintain your personal ideal body composition. And yes, results can and will vary based on your genetics, so the focus should always be on looking your best, without worrying about how you stack up with the uber-devoted genetic outliers that grace magazine covers.

JFW STRATEGIES

Today, it's possible to be a fully functional, highly productive member of society without moving much at all. Special thanks to Amazon Prime and Uber Eats! However, lest we romanticize our ancestors for their devotion to healthy, active lifestyles, we must acknowledge that humans have always been hardwired to find the easiest possible route through life. Anthropologist Marshall Sahlins's popular theory of the "original affluent society" contends that hunter-gatherers were able to achieve our modern notion of affluence by getting all their wants and needs met and desiring for little. Studies of the !Kung people in Africa, modern-day hunter-gatherers, reveal that they only hunt and gather for 5 hours a day, spend 6 hours a day in leisure time and group or family socializing, and sleep or rest for 10 hours a day. Hunter-gatherers were obligated to move and exercise to the bare minimum necessary in order to survive, and their comparatively harsh circumstances made this obligation fortuitous for their health. Everything they did was utilitarian and survival-driven; no one pumped iron or ran marathons to accumulate a collection of shiny medals.

Our hardwired quest for leisure and luxury is the driving force behind inexorable technological innovation. It has brought us very quickly (in the context of the evolutionary timeline) from a primitive hunter-gatherer existence—with a life-or-death obligation to movement and physical fitness—into the age of self-inflicted gluttony and sloth. Today, in order to honor our genetic expectations for health, we have to make concerted efforts to orchestrate artificial movement and exercise opportunities every day—none more important than walking. Following are an assortment of fun and convenient ways to get moving more every day.

Daily stroll: If you're a dog owner, honor yourself and your commitment to caring for your animal, and get out for a morning, and evening, walk every day. If you don't have a dog, pretend you do and make a daily stroll mandatory. To get into a good rhythm here, resolve to just get out for 5 minutes every single day no matter what, and see where that habit takes you. Perhaps you'll discover a sweet spot of 15 or 20 minutes, where you establish a favorite loop, cleanse your racing thoughts or pent-up emotions, and/or mitigate a postmeal glucose spike and insulin crash.

Obligatory walking: Walk your child to school every day. If inconvenient, drive to a spot a mile away and walk from there. On your commute home, stop at a nearby park, walk a lap, and continue on your drive. Find a venue around the halfway mark to break up yet another forced stillness period. If you take the bus or the subway, walk to the next stop before boarding. If you are falling short with JFW objectives, stop anywhere, anytime before you get to the vortex of sedentary living that is the modern home, and bag some JFW time.

Don't be a parking lot muppet: Andre Obradovic, Australian health and executive coach and serious amateur triathlete, uses the term "muppet" for someone who is content to follow the pack without engaging any competitive focus or critical thinking. Why do we all reflexively troll for the absolute closest possible parking spot at the shopping center, causing the annoying backup lines? Instead, enter the parking lot, turn away from the building, and claim the farthest possible spot from the store. Every time. Fewer door dings, too!

Don't be an elevator muppet: Implement a rule to avoid elevators and take the stairs instead. If your deals happen on the twenty-first floor and you're too lazy or too pressed for time to conquer that many flights a couple/few times every day, get off the elevator at seventeen and bank a few flights instead of zero. Descending stairs is great for preserving balance and bone density, too, and meeting interesting new coworkers.

Make the entry barrier low for your chosen endeavor(s) on the list by agreeing to complete a brief session once a week, then see if you naturally and enjoyably add more days over time. If you notice yourself succumbing to the powerful pull of ingrained bad habits and cultural norms, downsize your ambitions further until they feel ridiculously doable.

While familial genetics and personality characteristics might make certain people more naturally active or hyper than others, the good news is that by making a concerted effort to move frequently and avoid prolonged periods of sitting or other stillness (yep, even prolonged stints at your stand-up desk), you can rewire your brain to become more naturally and spontaneously active. Furthermore, adding more daily movement and developing these efforts into habits can reprogram your genes to favor fat-burning mode rather than fat storing. A simple and immediate step to take in the proper direction, especially if you are trying to drop excess body fat, is to commit to walking for 5 to 15 minutes after dinner every day for 21 days. See how great you feel when you take the edge off the postmeal insulin response, and perhaps even drop some body fat independent from any dietary modifications.

Don't be an athletic muppet: Fitness freaks are some of the worst examples of human laziness short of the professional couch potato. The fittest among us love to flash hall passes for couch time and hot fudge sundaes on account of the impressive entries into our training logs. However, emerging exercise science suggests that gentle movement can accelerate recovery better than complete inactivity. This can include anything from walking more and doing more flexibility/mobility exercises in the hours and days after your most strenuous workouts, to conducting sophisticated "Rebound Workouts" in the gym (see page 146). The next time you beg out of household chores because you're in an all-important "build" training phase, realize that raking the leaves and potting the plants is helping you become a better athlete.

DYNAMIC WORKPLACE STRATEGIES

Frequent movement breaks: If you follow a typical 8-hour office workday routine, or have other prolonged sitting periods during the day, honor the following template:

- 5-minute break every hour: Get up and leave your workspace, focus your eyes on assorted and distant objects (crucial for ocular health to balance extended gazing at a fixed-distance screen), and do some counterbalancing exercises against the hunched over desk position. For example, Katy Bowman's "wall angels": Stand with your back against a wall, extending arms sideways to form a T. Slowly and carefully raise arms overhead, keeping arms and hands against the wall, then return to a T-position. Repeat to make wall angels!
- 10-minute break every 2 hours: Change venue, change eye focus, do counterbalancing exercises, walk around the courtyard! Brain studies on the concept of *sustained attention* reveal that we only go for about 20 minutes of intense

focus and peak cognitive performance until we require a break to zone out. Without these recurring short breaks, your focus, attention span, and willpower to sustain them will drain like a smartphone battery.
- Midday break of at least 30 minutes: Get outside into fresh air, open space, and sunlight and start moving—JFW, or perhaps even pedal your bike around. This midday break is essential for refreshing depleted brain synapses, optimizing hormonal function (including fat burning), and reenergizing cells throughout your body that have been depleted after hours under artificial light, staring at a fixed-distance screen, and breathing energy-depleted recirculated air.

Create standing/sitting variation: To avoid the disease and dysfunction associated with prolonged stillness, strive to continually alter your body's positioning and functioning throughout the workday. This entails pairing the aforementioned breaks with a purposefully fidgety experience at your work desk. One popular strategy is to create a stand-up desk, where keyboard and screen are elevated through high-tech or low-tech means to operate comfortably from a standing position. When you're standing, there is much greater opportunity to vary your body load and engage different muscles. For example, you can rest one foot on a stool or other elevated perch, lean this way or that, switching legs frequently, or stand on a pebble mat or balance board. The goal is to avoid a static position for longer than a few minutes. Treadmill desks have become very popular, too—it's surprisingly easy to type or read the screen while walking at a slow pace. If you have sufficient freedom at your work environment, try putting your laptop on a very low table and sitting on the ground or on a Bosu ball (half an exercise ball with a flat base).

Engaging in bouts of stand-up work helps re-engage dormant muscles and promotes good posture and skeletal alignment. Alas, Katy Bowman is quick to remind us that standing in a fixed position all day is no better than sitting—you'll still create stiffness in the load-bearing muscles and joints, and in the arterial walls within those muscles and joints. Rather, you hereby have permission to frequently switch from standing to sitting, and seek out other creative opportunities to vary the position of your body, of course within the limitations of your workplace decorum. While correct ergonomics are important to avoid repetitive joint strain, the superseding goal is to achieve continual variation. Even the optimal ergonomic position is extremely unhealthy and will generate cellular dysfunction if you assume it for too long. Within the obvious constraints of your workplace duties, strive to be more cognizant of opportunities for variation that might otherwise be neglected. For example, can you take a significant number of your phone calls on the move? If you must engage with a screen during a call, can you at least do some of the following exercises while the other person is speaking?

BALANCING EXERCISES

Balance and *proprioception*—the awareness of your body moving through space—are among the most prominent markers of age-related physical decline. This decline is often imperceptible because we rarely challenge and expose our balance shortcomings directly, even when engaged in ambitious workouts or athletic events. Instead, we lament that we just seem to be a step slower on the tennis or basketball court, can't quite jump as high for the Frisbee, stumble more frequently when hiking or running the trails, or sustain mysterious injuries that have "never happened before."

Losing a set you should have won is one thing, but the statistics about the risk of falling and other accidents are more sobering. Our sense of balance actually starts to deteriorate as early as age 25, and one in three independently living people over age 65 fall every year—with 10 to 15 percent of those falls having serious morbidity consequences. Falling once doubles your chances of falling again. The US Center for Disease Control cites falling as the leading cause of injury and death in those over 65.

Good balance is dependent upon the complex interplay between your visual system, vestibular system (inner ear), and sensory-motor receptors in your spine, joints, connective tissue, and muscles. The sensory cortex in the brain processes all the information and allows you to function efficiently during a balance beam routine or descending a mountain pass on a bicycle at 50 miles an hour.

When these and other fun endeavors happen less frequently over the years, the use-it-or-lose-it principle kicks in and your aptitude for routine challenges like standing on one leg declines steadily to eventually put you at risk of demise. Time to have some fun in the privacy of your cubicle or office! If you become frustrated when trying the following challenges, relish the opportunity to make huge improvements with even a few minutes per day of devoted practice.

One-legged balancing: The description seems so easy, but you may find it incredibly difficult to remove your shoes, bend one leg, lift it slightly off the ground, and balance on the other foot. Bend your knee slightly on the balancing leg to form a nice supple anchor for your bodyweight. Rest arms comfortably at your sides, or extend them for balance if you need to. When you first go up onto one leg, you may discover that the small stabilizer muscles in your foot and calf are working furiously to keep you from falling over. Wow! Who knew?! Concentrate your gaze on a single spot and try to find a still point to quiet the wobbling. If you're able to get comfortable, close your eyes for a few seconds and see if you can hang in there. Yes, things get much tougher when you eliminate the visual input!

For athletic types who want an even more difficult challenge, try this: Get stable on one leg, then rise up onto the ball of your foot (the metacarpal bones, between arch and toes). This move is particularly functional to improve your stability for any form of explosive jumping. Get stable balancing on the ball of your foot, then gradually bend your weighted knee to lower into a squat, then rise back up to tall posture. Got it? Okay next, lower into a squat and then explode upward by driving the opposite knee to your chest. Once you master that, do the whole thing with your eyes closed!

Balletic karate kicks: Fantastic for improving balance and stability, this move also spotlights the hip flexors, which are a common weak and tight spot for fitness enthusiasts and desk jockeys alike. Stand tall with hands on hips. If necessary, gently hold onto a desk or wall for balance—but try to touch softly with just your pinky finger. Maintaining tall posture, balance on your right leg. Next, raise your left leg while bending the knee, tracking the knee up and away from the body as if getting your left adductor (groin muscle) parallel to the ground. Knee is fully bent. Then, straighten your left leg and extend it sideways. Try to form a 90-degree angle between the extended left leg and the grounded right leg. The closer you get to 90 degrees, the more your hip flexor will burn! Next, while maintaining a consistent knee position with the extended left leg, repeatedly bend at the knee, then straighten leg. Challenge yourself to eventually complete 10, or 20, repetitions on each side, with little or no hand support. Again, this takes all of a minute to complete a set, and is a great way to get blood flowing into those hip flexors after long sitting stints.

There are numerous similar movements that can boost your balance and mobility. From the same starting point, instead of kicking out, raise your leg with a bent knee to get your thigh parallel to the ground, then lower down while straightening the leg. Or, balance on one leg as described, then swing your free leg up and away from the body while keeping it straight. You're likely to need hand support for this one, but see if you can progress to doing these hands free someday!

Deep squats: Place feet facing forward or a few degrees out, shoulder width apart. Extend arms forward or in prayer position for balance. Lower deliberately, imagining that you are sitting down onto a chair. Use your quads and glutes to absorb the load both sitting and standing. Maintain a straight spine (it will travel from a 90-degree to a 45-degree angle), but resist the urge to lean forward—chest up!

If you are a squatting novice, actually use a chair to lower into. Otherwise, go as low as you safely can, and strive to make steady progress. Eventually, you want to achieve "ass-to-grass" position, as former Olympic 1,500-meter runner Michael Stember instructs his pupils. Don't use the excuse that your knees are creaky! More likely, you're inflexible. Gaining squat competency with stronger quads and glutes will actually minimize joint strain over time.

When you reach the bottom of your squat, raise up deliberately. Strive to rotate your knees outward to get them tracking directly over your feet at all times. Take care to avoid the common errors of caving the knees inward instead of tracking along the foot line, or tipping your torso forward to cheapen the load on the glutes. Try right now to drop for 20 ass-to-grass squats.

Desk dips: Model the popular gym exercise of bar dips, but using a desk for support. Face away from the desk and place your hands behind you. Grab the edge of the desk with your palms facing backwards. Lower down as far as you comfortably can, hopefully to 90-degree elbows or beyond. Exhibit good squatting form with your legs, but try to not engage the leg muscles. Isolate the effort on the upper body and let the legs go along for the ride. Engage the core for stability. Perhaps piggyback your twice-daily squats goal with a similar number of dips?

FLEXIBILITY/MOBILITY EXERCISES

There is no better way to start the day than to get the blood flowing with a deliberate sequence of gentle flexibility/mobility movements that promote functional fitness and help minimize injury risk when you participate in serious workouts or competitive sports. Functional fitness is the capacity to perform real-life activities like lifting, bending, and jumping that are essential to quality of life and longevity. Here again, it's essential to reject the flawed and dated mindset that only structured workouts of a certain duration count toward your fitness objectives. Spending a few minutes every morning lubricating your engine parts can offer fantastic injury prevention and set you up for fitness breakthroughs by allowing you to go harder in tough workouts.

Morning flexibility/mobility sequence: Do these as soon as you wake up to get blood and oxygen circulating throughout your body. You'll need flat ground with carpet or yoga mat padding, and sufficient space to swing your legs in assorted directions.

- Hamstrings + kickouts: Lie flat, elevate your legs 6 to 12 inches off the ground, and carefully extend left leg straight up in the air (leg straight), high enough to engage the hamstrings, then lower. Do a few reps to get the move right. Then, rotate the right hip open and bend the knee fully, as if doing a butterfly stretch with your right leg, while the left leg stays straight. While raising the left leg for another hamstring rep, extend the lower right leg outward, keeping the knee in a fixed position. When the left leg returns to the ground, the right leg returns from fully straightened to bent. Both legs should end the move a few inches off the ground. It might be tough to get the rhythm at first but soon you will achieve a smooth hamstring plus kickout pattern. After reaching the desired total, switch sides and repeat with legs doing the opposite move. Suggested reps: novice—15 each leg. Expert—30.
- Frog kicks: Lie flat with legs together, fully extended and 6 to 12 inches off the ground.

Initiate a frog kick pattern as if swimming the breaststroke: From extended legs, bring both knees up toward the chest, then extend the legs out to either side as far as possible while straightening them. Then sweep legs back to straight and fully extended. Repeat bringing knees to chest, extend to side, straighten sequence, to achieve desired total. Then, reverse the direction of your frog kicks and do an equal number in the reverse direction. That is, sweep legs out first, then bring them in while bending knees to chest, then bring legs together and extend fully. Bonus: Roll right into this from your hamstring + kickouts for a great core challenge. Suggested reps: Novice—10 each direction. Expert—20 each direction.

Advanced flexibility/mobility exercises: The aforementioned exercises should be safe and doable even for novices. Your abdominals will burn at first, and you can take a rest as needed. You will enjoy making steady progress and noticing your core become more resilient each day. The following exercises require a solid fitness foundation to protect you from what might otherwise be an injury risk if your core is unstable or muscles inflexible.

- Scissors: Lie flat and raise straightened legs together up to a 90-degree angle. Commence scissor sequence by splitting legs apart and then returning to 90-degree, legs-together position. Be deliberate with the lowering and raising of your legs to avoid straining the delicate adductor (groin) muscles.

- Bridges: Lie on your back with knees bent and feet flat on the ground, facing forward. Slowly elevate your hips to bring your thighs and torso into a straight line. Return to ground and repeat to achieve desired total. Suggested reps: Novice—10. Expert—20. Super expert: Raise entire back off the ground and form a complete arch with only feet and hands touching the ground, hold for 20 breath cycles.
- Alternating Bird Dog: On your hands and knees, carefully extend right arm and left leg to straight positions. From a side view at full extension, you should see a straight line from left leg, through torso, and out right arm. Repeat with opposite arms and legs to achieve your count. Suggested reps: Novice—10. Expert—20.
- Full Matty's: Make sure you are warmed up with some other movements, have a very strong core, and perform the exercise in a deliberate and controlled manner. Props to *Paleo Primer* coauthor Matt Whitmore for busting these out beautifully on Instagram @Fitterfood. Lie flat on ground with arms and legs fully extended. Bring legs 6 to 12 inches off the ground, then raise your arms and legs into the air, touching them together above your body. Lower carefully until arms and legs are 6 to 12 inches off the ground, and repeat. Take care to lower them in a controlled manner, to intensify the core stimulation and protect the lower back from strain. Do half of your count touching arms and legs together in the middle, then alternate reaching both arms across left leg, both arms across right leg, to engage the oblique abdominals. Suggested reps: Novice—10 straight, 5 left, 5 right. Expert—30 straight, 10 left, 10 right. Pro tip: Wrap both legs together with a 5-pound ankle weight.

Yoga sun salutation: The sun salutation is a sequence of postures and stretches that are fundamental to the practice of yoga. The sun salutation is ideal for first thing in the morning, because the movements are safe and gentle, and get blood and oxygen flowing throughout the body. These exercises also strengthen and stretch the major muscle groups of the body, massage and circulate blood to the internal organs, and improve balance and flexibility. Beyond the physical benefits, the sun salutation helps integrate mind, body, and breath, a concept that Eastern philosophy holds essential to happiness and general well-being.

Following are descriptions of the postures that comprise a basic sun salutation routine; this and other sequences are known as *vinyasas* in yoga. There are plenty of more advanced movements that you can add to your routine as you gain more flexibility, strength, and endurance. Check out a good instructional yoga book or video, or see a qualified teacher for ideas. The movements should be performed in a fluid sequence with no interruption between them. The postures should never be painful or cause your muscles to twitch or shake under strain. If you are inflexible or have muscle or joint injuries, modify the routines as necessary to avoid pain.

Control of breath is essential to the sun salutation experience. Establish a pattern of inhaling when you extend or elongate your body, and exhaling when you bend or compress your body. Pay close attention throughout the entire series of movements to be sure that breathing matches your physical movements. Strive to have nothing else in your mind than the correct execution of the movement and the integration of breath. All of these poses have authentic Sanskrit names like *samasthiti* (salutation) or *ashwa sanchalanasana* (horse stance). For the purposes of simplicity, we will use simple, Western terms.

1. *Salutation:* Stand erect with feet parallel to the ground for men, splayed out at a 45-degree angle for women. Place your palms together in front of your chest, elbows out as if you were praying. Press your palms together to feel your chest expand.
2. *Raised arms:* Inhale and extend your arms directly overhead as high as you can reach. Stand tall by imagining the top of your head being pulled up by a string. Advanced: Raise up on your tippy toes and hold the position for some extra beats.
3. *Hand to foot:* Exhale, sweep your arms in as wide a downward arc as possible, then touch the ground next to your feet. Bend carefully from the waist to fold into a diver's pike position at the bottom. Make sure that your knees are relaxed and legs are not locked straight.
4. *Straight back:* Inhale, grab your ankles with your hands, and extend upward, bending at the waist only. Let your hands drag up your shins to

assist in raising the upper body. Stop when your spine is parallel to the ground. Keep your spine as straight and elongated as possible, including the cervical area, which we tend to compress. Imagine extending your head forward as far as possible, and your tailbone backward as far as possible.
5. *Hand to foot:* Exhale and let your spine fold back down toward your legs. Try to compress further than you did on your first hand to feet movement.
6. *Return to salutation:* Inhale, sweeping your arms up in as wide an arc as possible all the way over your head, then exhale and drop your hands into the salutation position.

Repeat Positions 2 through 5 up to 4 times. After the appropriate number of repetitions, you may incorporate the following "triangle" movements to complete a more advanced cycle.

- *Side bend:* From Position 2 (raised arms), drop your left arm to your side. Exhale and bend your entire upper body to the left, taking care to keep the hips level so you don't compress the lower spine. Slide the left hand as far down your left leg as you can. Reach for the sky (not sideways, but up—important to protect your back) with your right hand. Hold this position for a cycle of 3 breaths. Return to center, raise your left arm overhead, and lower your right arm to the side. Repeat the movement in the other direction. The key here is to be gentle to protect against back strain.

- *Forward bend:* After returning to center from the right side triangle, clasp your hands behind your back and inhale. Exhale and bend forward from the waist. Keep your spine as straight as possible when you lower, and keep your legs slightly bent. Lower your forehead toward your knees while raising your clasped hands as high as possible above your body.

From here you can return to the salutation position, complete the basic sun salutation cycle. There are endless variations to implement as you become more experienced, such as downward dog, upward dog, and warrior poses.

Dynamic stretching: I recommend this sequence prior to doing my beloved all-out sprints or any other ambitious workout or athletic event. The following dynamic stretches are also a great stand-alone sequence to promote flexibility, mobility, and injury prevention. Strive to preserve a straight and elongated spine at all times when performing these stretches.

- Deep squat: This is the ideal warm-up move for anything—including first thing in the morning, or before any workout or athletic participation. It activates muscles throughout the lower body, including core and lower back. Lower to a safe and comfortable position and strive to improve over time to eventually achieve ass-to-grass position.
- Knee-to-chest: Stand tall and gently grab your shin, just below your knee, with both hands.

Pull your knee up toward your chest, hold for a beat, then release. Repeat with opposite leg as you walk slowly forward.
- Pull quads: Bend your knee so you can reach and grab the back of your foot. Gently pull your foot up toward your butt, hold for a count, then release with a forward step.
- Open hips: Face forward, then bend and rotate your knee out and away from your body, so your adductors are facing forward. Sweep your knee back toward the center line of your body as you eventually take a proper forward step with the rotating leg. Repeat with the other leg.
- Mini-lunge: Take forward strides of exaggerated length and depth, lowering your front thigh to near parallel on each stride. Take care to keep the knee over the ball of foot upon landing, but not beyond the foot.
- Leg swings: Fully extend one arm and brace against a wall, tree, or other stable support at or near shoulder height. Bend slightly at the waist and preserve a straight and elongated spine at all times. Lift one leg off the ground and commence a gentle side-to-side swing, keeping the weighted leg and trunk stable at all times. Don't allow your back to curve/compress with the swing. Don't add more force to the swing beyond the natural momentum created by the weight of your swinging leg. As you gain more competency, you can extend the outer swing to get your leg parallel to the ground (dynamically stretching the hamstrings and adductors), then extend through the por-

tion of the swing across your body to approach parallel on the opposite side (dynamically stretching the glutes).

SELF-MYOFASCIAL RELEASE (ROLLING)

Self-myofascial release is the act of "rolling" muscles with a hard Styrofoam cylinder, a rolling pin-style gizmo with protruding rubber spikes, a hard rubber or rubber-spiked therapy ball, or lacrosse or golf ball. Who knew that rolling out tired, stiff muscles could count toward your movement objectives? A quality rolling session of just 5 to 10 minutes has been found to increase blood circulation in the involved muscles by 50 percent for up to 30 minutes afterward, thereby qualifying as a movement practice. Self-myofascial release is a great postexercise or evening activity to unwind from stress and tension, a popular injury treatment modality for athletes or anyone seeking to combat muscle tension and soreness, and also a great morning or preworkout warm-up activity.

Beyond increasing oxygen delivery and blood circulation, rolling helps reduce inflammation and speed the removal of metabolic waste products in fatigued muscles, improves tissue hydration, improves range of motion in nearby joints, and enhances the function of the lymphatic system (which, like rolling, operates via compression mechanisms). Rolling is often lauded for breaking up adhesions and scar tissue, but this benefit is overblown because muscles are extremely difficult to manipulate or restructure in this manner. Rather, the most significant benefit of self-myofascial release is to generate a relaxation effect in tense, overstimulated, inflamed muscles.

Self-myofascial release helps you unwind from the stress of workouts or a busy day in general by stimulating the parasympathetic nervous system. As you apply pressure and breathe through mild-to-significant discomfort at your trigger points, calming hormones and neurotransmitters are released into your bloodstream. Even if you're amped up after a vigorous workout, you'll start to feel blissfully relaxed after just a few minutes of rolling. You'll also experience significant pain relief in the muscles themselves via the activation of mechanoreceptors that mute sensations of pain generated in the central nervous system. This painkilling effect of stimulating mechanoreceptors is why we have the instinct to rub the affected area when we bump our head or stub a toe.

Self-myofascial release entails using your chosen device to apply deep pressure to muscle groups throughout the body. Experts recommend initiating rolling from the pelvis and working outward, either down the legs or up the torso. Work at a slow pace, going forward for a few seconds, then backward for half that time, then forward. Stay away from joints and connective tissue; for example, rolling along your calves, skipping your knees, and then continuing up your hamstrings. As you apply pressure, you'll discover stiff, sensitive spots known as *trigger points* that represent the origination of injuries and imbalances that might be symptomatic elsewhere. For example, tight calf muscles might be causal to your inflamed Achilles tendons. The painful IT band syndrome that many runners suffer from typically presents as pain on the outside of the knee, but can be treated by working trigger points higher up on the lateral thigh, where the quads, glutes, or hamstrings connect with the IT band. Note that a direct attempt to loosen the IT band does no good—it's a superstrong tendon capable of absorbing 2,000 pounds of pressure per square inch. It will not contract or stretch even with your hardest efforts. Rather, it is working to loosen the muscular adhesions to the IT band that will facilitate healing.

All fitness enthusiasts can benefit greatly from rolling sessions, because ambitious workouts simply don't pair well with the prevailing inactivity patterns of modern life. Consequently, it's easy to develop recurring soreness, stiffness, imbalances, and mobility limitations from an otherwise well-meaning fitness program. Strange as it may seem, you should absolutely be able to lie face down onto a foam roller, roll along the length of your anterior quadriceps (with your bodyweight applying substantial force onto the roller), and not wince in pain. Ditto for grinding a ball into those commonly touch-sensitive calf muscles, or lying down and rolling your trapezius muscles running from your neck through your thoracic spine area. If, for example, your calves are too sensitive to roll under pressure, this indicates dysfunction and an increased need for myofascial release.

Be sure to spend the most time and effort on the trigger points, even if they are the most painful spots. When you find a trigger point,

apply static pressure for 15 to 30 seconds and then continue with your back-and-forth rolling pattern. Be sure to breathe through the discomfort! You will often experience immediate relief from muscle tightness when you finish your work. Effective self-myofascial release will definitely be uncomfortable, even painful, but in a good way. Be consistent with your practice and soon you'll go from an immediate "ouch" upon a light application of pressure, to catlike suppleness, where you can press deeply into your muscles without pain.

Be sure to devote proper attention to opposing muscle groups, so that you address the cause of pain and dysfunction instead of just treating the symptoms. For example, if you have pain in the thoracic area from working in hunched-over positions while texting, typing, driving, and so forth, this represents muscle imbalances between your chest and back. You may have short, tight chest and shoulder muscles, and weak, loose, and elongated back muscles. Rolling those back muscles will make them even longer and looser, perhaps providing immediate relief but exacerbating the muscle imbalance. Instead, attack the cause by rolling out your pectorals, shoulders, and lats.

Know the difference between the desirable pain of working hard to release trigger points and the undesirable pain that comes from overdoing inflamed/injured areas, or hitting nerves, bones, or joints. Be gentle rolling your lower back muscles, because there is minimal muscular protection for the spine in that area. If you have low-back tightness, work on the trigger points in midback, quads, glutes, and even the abs. Don't hesitate to roll all through the abdominal cavity, as this is believed to assist with digestion, healthy circulation in your organs, and also be particularly effective for parasympathetic stimulation. Rolling is an absolute pleasure to integrate into your morning longevity routine, or while relaxing in front of the TV or social time in the evening. A few minutes a day can pay great dividends, so get started right away!

FORMAL MOVEMENT PRACTICES

When you get immersed in the wonderful world of yoga, Pilates, tai chi or the many other formal movement practices that have exploded in popularity in recent years, you are accessing some of the most potent longevity tools known to mankind. These workouts stimulate parasympathetic function by directing your focus inward, and emphasizing diaphragmatic breathing, precise body movements, and soothing music in a relaxed, noncompetitive atmosphere. You feel relaxed and refreshed afterward, and can build upon this momentum to feel great all day long.

In contrast, workouts that emphasize raw energy expenditure—lively group classes with pulsating music, cardio machines with calorie counters, and endurance workouts on the road—stimulate sympathetic fight-or-flight nervous system activity. You may briefly experience a pleasurable postexercise endorphin buzz, but the net effect

of the workout is to add to your overall life-stress levels of all forms. Hence, these raw energy expenditure workouts fall into a different category than the restorative nature of formal movement practices, as well as the distinct recovery-based workouts that I'll detail in the following section.

Your best bet with formal movement practices is to enroll in a program with a qualified teacher at a studio or health club in your area. You'll gain the dual benefits of expert instruction to develop proper technique, and also the motivation and compliance benefits of being compelled to get your butt to the 5 p.m. yoga class instead of lingering at work for another hour on Tuesday evenings.

Yoga: With a 5,000-year track record, yoga is now being integrated into mainstream medical treatments for mental illness, chronic lower back pain, and many other maladies we've traditionally treated with prescription medication and surgery. You can indulge in a tremendous variety of programming, from mini-sessions in your own home, working off a sun salutation baseline, to group classes that range from gentle and restorative to incredibly challenging.

Pilates: Pilates is celebrated for helping you develop a strong and flexible core and excellent posture and functional movement techniques. Joseph Pilates created the original program in the 1920s as a means of rehabilitating feeble hospital patients and wounded soldiers. You can conduct Pilates with just a floor mat, engaging in a variety of creative prescribed moves, or use the Pilates Reformer machine in a group setting with a certified instructor. The Reformer looks like a small bed with an assortment of straps and springs to provide resistance, and a sliding carriage to move your body through space as a component of the exercises.

Whatever you may have heard about Pilates or think when you see a room full of Reformer machines ready for new victims, don't be intimidated. The program is appropriate for all ability levels and scalable to your current level of fitness. Being low-impact and intently focused on safety and stability, Pilates is great for everyone from serious athletes to seniors, pregnant women, and those interested in injury rehabilitation. Try a class with a good instructor and see if you can catch the bug!

Tai chi: The ancient movement popular in the East originated as a martial art, but is today recognized as the preeminent mindful movement exercise in the world. Literally billions of people on the planet make tai chi a daily ritual to achieve calmness and focus, and improve balance and proprioception. Dr. Peter Wayne, director of research for the Osher Center for Integrative Medicine at Harvard Medical School and author of *The Harvard Medical School Guide to Tai Chi*, describes the benefits of tai chi: "A growing body of carefully conducted research is building a compelling case for tai chi as an adjunct to standard medical treatment for the prevention and rehabilitation of many conditions commonly associated with age." Tai chi is also a great choice for those who struggle with sitting meditation. Dr. Wayne and others are fond of the nickname "meditation in motion." At UCLA's Mindful Awareness Research Center, numerous studies have been published touting tai chi's benefits to treat arthritis, depression, digestive disturbances, inflammatory and autoimmune conditions, insomnia, and basically all other conditions associated with hectic, overly stressful modern life.

CARDIOVASCULAR EXERCISE

When you add a few hours of structured cardio workouts per week to your general everyday movement efforts, you are doing a great job honoring your genetic expectations to live an active lifestyle. Your cardio workouts can happen in any activity that you enjoy, such as brisk walking or jogging, exercise machines such as the treadmill, elliptical, stair climber, stationary bike, or Versa-Climber (my personal favorite machine—like a moving ladder engaging both arms and legs!), swimming, or any other activity that elevates your heart rate into the aerobic, fat-burning zone for a sustained period.

Cardiovascular exercise that emphasizes fat burning helps turbocharge fat metabolism around the clock. At a comfortable pace, you have plenty of oxygen available to make fat your predominant fuel source, which prompts the huge longevity booster that is mitochondrial biogenesis. Comfortably paced aerobic workouts also help optimize immune and hormonal function, stabilize appetite and mood, stimulate brain-derived neurotropic factor to build new brain neurons, and leave you feeling refreshed and energized for the rest of the day.

Contrary to flawed "no pain, no gain" fitness concepts, you don't have to worry about maintaining a certain minimum heart rate for your effort to qualify as an aerobic workout. Even JFW delivers a cardiovascular training effect, because you are more than doubling your resting heart rate when you so much as walk around the block or up a couple flights of stairs. The bigger concern is to be absolutely sure that you maintain a heart rate in the aerobic zone for the duration of your workout. The upper limit of your aerobic zone is "180 minus age" in heartbeats per minute, a calculation promoted for decades by legendary endurance coach Dr. Phil Maffetone. You simply subtract your age from 180 and stay at or below this heart rate for the duration of your workout. For example, a 50-year-old exerciser would calculate an aerobic max of 130 beats per minute (180 minus age 50).

During an aerobic session, you are burning mostly fat for fuel and the effort feels easy to moderate. At the "180 minus age" upper limit of your aerobic zone, you are achieving peak fat oxidation—burning more fat calories per minute than at any other heart rate. Hence you are experiencing maximum aerobic benefits with a minimum amount of anaerobic stimulation. If you were to increase your effort beyond your maximum aerobic heart rate, you would of course burn more total calories per minute, but your fat-oxidation rate would decline in favor of increased glucose burning. You would also prompt more fight-or-flight hormone production and cellular waste products that can lead to longer recovery times and more risk of breakdown and burnout. The main objective of aerobic exercise is to increase energy, enhance fat metabolism, optimize immune and hormonal function, and allow you to improve your conditioning steadily over time without accumulating fatigue. Note: You must maintain aerobic heart rates for the entirety of your workout. If you go too fast, even for a bit, and stimulate increased glucose burning, it's hard to return to a lower-stress, fat-burning state.

BEWARE OF THE BLACK HOLE

Unfortunately, the invigorating sensation of getting into that medium-to-difficult intensity zone, combined with the flawed mindset that you aren't getting a productive workout unless you're suffering a bit, combined with the surprisingly easy perceived exertion of an aerobic workout, prompts exercisers of all levels to habitually and often unknowingly make the mistake of exceeding aerobic maximum heart rate. Besides compromising your fat-burning goals, overly stressful workouts can trash your health and compromise longevity in many other ways.

When you engage in a pattern of workouts that are of medium-ish intensity—not challenging enough to be considered truly explosive, high-intensity sessions, but too strenuous to qualify as aerobic, fat-burning workouts—you enter what exercise scientists call the "black hole." Black hole sessions put you into a different metabolic and hormonal state—burning more glucose and less fat, and increasing stress hormone production and muscular fatigue. While it's okay to challenge yourself with a lively group class or an outing with the fast pack on the road once in a while, it's a sustained pattern of these slightly too difficult workouts that becomes overly stressful, depleting, and immune-suppressing, and that accelerates the aging process.

Black hole training has been shown conclusively to increase the risk of cardiovascular disease, mitochondrial damage, and accelerated aging. That's right, that neighbor of yours who's up before dawn faithfully putting in road miles and accumulating marathon finisher medals, can also be accumulating risk factors at a similar rate to your other neighbor, the Cheeto-chomping couch potato. A phenomenon called the *excessive endurance exercise hypothesis* is gaining traction in scientific circles. One of the leading voices is Dr. James O'Keefe, a sports cardiologist in Kansas City (view his TEDx talk titled "Run for your life! At a comfortable pace, and not too far") and co-author of *The Forever Young Diet & Lifestyle*. Dr. O'Keefe mentions how droves of seasoned marathon runners with ideal body composition and healthy blood profiles nevertheless have increased scarring, thickening, and a searing of their arterial walls caused by chronic exercise-driven inflammation. Their six-pack physiques belie the markedly elevated levels of calcified and noncalcified arterial plaque inside their rapidly aging hearts and cardiovascular systems.

Dr. Peter Attia is one of the world's leading experts on longevity, ketogenic eating, and fat-adapted athletic performance, and host of a fabulous podcast launched in 2018 called *The Drive*. He describes how mitochondria become damaged by chronic exercise, a scary story of accelerated aging and health destruction to ponder: "When mitochondria are heated up too frequently for too long, proteins become denatured (destruction of the tertiary elements of the molecule, causing dysfunction) and mitochondrial DNA leaks out of cells." This is highly problematic because mitochondrial DNA is a foreign agent to your body. The issue is that mitochondrial DNA are different from cellular DNA, and strikingly similar to bacteria cells. When mitochondrial DNA leaks into the bloodstream (this is particularly prevalent in the intestinal tract via a leaky gut), your immune system is confused into launching an attack against a perceived invader. This triggers an inflammatory autoimmune response (essentially the body attacking itself), a sustained pattern of which accelerates aging and disease risk.

These issues have touched the CrossFit community as well, as the occasional exhausted, dehydrated WOD enthusiast (CrossFit speak for "Workout of the Day," challenges that are presented on their website for followers to strive for) has presented in the hospital with the rare condition known as rhabdomyolysis. "Rabdo," which occurs when traumatized muscle cells burst, and contents leak into the bloodstream, bring risk of serious complications in the kidneys, heart, and lungs.

Dr. O'Keefe's firm conclusion is that moderate cardiovascular exercise is healthier than extreme exercise. He offers a specific recommendation of running just a couple hours per week at an aerobic pace to optimize cardiovascular health, noting that anything beyond starts to travel along that bell curve path into the danger zone of increased disease risk. Because it's so easy to drift into the black hole without feeling strain, it's essential to use a heart rate monitor with a limit alarm to help you stay aerobic. The highest accuracy comes with a high-quality wireless heart rate monitor with a chest strap, which you can get for less than 50 bucks these days. In contrast, the Apple Watch delivers a reported 91-percent accuracy in measuring wrist pulse, while other smart watches have been tested to be less than 80 percent accurate. A 10-percent margin of error is decidedly insufficient for the purpose of staying at or below maximum aerobic heart rate with complete certainty during a workout.

If you refuse to use a heart monitor, you should at least apply the low-tech strategies of nose breathing or the talk test. If you are exercising in the aerobic zone, you should be able to recite the alphabet out loud without gasping for air. Or, you should also be able to exercise with your mouth closed, drawing sufficient air through your nostrils only. Nose breathing during workouts provides the added benefit of facilitating deep, diaphragmatic breaths, where you engage the oxygen-rich lower lobes of the lungs for maximum respiratory efficiency. Exhibiting the patience and discipline to slow down and develop the aerobic system properly will pay tremendous dividends to everyone from elites to novices. While slowing down may not be as much fun as the endorphin buzz you get from a vigorous workout, you can enjoy the satisfaction of making steady and quantifiable progress with your aerobic fitness over time, without the usual interruptions of breakdown, burnout, illness, and injury caused by chronic exercise. As your fat-burning efficiency improves, you'll discover that you can maintain a faster pace at the same aerobic heart rate. For example, you'll transition from brisk walking to smooth jogging without the limit alarm sounding, or be able to pedal uphill at 11 mph instead of 8 mph.

The best way to quantify your aerobic improvement is through the MAF test (stands for Maximum Aerobic Function, but also a play on Dr. Maffetone's name—the originator of the test). Here, you find a measured course that you will repeat for every test, such as a running track, a measured bike path, or a bicycle hill climb. You can also use GPS technology outdoors or a cardio machine that measures output. Commence your timed test over the desired distance, such as 8 laps around a running track or 1.5 miles on the GPS watch. Do your best to stabilize your heart rate right at your aerobic maximum (130 beats per minute in the example of the 50-year-old), and record your finishing time. As your aerobic fitness improves, you will be able to complete the same course, at the same heart rate, more quickly.

For your overall cardiovascular fitness objective, strive to land in the very modest sweet spot described by Dr. O'Keefe—a bit of easy jogging, pedaling, or paddling each week, and some ambitious weekend hikes or urban adventures. It's great to do an occasional challenge like a community 10k run where you significantly exceed your aerobic maximum heart rate, stimulate a fitness adaption, and take appropriate recovery afterward. Don't worry about following strict guidelines or time minimums with your aerobic workouts. Even short-duration stuff is great, such as trotting a few laps around the park during your kid's soccer practice. Coupled with your devoted efforts to increase general everyday movement, a modest commitment to structured cardio sessions will help you nail the cardiovascular fitness objective that is so important for longevity.

STRENGTH TRAINING

Modern humans pretty much suck at strength training because of the never-ending innovations and luxuries that minimize the need to expend physical effort. This is what I refer to as a *disconnect* from our genetic expectations for health, informed by our long history of hardworking, heavy-lifting, constantly moving hunter-gatherers. Unless you're huffing and puffing in a busy warehouse, loading dock, or construction site, you'll have to join me in orchestrating opportunities to lift heavy things in comfortable modern life.

Let's lower the bar, pun intended, and make your foray into strength training simple and enjoyable. No matter how weak and/or uninterested you are currently in strength training, I can help you get started with a fun, safe, time-efficient program to get stronger. Even longtime cardio kings and queens often fall in love with strength training as soon as they start a program. I know I did. After my marathon and Ironman triathlon days ended and I was looking to preserve an athletic physique with a minimal time commitment, I got off the road for the most part and hit the weights hard. What I experienced was an immediate improvement in mood, energy, appetite stability, muscle mass, posture, sleep quality, and libido. The connective tissue pain I'd had for decades—caused by my high mileage on the road—nearly vanished. Most shocking of all: I maintained a high level of endurance despite cutting my training hours back drastically. Granted, I had an excellent aerobic

base built over decades, but the return on investment from my explosive, short-duration sessions was phenomenal.

The good news is that strength training takes only a fraction of the time that your movement and cardio objectives require. There is a popular concept among biohackers called Minimal Effective Dose (MED)—a threshold where you obtain the vast majority of benefit in the most time-efficient manner, and in this case without the health risks of excess exercise. With aerobic exercise, the MED would be Dr. O'Keefe's recommendation of a few hours a week of easy-paced cardio. For strength training, I hereby set the MED at 2 workouts per week, lasting as little as 10 minutes and no more than 30 minutes each. Believe it or not, this is sufficient to get exceptionally strong and trigger potent antiaging hormonal signals. Since so many fitness enthusiasts are immersed in chronic exercise patterns, and/or do too much cardio and not enough strength training, this requires a fundamental change in mindset. You don't have to suffer through prolonged workouts that lead to exhaustion in order to get fit. You can perform short duration, high-quality, high-intensity sessions that are challenging to be sure, but leave you relaxed and satisfied over a job well done at the end—not fried.

The reason you want your formal strength training sessions to be 30 minutes or less is so the fight-or-flight hormonal response is brief and you are able to quickly return to homeostasis. This aligns with our genetic expectations for health, framed by our ancestors' brief life-or-death stressors and utter lack of modern chronic stressors. If your strength sessions last too long or are too frequent, they can have a depleting effect and cause cortisol and other stress hormones to linger in the bloodstream too long, with catabolic consequences. Depleting workouts will prompt brief euphoria afterward, followed by hours of mood, energy, and appetite fluctuations, increased sugar cravings, sleep disturbances, immune disturbances, and eventually diminished motivation and performance. Even if you don't fall apart with illness and injury like many well-intentioned fitness enthusiasts who get stuck in chronic patterns, you'll likely become mediocre instead of stronger and more explosive over time. If you're already quite fit and motivated to make rapid strength gains, strive to increase the degree of difficulty of your workouts rather than extend the duration.

Any form of strength training that you enjoy will deliver fantastic benefits, so strive to keep things simple, enjoyable, and convenient. Reject the massive amount of hype and marketing glitz in the fitness scene that attempts to manipulate you into thinking you must join a gym, hire a trainer, use free weights instead of machines, or switch up your workout routine every week to achieve muscle confusion and prevent stagnation. If you do nothing more than a few sets of squats and pushups in your living room on a regular basis for the rest of your life, you are grabbing the low-hanging fruit in this category.

Generally, your strength sessions should feature a small number of exercises, with a weight or resistance level allowing you to complete 8 to 12 repetitions until the relevant muscles become temporarily exhausted. Take sufficient recovery between each set so that the entirety of your workout is explosive, and all moves are conducted with impeccable form. Emphasize sweeping, full-body, functional movements such as squats, deadlifts, pushups, pull-ups, planks, and Olympic lifts, or compound movements using resistance bands, straps, or machines. These big moves have better real-life application than the isolation or "vanity" exercises that work fewer muscle groups. There are endless methods of putting your body under resistance load while honoring these philosophical guidelines, including gym machines, free weights, home fitness machines such as Bowflex, resistance bands and straps such as TRX or StrechCordz, fitness routes in the park with challenge equipment placed at regular intervals, and so much more. Thank you, Thighmaster!

PRIMAL ESSENTIAL MOVEMENTS (PEMs)

The PEMs comprise four of the simplest and most effective exercises ever known to humankind: pushups, pull-ups, squats, and planks. There are easier progression exercises in each movement to allow novices to load the same muscles and work toward competency in performing the baseline essential movement. For example, chair-assisted pull-ups or incline pushups. Search YouTube for "Mark Sisson Primal Essential Movements" to learn correct technique for the baseline movements of the progression exercises. Following is a brief overview describing the PEMs and their progression exercises.

Pushups (lats, pecs, triceps): Assume pushup plank position (arms extended below you, hands forward, body straight from head to toe). Lower to ground—chest touching first! Keep body dead straight, core and glutes tight, head and neck neutral to torso. Elbows bend backward at 45-degree angle as you lower. Mastery level: male 50, female 20

Easiest progression—wall pushups: Stand with your arms extended and hands resting against a wall. Maintain plank position as you lower to the wall and reextend your arms to starting position.

Next progression—incline pushups: Rest your hands on a bench, chair, or other elevated surface. Maintain plank position as you raise and lower.

Pull-ups (back, lats, pecs, biceps): Grasp bar at shoulder width with overhanded grip. Elbows tight, chin tucked, shoulder blades retracted to protect spine. Lead with chest up, keeping lower body quiet. Raise your chin over the bar and gradually lower all the way until your arms are just before straight but not straight. Mastery level: male 12, female 5.

Easiest progression—chair-assisted pull-up: Start with one leg loosely positioned on a support chair underneath the bar. Engage your upper body muscles and raise yourself up to the bar, using the minimum leg force necessary to get your chin over the bar. You probably need to use only one leg, but can use two if necessary. Yes, everyone can do pull-ups!

Next progression—chin-up: Invert your grip on the bar so your palms face you, and raise yourself until your chin is over the bar. Many people find the chin-up to be slightly easier than a pull-up, particularly if you have wrist, elbow, or shoulder issues.

Squats (lower body): Remember the technique pointers described in the movement section: feet straight, spine straight, keep chest up, and lower as if sitting in a chair—loading quads and glutes. Screw feet into the ground—left foot turning counterclockwise, right foot clockwise—always tracking over the feet, never caving in. Mastery level: male 50, female 50.

Easiest progression—assisted squats: Hold a pole or support object while lowering into and raising up from squat position. As with the chair-assisted pull-ups, try to use the support object as little as possible.

Planks (core and lower back, as well as shoulders, triceps, hip flexors): Hold pushup plank position while resting your elbows on the ground for as long as possible until your body sags or arms and shoulders fatigue. An optional movement to stimulate the oblique abs is to lean on one extended arm and rotate body into sideways plank position, preserving a straight line from your head to toe. Hold until failure, and then repeat on other side. Mastery of straight plank: male 2 minutes, female 2 minutes.

Easiest progression—forearm/knee plank: Assume plank position with forearms and knees resting on ground. Engage core muscles and glutes during exercise.

Next progression—hand/feet plank: Assume plank position à la pushup starting point, with arms extended and hands and feet on ground. Yes, this is easier than the forearm plank!

MAXIMUM OVERLOAD TRAINING

One example honoring the explosive, high-quality, minimally stressful workout is called Maximum Overload Training, developed by Jacques DeVore, coauthor of *Bicycling Maximum Overload for Cyclists* and founder of Sirens & Titans Fitness in Southern California. Maximum Overload sessions entail lifting a heavy weight/difficult resistance load and conducting shorter, more numerous sets. This allows you to hoist the same load over and over (instead of having to go lighter), rest more frequently, and thereby minimize the cumulative fatigue of the workout. In contrast, a typical no-pain, no-gain session might entail loading up a deadlift bar with 80 percent of your one-rep max (the most weight you can lift in a single effort) and performing numerous sets until failure. Let's use 200 pounds for this example. Perhaps you'll achieve 12 reps to failure on your first set, 8 on the second set after a short break, and 5 on the third and final set—the decline in reps due to the challenge of repeatedly

going until failure with minimal rest. Maybe you'd repeat this template for assorted other exercises like squats, bicep curls, bench press, overhead press, and so on. By the end of an hour-long session like this, you might feel pretty cooked from maxing out so many times and soldiering on amid mounting fatigue.

For a Maximum Overload session using the same 200 pounds, you might perform 6 reps at first, dropping the weight for rest before your form cracks even a bit or extra strain is required to continue to temporary exhaustion. After an extended rest period, you'd return to the bar feeling fully refreshed and energized. You might feel even better than the first set because the moderately strenuous first set primed your central nervous system for explosive effort, bringing greater motor unit recruitment and force production to the next set. This concept of feeling more explosive after an initial priming effort is called *post-activation potentiation*. You'll easily get another 6 reps on your second set, then drop for more rest. Perhaps you'll get 5 reps on the ensuing set, then 4, then another 4, then 2, then another 2, and a final 2 before you realize that any further effort might compromise form or require a substantial increase in effort.

In the first example, you've completed 25 total reps of 200 pounds, lifting 5,000 pounds. In the Maximum Overload example, you've completed 31 reps, lifting 6,200 pounds. You are quite likely less fried, because no single bout of explosive performance was overly taxing, but you have lifted nearly 25 percent more total weight! Maybe you'll apply the same Maximum Overload protocol to one or two other exercises, and wrap up your workout in less than 30 minutes.

When you preserve explosiveness throughout your workout, you send the right signals to your genes to build muscle and accelerate fat-burning, without the risks of burnout, inflammation, and immune suppression that happens with the comparative pattern of overly stressful, blended workouts.

SPRINTING

Sprinting is the ultimate antiaging workout, honoring the natural law of longevity that is, "use it or lose it." When you occasionally push your body to perform at maximum capacity for brief bursts, you experience a host of positive hormonal, psychological, neuroendocrine, and structural benefits similar to those described with strength training. After all, humans evolved amidst the occasional brief life-or-death threats calling for superhuman physical efforts—to kill or be killed! When we hone our fight-or-flight attributes once in a while as our genes expect us to, we stay youthful, powerful, vibrant, and self-confident. Conversely, when you indulge in endless modern comforts and conveniences, stay constantly warm and well-fed, and never stress the organism to spur hormesis, your mind and body atrophy across the board and you become less resilient to all forms of life stress.

Sprint workouts turbo-charge fat-burning around the clock, enhance oxygen utilization and maximal oxygen uptake in the lungs, enhance insulin sensitivity and the ability to store and use glycogen, and improve your muscle buffering capacity (better lactate clearance and less acidosis during exercise). Exercise physiologists have known for decades that even a single all-out sprint of 10 to 30 seconds triggers mitochondrial biogenesis and assorted other benefits through the spiking of the AMPK (adenosine monophosphate–activated protein kinase). AMPK is an enzyme lauded for its wide-ranging beneficial functions relating to cellular energy production.

Psychologically, sprint workouts reduce your perceived exertion and extend your "time to fatigue" threshold at all lower levels of intensity. When you become competent at sprinting, all of your other workouts seem easier. Sprinting also elicits that treasured spike in adaptive, antiaging hormones, which work their magic to keep your brain neurons, mitochondria, organs, muscles, joints, and connective tissue youthful and resilient.

Sprinting can help accelerate fat loss more than any other workout, because the intensity of the effort has an extreme impact on your metabolism for many hours afterward. Sprinting has been found to elevate your metabolic function up to 30 times higher than resting baseline, a measurement known as metabolic equivalent of Task (MET). A 30 MET workout sends a strong adaptive signal to your genes to shed excess body fat, because excess weight is a tremendous hindrance to sprinting performance—unlike with jogging or easy pedaling (these workouts range from 6 to 10 MET). This is another genetically programmed survival mechanism to prepare for future (perceived as life-or-death) maximum physical efforts. If you are stuck in the flawed and dated calories in/calories out fitness mindset, it might be hard to imagine how a brief workout that you only conduct a few times per month can have a measurable impact on your fat loss and fitness progress, but this is how genetic signaling works. Throw some 30 MET fuel into your fat-burning machine and it kicks into high gear for up to 72 hours after the workout.

HOW TO CONDUCT A SPRINT WORKOUT PROPERLY

Because sprinting is so physically stressful, you have to honor numerous important elements that will help you maximize benefits and minimize the risk of overstress and breakdown. Since a little goes such a long way with sprinting, one quality session every 7 to 10 days is ideal. The first guideline is to only attempt these sessions when you are *100 percent rested and motivated* to deliver a peak-performance effort. This means you are chomping at the bit as you jog over to the track, or find yourself daydreaming about your evening session while working in your office. This also means there will be occasions where you do your warm-up, launch into your first sprint, and feel a little off. Perhaps it's muscle tightness, technique deficiencies, or an abnormal sensation of fatigue. At these times, it's best to pull the plug and return another day when your muscles and brain are ready to perform.

The next essential element of a quality sprint session is to complete an *extensive warm-up and preparatory drills* before you commence the main set of sprints. This is especially important with high-impact running sprints to protect your muscles and joints from injury. A proper warm-up gets a light sweat going, along with elevated body temperature, respiration, and heart rate. From there, you can perform some dynamic stretches, such as the mini-lunges and knee-to-chests that ensure joints are lubricated and muscles are flexible. Next, you can conduct a few "wind sprints" where you focus on excellent technique, steadily accelerate into just a few seconds at top speed, then stride (or pedal, paddle, or row) back down to a gradual stop. After an excellent warm-up, you should feel supple, focused, and ready for some explosive efforts.

When it's time for the main set of sprints, it's essential to choose the *optimal duration, rest interval, and number of repetitions*. Remember, the goal is to stimulate an adaptive hormonal response without the risk of overstress, depletion, or injury from doing sprints that are too numerous or last too long to qualify as truly explosive. Recent science makes a compelling case for staying in a narrow range of 10 to 20 seconds duration for your sprints. This is where maximum fitness benefits can occur with a minimum amount of cellular damage. After all, it's impossible to maintain maximum output for longer than 20 seconds anyway, and attempting to do so can cause some adverse physiological reactions.

For each sprint of 10 to 20 seconds, you must

deliver a *consistent quality of effort*. This will inform the quantity of sprints you perform within a tight range. Consistent quality means both your performance standard and level of perceived effort are nearly the same for each sprint. A tiny bit of attrition is expected, but again—no suffer-fests allowed. For example, if your first sprint across a football field takes 18 seconds and you rate the effort 85 (on a scale of 1 to 100), your final sprint should be no more than 19 seconds with a difficulty rating of 85 to 90.

The duration of your rest interval between each sprint should be sufficient for your respiration to return to near normal (not heart rate, which will stay elevated well above resting level) and for you to experience renewed enthusiasm and complete focus for another effort. Take what sprinting expert Dr. Craig Marker calls "luxurious" rest intervals. Even elite athletes have been known to rest for several minutes after brief sprints. This ensures an optimal replenishment of the key sources of cellular energy for explosive performance: ATP (adenosine triphosphate) and creatine phosphate.

As you catch your breath and shake out muscle tension, also pay attention to signs of mental fatigue caused by the extreme demand placed on the central nervous system to fire motor neurons for explosive efforts. If you find yourself staggering around, taking shallow panting breaths, or whining and complaining during the recovery period, these are signs that your nervous system is getting fried (could be from ammonia toxicity, which brain neurons are especially sensitive to) and it's time to quit. Knowing you crossed the line with symptoms like these, you can then revise future workouts to be more sensible and less destructive.

You should be able to perform at least three or four good sprints before your quality control drops. If you can't, you're going too long or too hard out of the gate. If you can deliver 6 to 10 reps of consistent quality, strive for faster times at future sessions instead of adding reps. With sprinting, more is not better, and 6 to 10 reps is plenty for even a supremely fit athlete. Indeed, 6 to 10 sprints of only 10 to 20 seconds' duration is all you ever need to become a competent sprinter. (Hit the lower reps and duration for running; upper ranges for low-impact exercises.) Keep this in mind when you commonly hear the term "sprint" misappropriated by athletes and trainers. For example: "We did six times 400-meter sprints on the track today!" or, "We did twenty sprints at the end of Spinning class today, it was tough!" In these and endless other examples of high-stress interval workouts, the volume and/or duration is far too excessive to qualify as a true sprint workout.

The final component of a successful sprint workout is the cooldown, where you want to gradually transition from an elevated metabolic state back to a resting state. This entails some light jogging or other activity for 7 to 10 minutes. After your final sprint, gradually diminish your activity until you stop sweating and your breathing rate returns to normal. You can end with some dynamic stretches to address tightness in problem areas, or even static stretches if you have an injury prevention protocol. As with a good warm-up, a gradual cooldown will minimize the stress of the workout.

This is because fight-or-flight mechanisms are activated when you abruptly transition from an inactive into an active state (obviously, as when a predator pounces), and also vice versa.

If you neglect a cooldown, clearance of muscular waste products can be compromised, fight-or-flight hormones can linger (instead of being replaced by calming hormones like dopamine and serotonin, produced during the cooldown), and blood can pool in the extremities. Your recovery continues after you leave the track or the gym. For the next 24 to 36 hours, it's essential to be more active and less sedentary. This will ensure that you keep inflammation under control, leverage all the fat-burning benefits triggered by the workout, and enable your circulatory and lymphatic systems to efficiently clear waste products from muscles.

In summary, the components of an effective sprint workout are as follows: Pick the *right day* (100 percent rested and energized) and the *right exercise* (high-impact sprinting delivers the best weight-loss and musculoskeletal benefits; if low- or no-impact sprints are more appropriate, know they are still beneficial). Complete a deliberate and focused *warm-up and preparatory drills*. Choose the appropriate *work efforts* (10 to 20 seconds), *rest intervals* (luxurious, to ensure your cells and brain are refreshed for the next effort), and *reps* (minimum 4, maximum 10). After your final sprint, conduct an appropriate *cooldown* (gradual transition from peak state to resting state lessens stress impact), *keep active* over the next couple days, and *recover completely* before ensuing workouts, at a frequency of once every 7 to 10 days.

PLAY

The category of play is included in the Movement and Physical Fitness Pillar, because you can get a fantastic workout by engaging in an endless variety of outdoor, unstructured physical fun, including both brief interludes here and there (a few minutes of roughhousing in the yard with your dog) and grand weekend outings to learn surfing, rock climbing, orienteering, or stand-up paddling. A quality play session will include one or all of the aforementioned fitness endeavors. For example, my favorite activity in recent years has been a weekly Ultimate Frisbee match where I mix it up with hotshots like my son and others half my age.

I give it all I got during these 2-hour sessions, featuring nonstop movement, tons of brief explosive sprints to catch, or defend, a scoring pass, and all manner of body contortions, quick change of direction moves, and explosive jumps requiring muscular strength, balance, and flexibility. I'm having so much fun competing that I don't realize I'm putting in a few miles of aerobic jogging, along with getting what amounts to an excellent sprint workout and strength training session. Actually, I must admit that much of my motivation for working so hard at sprint workouts and lifting sessions in the gym is to prime me for my Ultimate matches, and minimize the risk of injury when I engage in any other form of athletic activity.

The epiphany about the importance of play came to me later in life, after retiring from marathon and Ironman triathlon competition and allowing myself to explore more diverse fitness endeavors. Reflecting upon my decades of racing, a profound insight occurred to me: At no point during any of the hundreds of hours of endurance competitions could I ever admit I was actually having fun. Sure, I obtained plenty of self-satisfaction from working hard to achieve lofty competitive goals, and had plenty of blissful flow-state experiences during epic workouts. But endurance sports, at least at a competitive level, are all about pain management and preserving focus to outlast your competitors at a grueling pace. We talked about avoiding suffer-fest workouts, but endurance races are exactly that from start to finish!

Here are your two assignments in this category: Take some time every day to unplug from the office or daily chores for some unstructured outdoor physical fun. Even a few minutes of play here and there during a busy day makes a big difference. Dogs or kids can get you in the groove, as they require these opportunities more than ever in our new hyperconnected world. You can also learn a thing or two from these naturally playful canine or human companions. Second, get yourself or the whole gang out for a grand outing once a month, such as a hike, mountain bike ride, stand-up paddling, golf round, or rock-climbing adventure. Constantly explore new places and novel adventures—it's the essence of your humanity!

If your Type A voice is whispering self-critical words into your head while you're trying to carve out time for play, realize that play has been scientifically proven to help you return to life responsibilities with more focus and productivity. Speaking of Type A, did you know that this term—one that is often used in a complimentary manner to describe busy, seemingly productive types—was originally used to describe those in the highest risk category for heart attacks?

PILLAR #3
MENTAL FLEXIBILITY

For many highly motivated, goal-oriented health enthusiasts, it's often easier to carry out distinct marching orders (ditch sugars and grains!) than it is to engage in honest self-reflection about your belief systems and automatic behavior patterns, catch yourself when you regress, and recalibrate in the heat of the moment. In this pillar, we will cover an assortment of topics requiring an open mind, a willingness to grow, and a devotion to taking practical steps to break free from the mental ruts in which we may have unknowingly existed for decades.

You'll start by honing the valuable skill of "pivoting"—expertly recalibrating and persevering through life's ups and downs. Next, you'll reject self-limiting beliefs and behavior patterns and start living a life of passion and purpose. You'll practice being mindful and appreciating the present, instead of ruminating about the past or the future. You'll cultivate a formal gratitude practice, retraining your brain to appreciate what you have instead of succumbing to the forces of FOMO and consumerism. You'll nurture loving, reciprocative social connections, being especially vigilant to prevent digital connections from crowding out real ones.

LEARN TO PIVOT

This is my favorite word to describe perhaps the single most essential entrepreneurial attribute, not to mention personal life attribute that represents the essence of mental flexibility. Pivoting means you are highly adaptable to ever-changing life circumstances and challenges. You are committed to self-awareness, open to constructive feedback, and willing to say "I'm sorry," "My bad," and "I was wrong." You learn from your mistakes and failures, embracing everything as growth opportunities. You are always focused on the appreciation of the process, and release the attachment of your self-esteem to the outcome.

Pivoting enables you to access your highest peak-performance potential, because it makes you fearless against the rigidity of beliefs and behavior patterns that cause us widespread pain and suffering. Instead, you are able to maintain an open heart, an open mind, and live in radical acceptance of whatever life has in store for you. Finally, you understand the distinction between pivoting as recalibrating your competitive intensity versus pivoting so that your doormat can welcome people trampling on you from all directions.

Perhaps the best application of pivoting is with the matter of aging gracefully. I'm a firm believer in the importance of maintaining competitive intensity throughout life, but you must continually recalibrate your goals and mindset

so you rage against the dying of the light with a smile instead of with a chip on your shoulder. I remember a watershed moment in my journey as both a parent and an athlete. It came at the end of an epic day of snowboarding in Colorado with my then-teenage son, Kyle. We'd bonded over athletics and adventure since he was a child, chalking up numerous experiences that are among my most precious life memories. On our final run of the day, I decided to open up the throttle a bit and test my limits. I'll admit that there were more than a few competitive juices flowing between us that day as we pushed ourselves to performance breakthroughs on double black diamond slopes. Nearing the bottom of our final run, adrenalin flowing, in the flow state, I reached what was likely a new personal speed record. I felt like the king of the mountain! Just then, out of the corner of my eye a blurry streak appeared on the other side of the ski run. Yep, it was Kyle blowing past me!

My immediate visceral sensation felt like a punch to the gut; I simply could not believe *anyone* could blow by me at that speed, let alone the little squirt whom I strapped into his first board a decade earlier. As I backed off and cruised into the lodge area, profound revelations flooded my consciousness. First, I had ceded the Sisson throne to the kid. Not only was I not king of the mountain, I wasn't even in control of my own mortality. The stylized reaction of my ego quickly faded, and a big smile appeared. What better way to get your butt kicked than by your own protégé? What better representation of aging gracefully than to set the pace for as long as humanly possible, allow a new frontrunner to emerge, and then assume a position in the pack—knowing you will soon be fighting just to hang on?

This brings to mind another nuance to pivoting that is less appreciated but perhaps just as important as changing tactics in pursuit of a specific goal: quitting. Yes, eating your losses, swallowing your pride, and pivoting on a dime into an entirely new direction. I must admit that every time I've quit something important in my life, I've experienced some level of remorse. This was, and still is, disturbing to me. I knew it was the right decision to make, so why did I feel remorse? I speculate that it's from our unhealthy modern attachments to possessions and status quo. As Dr. De Vany's previous insight reminds us, we've drifted so far from our evolutionary baseline of "another lifeway in which material goods do not matter," that our "restless, underutilized" minds manufacture nonstop drama today. The tragedy that is today's closed restaurant, divorce, bankruptcy, stock market slide, or family dispute is largely laughable at the *Homo sapiens* genetic level. After all, our ancestors were bathed in routine daily uncertainty, struggle, and suffering to an extent that's unimaginable today. At those times when you experience emotions that are illogical or difficult to rationalize upon major life changes, it's best to be kind to yourself, refrain from judgment or shame, and realize that "this too shall pass," perhaps without a great explanation.

When I look back at the twists and turns of my athletic and entrepreneurial journeys, I realize that every time I quit something when I wasn't feeling the magic, it eventually propelled me toward my true calling (at that time) in my life. Perhaps you can relate to similar pivot points in the journey that made you the person you are today. When I was (finally) able to whole-heartedly pivot in the direction of my unique talents and vision, I had no problem going all in—even amidst some "Are you crazy, Mark?" feedback from the world. And I had absolutely no problem making it through the extremely tough times that would have buried me had I not believed I was serving my destiny. Conversely, whenever I stubbornly stayed the course on stuff that didn't feel right—head down, prideful, stubborn, and with those endurance-athlete genes willing to suffer through whatever—I went down in flames.

With my restaurant chain venture, there were at least seven times along the route where I knew I should have bailed, absorbed a significant financial loss, and redirected my attention to the stuff I do best. But, as my flawed thinking went, I was so heavily invested at those checkpoints that I couldn't bear to pivot. Instead, I invested even more heavily. Indeed, the opposite of pivoting is getting stuck in a career or relationship rut and drifting toward Einstein's theory of insanity: doing the same thing over and over and expecting a different result. As you might imagine, insane behavior is not good for gene expression, so developing the skill to pivot is absolutely essential to your health, happiness, and longevity. Following are some exercises to hone your pivoting skills:

- Play the "WhaT WiTCH" game. When faced with dilemmas or life crisis, it may be helpful to perform an exercise called, "What's the Worst that Can Happen?" Interestingly, whatever sequence of worst-case scenario answers you come up with, the game ends up at the same destination for everyone: That's right, your eventual final answer is that you die. For a high-speed example, let's say you're thinking of quitting your miserable job. What's the worst that can happen? You won't find another job. Then what's the worst? You lose your house and get kicked to the street. Then what? You run out of food, starve, and die. It's a morbid exercise to be sure, but the idea is to give you a sense of comfort and liberation at how preposterous it is to worry yourself into paralysis instead of pivoting.
- Make the tough choices. It's okay to respectfully resign from your role as wine club treasurer when you start feeling overstressed and underappreciated. It's okay to bail on book club when the drinking starts to predominate over the reading. Sometimes, you just pivot and walk away; you don't even have to say anything.
- Pivot in relationship dynamics. Open your heart, seek first to understand, then be understood. Realize that if you pivot with your relationship dynamics, the relationship itself transforms.
- Know when to quit. Bestselling author Seth Godin recommends that you learn how to quit early and quit often. Pivoting means both changing tactics in pursuit of the same goal, but also knowing when to quit. Quit early and quit often in pursuit of the highest expression of your talents. When you lock in, strive to be the best in the world, pivoting as necessary to make it through the dip. Adopt the strategy of entrepreneur and author Derek Sivers, who says to say "no" to everything short of "hell yes!" No more "sure," or "okay," or even "yes"; it's either hell yes or no.

LIVE A LIFE OF PURPOSE

As we've touched upon frequently throughout this book, more science is emerging every day to validate how "soft" stuff such as defining and pursuing a purposeful life ranks right up there with food choices as drivers of happiness and longevity. Consider the Midlife in the United States (MIDUS) survey, a longitudinal study of health and well-being that looked for "patterns, predictors, and consequences of midlife development in the areas of physical health, psychological well-being, and social responsibility." The study data revealed that having a strong life purpose correlates with a lower *allostatic load* (the accumulation of age-related wear and tear on the body) 10 years later. Those with a strong life purpose also believed they could exert more influence over their health in general.

The study data contradicts the popular notion that hard-driving peak performers are unequivocally wearing themselves out and accelerating aging. In reality, those living a life of passion and purpose, making a contribution to the world through the highest expression of their unique talents, seem to magically avoid many of the potential adverse health consequences of high-energy, high-intensity living. Granted, this insight is obviously subject to reasonable constraints, for there are many happy, purposeful athletes, corporate workaholics, and public servants who trash their health with an extreme and unbalanced approach. What we are striving for here is a graceful integration of objectives from each of the four pillars.

DON'T RUMINATE!

Compartmentalizing your various life roles and releasing the attachment of your self-esteem to the outcome of your peak performance endeavors is difficult; the measuring and judging forces of the modern world conspire to push you in the opposite direction. However, competing hard while releasing attachment is very likely the secret to accessing the health benefits of a purposeful life without risking the stressful effects of becoming consumed by your work—

ruminating over past failures, stressing about the future, or doggedly plowing ahead at the expense of your health.

Rumination is the act of engaging in obsessive and destructive thoughts about the past or the future that cause you to feel anxious, irritable, overwhelmed, and downright sad. The negative connotation of ruminating sets it apart from many aspects of daydreaming, reflective thinking, and executive planning that are healthy and productive, as well as occasional short-duration negative thinking about a disturbing past or future incident. Ruminating is when you keep replaying a past trauma or future scenario in your head until it eats away at you. Just like consuming inflammatory foods or engaging in overly stressful workout patterns, ruminating thoughts are a dangerous form of chronic stress. All day long and continuing into bedtime, your ruminations prompt the chronic overstimulation of fight-or-flight hormones, leading to hormone dysregulation (cortisol antagonizes testosterone, for example), immune suppression, fatigue, burnout, and ultimately disease and compromised longevity.

When you replay the conference room showdown in your head over the ensuing hours and days, or fret about your precious child's college prospects, grade-by-grade, throughout four years of high school, you activate genes that protect you from immediate life-or-death threats, and deactivate genes that promote happiness and longevity. Remember, cells are either in protection mode or growth mode, and it's your choice at all times. By now, you should appreciate the scientific validity of your genetic functions being largely under your control.

Dr. Ronesh Sinha runs an innovative corporate health program in California's Silicon Valley. In caring for some of the most affluent employee populations in the world, Sinha has become an expert in rumination due to its recurring emergence as a marker for mental and metabolic disease. He explains that rumination drives excess cortisol, which drives chronic inflammation, which drives depression, anxiety, heart disease, and much more. "Regardless of how calm you appear on the outside, your body still recognizes rumination as a threat and mounts a physiological response. On a chronic basis, this can lead to mental and physical disease." While rumination can definitely ruin your day, it can also compromise the health of your offspring, along with your entire social network. Referencing findings from the field of behavioral epigenetics, Sinha describes a concept called *intergenerational stress* whereby children inherit their parents' ruminating, hard-driving, overworking ways. Indeed, Sinha says he is treating a generation of mini-stressheads in his clinics, instead of happy, well-adjusted kids leveraging their incredible economic advantages.

Overcoming your propensity for rumination requires heightened awareness, repetition, and endurance. Realize that dwelling on the future prompts anxiety, while getting stuck in the past prompts depression. If you are simply able to notice yourself ruminating, you have achieved a small victory by disengaging the subconscious and engaging the conscious mind. Sinha suggests actually saying out loud, "There I go ruminating again." Instead of scoffing at this suggestion, commit to doing this again and again. Take inspiration from Viktor Frankl, esteemed Austrian neurologist, psychiatrist, Holocaust survivor, and author of the classic *Man's Search for Meaning*, who explains: "Between stimulus and response, there's a space. In that space lies our power to choose our response. In our response lies our growth and our freedom."

Frankl's body of work reveals that when you are able to take control of your thoughts and choose your response to life, this represents the secret to happiness and fulfillment. As you commit to a different kind of work in this pillar, be sure to never, ever beat yourself up over your ruminations, for this is exactly how you remain stuck instead of transforming. Instead, as Dr. Sinha counsels his patients, "If you can't stop the thoughts, then take out the popcorn and start watching them like you are watching a movie."

THE POWER OF JOURNALING

First, put down your mobile device for a moment and bring your dreams into focus. Write down with as much specificity as possible how you might spend your day, your year, and the next five years, if you had 10 million bucks, or otherwise had your druthers. Go beyond daydreaming and take the written exercise seriously. Neuropsychologists explain that when you put pen to paper (yes, writing by hand gets higher marks than typing), the material takes on greater significance and is better retained for numerous reasons. First, you enlist more cognitive powers to organize your thoughts and transfer them into written form. Second, you now have an easily accessible resource to review and reconnect with the information any time you want. Placing a small note with summary bullet points in a prominent location for frequent viewing also helps strengthen your connection to and appreciation for the material. Third, your hippocampus does a much better job encoding and retrieving written information than it does with mere passing thoughts.

Now that you have a written plan, it's time to acknowledge the self-limiting beliefs and behavior patterns that have prevented you from being all that you can be to date. Acknowledge these hard truths with as much vulnerability and honesty as you can muster. Take a break and then come back to the page with ideas to overcome these barriers. Remember that the mere act of forming a new, empowering belief will become a chemical signal that influences cellular function throughout your body. Remember the adage that your brain doesn't know the difference between what's real and what's imagined. When you imagine asking that girl in the elevator out for coffee, telling the boss to take this job and shove it, moving in with your boyfriend after a long hesitancy, or meeting the income projections for your fledgling business, actually making things happen becomes that much easier.

The next step is taking decisive action for lifestyle change. Remember, we have most success achieving our goals when we cultivate intrinsic motivation from complete understanding, trust, and buy-in for the entire process. This insight that intrinsic motivators are the most resilient and effective has been proven true again and again for me during my entrepreneurial journey. My most successful ventures were certainly undertaken with consideration of the economic prospects, but I was always driven by something much deeper and more meaningful than mere financial success. With my career failures and mistakes, I clearly strayed from passion, purpose, and contribution every single time. Instead, I succumbed to lowest common denominator stuff such as greed and ego demands. You've heard about my train wreck café, but I also blew a million bucks on an ill-fated television show venture—perhaps in part due to the allure of Mark Sisson hosting the show and elevating his health expert status. For a brief period during the dotcom craze, I got deep into day trading, lured by the dopamine hits and the extrinsic motivation of making some quick cash.

Eventually, I lost my shirt, and my passion for it. Imagine that.

Indeed, it takes some resilience these days to avoid temptation and distraction and stay connected to your calling. That's why the final step here is to extricate yourself from your present rut by doing something outrageous. Say WTF to yourself and to the world, take some risks, and refuse to go back to your old dysfunctional patterns and flawed beliefs no matter what. Be sure to journal any forward progress that you make, and commit to making continued brush strokes toward your finished masterpiece at a comfortable pace. Seek to be in service rather than to see how much you can take from the world. With this mindset, even when you fail, it will serve as leverage for further progress on the path of your destiny.

PRACTICE GRATITUDE

Gratitude asks us to resist the temptation to judge the height of our own fortune (or the depths of our misfortune) by comparison with others. Gratitude is self-referencing, which is the seat of its power. So many things become possible when we operate from that place, particularly being able to stay the course with passion, purpose, and contribution. With the increasingly destructive influence of FOMO and consumerism in hectic modern life, it's time to implement a gratitude practice. This entails the important physical act of putting pen to paper and writing

down things, people, or circumstances you are grateful for every day.

For years, I've heard enthusiasts extol the magical benefits of this seemingly rudimentary act, and have long dismissed gratitude journaling as not really my thing. Fortunately, in recent years, inspired by Carrie's longtime devotion to gratitude exercises, I've become a convert, to my great benefit. My daily gratitude journaling session helps tone down the latent competitive intensity that I am compelled to unleash all day long in my career endeavors, because it can often get the better of me if I don't continually balance that yang energy with yin outlets like gratitude journaling. Most every morning these days, I spend a few minutes jotting down some free-form thoughts of gratitude. No grammar rules or complete sentences necessary, I just write down whatever comes to mind. Sometimes it's high-minded stuff; I'm grateful to be alive and have a loving family. Other times I'm rambling on about my new electric hydrofoil surfboard (check it out on my Instagram @marksissonprimal)—all within the rules!

As you learned in the previous section, actually putting pen to paper is the essential centerpiece of your practice. Science confirms that gratitude delivers an assortment of health benefits. Gratitude journaling has been shown to boost one's general level of happiness ("Hey, my glass is half full, that's awesome!"); increase success with making new friends; reduce aggression while improving empathy; neutralize the destructive effects of negative emotions like envy, resentment, frustration, and regret; help soldiers better cope with PTSD; help those affected directly by the 9/11 attacks become more resilient; and improve self-esteem in athletes by reducing the anxiety-producing penchant for social comparison.

On a cellular level, gratitude journaling has been shown to activate parasympathetic function, lower cortisol, reduce inflammation, and boost oxytocin, the so-called love hormone. Biohacker extraordinaire Ben Greenfield is a big enthusiast (he wrote and published the *Christian Gratitude Journal*), and reports that he is able to generate a significant increase in his heart rate variability (an indicator of healthy cardiovascular function and optimal sympathetic-parasympathetic balance) while he is engaged in the act of gratitude journaling. Yes, he wires himself up to an HRV monitor while writing! Greenfield also cites research revealing that gratitude can act as a natural antidepressant: "Specific neural circuits are activated that result in increased production of dopamine and serotonin, and these neurotransmitters then travel through neural pathways to the 'bliss' center of the brain—similar to the mechanisms of many antidepressants. Not surprisingly, gratitude also increases blood flow and activity in the hypothalamus. This is the master gland that controls feel-good hormones such as oxytocin, which delivers positive physical and psychological effects."

Of particular note are gratitude's benefits for sleep. Numerous studies suggest that thinking positive thoughts at bedtime assists with a smooth transition into better-quality and longer-duration sleep. Dr. Robert Emmons, a UC Davis psychology professor, founding editor-in-chief of *The Journal of Positive Psychology*, author of *Gratitude Works!: A 21-Day Program for Creating Emotional Prosperity*, and widely regarded as the world's leading scientific expert on gratitude, says, "gratitude promotes physiologically restorative behaviors, chief of which is better sleep." Emmons cites research that a few minutes of gratitude journaling before bed can help you sleep 30 more minutes per night, wake up feeling more refreshed, and have more stable daytime energy levels in comparison to those who don't practice gratitude.

Gratitude might be considered the antidote to rumination, because you are actively redirecting your attention away from past traumas and future anxiety and into the realm of the present and the positive. As with overcoming rumination, living in gratitude requires heightened awareness, repetition, and endurance. Unfortunately, our jam-packed daily schedules often push good intentions like gratitude journaling to the back burner, and eventually off the to-do list entirely. I know it did for me. Hence, I challenge you to sit down at the start, or end, of every day, put pen to paper, and write down a few things that you're grateful for. Even if you have only 2 minutes to spare, make the commitment to doing this—then you'll be ready when that challenge arises during the 21-Day Biological Clock Reset!

Some of my favorite practical suggestions from Dr. Emmons to get your gratitude practice on point include:

- Keep a handwritten journal.
- Remember some worse times and be thankful that you're past them today.
- Use visual reminders: Forgetfulness is the enemy of gratitude, so populate your world with grateful sticky notes!
- Go through the motions of smiling, saying thank you, and writing thank-you notes. Fake it till you make it if you have to; you will still trigger gratitude emotions!
- Discover new circumstances, situations, and perspectives whereby you can cultivate gratitude.

NURTURE SOCIAL CONNECTIONS

Nurturing meaningful, reciprocative interpersonal relationships is one of the most important health and longevity objectives in the entire book. It also might be the most blatantly disrespected and rapidly declining objective in modern life, thanks to the explosion of the Internet and mobile connectivity in recent years. Our connection to people has been replaced by a connection to machines, and this has come at an extreme cost to our physical and psychological health. We evolved for 2.5 million years in hunter-gatherer bands, becoming hardwired to depend upon a cooperative social network for our survival. Our ancestors' sense of self was determined by how they were accepted and supported by the clan. Our genes crave connection, yet modern life is organized to promote antisocial behavior.

The statistics on loneliness and isolation are distressing. Blue Zones and other experts define loneliness as having fewer than three good friends you can count on when having a bad day, thereby categorizing an estimated 26 percent of the US population as lonely. Sociologists at Duke and University of Arizona conducted 1,500 face-to-face interviews to conclude that half of Americans have no one outside of immediate family with whom to discuss personal struggles and triumphs.

More disturbing stats came from a survey of 1,000 Americans by the friendship website Not 4Dating.com: Two-thirds of Americans have lost 90 percent of their friends over the past decade. Common reasons include moving to a new city, entering an all-consuming romantic relationship, or simply drifting apart. Thirty-three percent of Americans admit to having had a falling-out with a close friend or extended family member such that they are not on speaking terms. Thirty percent more people live alone in the United States than did in 1980, many of them elderly and thus less likely to engage socially outside the home.

The disastrous health consequences of loneliness and isolation are widely acknowledged. Social isolation is strongly associated with increased risk of dementia. Lonely people have a 20 percent increased risk of early death by cancer, heart disease, and stroke. These are about the same as obesity risks! Loneliness and isolation can actually change your personality whereby you become more selfish and less sensitive to others. This is a genetically programmed survival mechanism against the very real survival threat that isolation posed in primal times. John Cacioppo, PhD, director of the University of Chicago's Center for Cognitive and Social Neuroscience, and author of *Loneliness: Human Nature and the Need for Social Connection*, describes the phenomenon as fol-

lows: "When you feel lonely, you get more defensive. You focus more on self-preservation, even though this is not done intentionally. Completely unbeknownst to you, your brain is focusing more on self-preservation than the preservation of those around you. This, in turn, can make you less pleasant to be around."

In his book *The Honeymoon Effect*, Bruce Lipton explains, "Human beings are not meant to live alone. There is a fundamental biological imperative that propels you and every organism on this planet to be in a community, to be in relationship with other organisms." Society is in decline in this area but we hardly notice it, because our attention has been diverted by digital stimulation—the driving cause of the decline in the first place! It's important to recognize how easily you can fritter away precious time and energy engaging in superficial digital relationships to the detriment of your real-life interactions with close friends and family.

It's also important to recognize that you are battling a formidable foe: the brightest tech minds working for the richest companies in the history of the world (by orders of magnitude over the industry giants of a few generations ago) to grab some of your precious mindshare by any means necessary. If you are not inclined to go off the grid and into the wild, at least you can resolve to use digital communication primarily as a way to leverage close connections. For example, sharing home videos with distant family members, or enjoying lively email chains with your college pals who live all over the place, but gather annually for reunions.

YUIMARU AND YOU

Those who aren't hyperconnected are better able to live communal lives of great richness and meaning, which of course greatly enhances longevity. Realize that three of the Blue Zones Power 9 list of evidence-based common denominators relate to social life! One of the Power 9 attributes is being part of a faith-based community, which adds 4 to 14 years to life expectancy alone. Another is putting family first, which encompasses caring for elders, committing to a life partner (adds 3 years), and devoting time and love to child-rearing. Also on the Power 9 list is having a strong social network. Okinawa has long been the reigning champ here among longevity researchers, for they have a deep sense of social obligation to family, friends, and neighbors, something they call *yuimaru*. Accordingly, there is tradition on the island dating back hundreds of years whereby small groups of friends—called *moai*—commit to one another for life, providing social, financial, spiritual, and economic support.

Thanks in large part to *yuimaru* and *moai*, there are some 400 centenarians on Okinawa. Furthermore, Japanese females on the whole are the longest-lived population group on the planet, with an average life expectancy of 90—8 years more than American females. Perhaps the most revealing Okinawan statistic of all is that natives who move away live an average of 20 years less than those who live their entire lives on the island!

Research from Dr. Lisa Berkman, epidemiologist, longevity expert, and director of the Harvard Center for Population and Development Studies (HCPDS), suggests that the details and logistics of your social network are inconsequential—all that matters is that you are deeply connected. Your social centerpiece could be your bowling team, your long-term marriage, the elderly parents or even the elderly neighbor you care for, or your globe-trotting, hard-partying homies.

Dr. Cacioppo has conducted decades of research to discover what does and doesn't work to overcome loneliness. For example, immersing into group environments won't guarantee success, because loneliness isn't the same as being alone. Ditto for improving social skills; most lonely people have good social skills—they just aren't using them. Even having a strong support system may not help, as Dr. Cacioppo elaborates: "If you are only receiving aid and protection from others, that doesn't satisfy this deeper sense of belonging. Being a client of a psychotherapist fulfills some needs, but it doesn't fulfill that real need to have a rich reciprocal bond." The opposite is also true, where busting out with a big smile and giving to others all day without receiving can feel lonely. What Cacioppo has found effective is reprogramming lonely people to achieve "reciprocity in communication" by developing empathy, reading body language and social cues, and getting out of self-absorption and into connection.

YOUR SOCIAL AND INTIMATE CIRCLES

It's important to create a social network that feels comfortable and sustainable with respect to your unique personality and lifestyle preferences. Oxford University anthropologist and evolutionary psychologist Dr. Robin Dunbar defines a "meaningful, reciprocative relationship" as being ready and willing to do each other big favors at a moment's notice. For example, dropping your weekend plans to help someone paint their new apartment, jumping into action to help find a lost dog at midnight, and the like. The "Dunbar's Number" theory draws a correlation in the primate world between prefrontal cortex size and maximum number of social connections an individual of a particular species can manage. Dunbar's research proposes that humans are capable of sustaining meaningful social connections with a maximum of 150 people; primates with less cognitive capacity can sustain far fewer connections. Dunbar further asserts that our human brains can sustain an "intimate inner circle" of no more than 12 people.

History supports Dunbar's calculations, for the 150 maximum group size has been observed when our ancestors faced intense environmental or economic pressures for survival. While our Paleolithic ancestors roamed in hunter-gatherer bands of 25 to 50 members (big enough to avoid vulnerabilities but not too big to compromise mobility), multiple bands would gather to hunker down in wintertime, commonly in a total group size of around 150. In early civilization, Roman maniples (military companies) contained around 160 men, while Neolithic farming villages typically had around 150 residents (as do modern-day Amish). These numbers are just meant for reference as you custom-design your own social and intimate inner circles, but personal preference will drive the specifics of how you socialize.

See if you can identify and nurture a *social circle* of people you sustain meaningful, reciprocative relationships with at some level; as well as an *intimate inner circle* of family, cohabitants, lifelong friends, and anyone else with whom you are super tight and have frequent meaningful and time-intensive personal encounters. While the liveliest among us might be able to keep it real with 150 friends, perhaps a social circle of 50 folks might sound more reasonable to you. For an intimate circle, 12 seems like an accurate maximum here, and you may feel more comfortable with a smaller number. Dr. Cacioppo says, "one is hugely better than zero, and two is probably better than one."

Family would seem to be a natural inclusion into your intimate circle, but there are no hard and fast rules here—everything is subject to your approval and ongoing modification. The late Jim Rohn, motivational guru, inspiration for Tony Robbins, and reliable quote machine once said, "You are the average of the five people you spend the most time with." This quip has been indoctrinated into self-improvement gospel for decades, and gone global to boot. The popular Spanish saying goes, *"Dime con quien andas y te diré quien eres"*—tell me who you hang out with and I'll tell you who you are.

Science strongly supports these aphorisms. Research from Harvard social psychologist Dr. David McClelland suggests that the people you habitually associate with—what he called your *reference group*—determine as much as 95 percent of your success or failure in life. McClelland studied the effects of reference groups over a 30-year period to deliver that lofty conclusion, going so far as to say that being in a negative reference group will essentially condemn you to a lifetime of failure and underachievement. No wonder parents are so keyed up about the dates their kids bring home in high school! What's more, with social clusters being contagious up to three degrees per the Framingham Study, you are actually an amalgam of not just the five people closest to you, but of everyone in your larger social circle.

While going with the flow is a great suggestion for so many aspects of life, nurturing healthy, vibrant social and intimate circles requires you to be mindful, proactive, and highly disciplined. Perhaps you can relate to the disparate influences of hanging around a group of good students versus a group of good partyers—especially if they are randomly placed together as roommates. Ditto for neighbors, coworkers, and others who float into your social or even intimate circles without you necessarily orchestrating or approving it. Medium.com psychology columnist and PhD candidate Maarten van Doorn urges you to "actively construct your social environment. Don't let it depend on proximity or chance or on how it has always been, but consciously plan which opinions, attitudes and life-philosophies you do and do not *allow* to be in your life."

I can identify a few occasions in my life where tapping into emotional self-sufficiency and severing dysfunctional relationships helped me grow and transform in a way that I could never have imagined. Van Doorn describes the phenomenon as follows: "The dream in your heart may be bigger than the environment in which you find yourself. Sometimes you have to get out of that environment to see that dream fulfilled." Indeed, humans are creatures of habit. We are comfortable in our ruts, even if we bitch and moan about them. We must acknowledge that at our core, we are hardwired for survival and reproduction, period. We have been so preoccupied with survival for the duration of our existence as a species that we never had a free moment to ponder the nuances of relationship intimacy or healthy reciprocity of friendships. Even in civilized life, marriage and family have been more influenced by economic concerns than matters of the heart. Only in the last few generations have we finally become affluent and safe enough to try to climb further up Maslow's Hierarchy of Needs pyramid.

This climb toward self-actualization—the top of the pyramid—is so intertwined with healthspan that the terms might as well be interchangeable. Why? Because it takes only a couple decades to fulfill the destiny that is coded into our DNA: to survive long enough to pass our genes onto off-spring. Then, according to the instructions on our blueprint, our mission is accomplished and we might as well die. The only way to transcend our genetic destiny is to sustain passion, purpose, and contribution, in all areas of life, for the rest of our lives.

LOVE FOR LONGEVITY

With a healthy social network and reference groups at the highest priority for health, happiness, and longevity, arguably nothing can make or break your healthspan like your intimate love relationship. Consequently, modern culture has evolved progressive and lofty relationship ideals, while facing more complexity and logistical challenges than ever before. Today, males are expected to be not just breadwinners per usual, but also sensitive and vulnerable partners, and hands-on superdads. Females are expected to honor their genetic predisposition as nurturers, but also kick ass in the competitive workplace. Next, as affluence and technology afford more isolation and privacy, we expect our romantic partnerships to meet disparate needs that were once provided by the community at large. The final ingredient in this recipe for relationship "issues" is the jam-packed daily schedule. A UCLA study of DIWK families (double-income, with kids) revealed that these couples converse for a grand total of only 35 minutes per week, and most of that conversation time is devoted to logistics instead of intimate topics.

Even if you self-proclaim to be cruising clear of the dreaded toxic/dysfunctional relationship category, today's "normal" love relationship seems to be rife with reactivity, resentment, and petty conflict, and deficient in joy, laughter, kindness, and deep connection. John Gray, PhD, author of the *Men Are from Mars, Women Are from Venus* book series that has made him the best-selling relationship author of all time, explains how the innate hormonal differences between testosterone-dominant males and estrogen-dominant females set us up for pain and suffering when we try to evolve beyond our primitive genetic wiring and the dated archetypes of male breadwinner and female caretaker: "We must acknowledge that men and women experience stress, love, and success in different ways, through different filters. Males are wired to pursue goals, and analyze and solve problems. Their driving purpose in life is to make a difference and be appreciated for it. Females thrive on happiness, gratitude, appreciation, and respect. Their driving purpose is to give and receive love."

Knowing how our subconscious is in charge of day-to-day operations (especially in high-stress modern life), it follows that most of us, most of the time, are merely re-enacting childhood dramas with new characters. When we allow subconscious programming to dominate, we can easily lack sensitivity and appreciation for the needs of our partner and destroy relationship intimacy. Instead of optimizing hormones to be the best man or woman we can be, we get stuck in fight-or-flight mode. Overstressed, testosterone-deficient males will become angry, emotional, demanding, depressed, and exhausted. Overstressed, estrogen-deficient females will become detached, cold, critical, resentful, anxious, and depressed. To avoid this sort of suffering, we must constantly strive to minimize relationship stress and support hormone optimization in ourselves and our partners. Healing and evolving involves bringing dysfunctional patterns into conscious awareness, being accountable for your role in relationship conflict instead of adopting a victim mindset, and embedding healthy new programming and daily habits.

Gray urges males to indulge their partners in what he calls, "Venus talks." This is where the female gets to vent about her busy day while the male listens intently, does not interrupt, and does not offer advice or solutions—expertly suppressing his male problem-solving instincts in the process. Males are also urged to never speak if they feel angry or have any sort of negative emotional charge. Instead, they are to take Gray's iconic "cave time" and engage in testosterone-boosting activities such as sports. Gray urges females to realize that the male's intense biological drive is to be the hero and protector to his partner. Resolve to never address your male in a complaining tone of voice, instead expressing everything as a preference. This will inspire peak relationship performance and increase the male's attraction to the female.

We can take guidance and inspiration from studies of couples who have proven in recent years what was previously thought to be next to impossible: maintaining that romantic spark of being "in love" even after decades together. Functional MRI imaging of happy couples together for 20-plus years reveals elevated activity in a dopamine-rich area of the brain called the *ventral tegmental area* (VTA). They appear similar to those who have just fallen madly in love. These model couples also show high activity in the thalamus and the *substantia nigra*, areas that have high oxytocin and vasopressin receptors and that are associated with monogamy, bonding, and attachment.

Dr. Helen Fisher, biological anthropologist and author of *Anatomy of Love*, offers up three ways to sustain romantic love: Do exciting, novel things together (a dopamine rush never hurt any couples outing!); stay in touch by sitting together, holding hands, and kissing (boosts levels of oxytocin, aka the "love hormone" in both parties); and make love regularly (prompts the ultimate feel-good hormonal cocktail of oxytocin, dopamine, serotonin, vasopressin, and a boost in testosterone or estrogen, according to gender). Yep, sex is a big deal—so much so that I've been brazenly taking a survey over the past decade among friends and acquaintances regarding a parallel between the quality/frequency of their sexual interactions and the quality of their relationships in general. Wouldn't you know it, they seem to go hand in hand almost without exception.

As you probably already know, tons of studies associate a healthy sex life with longevity. An interesting conclusion emerged from a study by Dr. David Weeks at the Royal Edinburgh Hospital, who discovered that sexually satisfied couples can appear up to 7 years younger than those who are lacking. A study published in the *British Medical Journal* showed that regular sexual activity prompts a 33-percent increase in immunoglobulin levels, an antibody that boosts immune function and protects you against the common cold. Frequent intercourse is also confirmed to lower stress hormones, lower blood pressure, and boost brain function. A 2002 study of 1,000 British men revealed an incredible 50-percent reduced risk of mortality among those who had at least two orgasms a week versus those who had sex once or less per month. Researchers also noted a "dose response"—the more orgasms, the greater the health benefits.

Sex is also good for the brain, boosting cell growth and neuron function in the hippocampus. This improves both long-term and short-term memory, reduces anxiety, and improves your ability to handle stress. Researchers at Rutgers University discovered that orgasm actually eclipses the often-touted cognition and memory preservation benefits of doing crosswords, brainteasers, and sudoku. Study coauthor Barry Komisaruk, PhD, explained that doing puzzles increases brain activity only in localized regions, while orgasms boost oxygen and blood circulation throughout the brain. The reliable oxytocin boost from sex not only increases bonding with your partner but delivers a pain-relieving endorphin rush. Dr. Beverly Whipple, acclaimed sexologist at Rutgers, reports that when women masturbate to orgasm, their pain tolerance threshold spikes by 75 percent and pain detection threshold spikes by 107 percent. Whew!

PILLAR #4: REST AND RECOVERY

It's time to get out of the disastrous modern epidemic disease state of recovery debt and develop some empowering new habits emphasizing rest and recovery as a true pillar of healthy living and longevity. We've paid enough lip service to the importance of sleep, disconnecting from technology, and balancing stress and rest. Now it's time to shatter destructive habit patterns and implement new ones. This will happen through heightened awareness, discipline, and repetition. If you feel FOMO kicking in when you knock off early for the night, or press the power down button on phone, tablet, or laptop, remember the overwhelmingly conclusive scientific evidence that you are more productive, more efficient, and more creative when you have sufficient sleep and downtime. In this pillar, we'll cover how to optimize your sleep habits and sleep environment, how to emphasize recovery instead of just take it for granted, and how to discipline your use of technology so you remain in control instead of becoming an addict.

SLEEP

Prioritizing sleep entails reconnecting your circadian rhythm with the rising and setting of the sun. The greatest urgency is to commit to evening patterns of minimal artificial light and digital stimulation, as this is one of the worst offenses to our genetic expectations for health in modern life. With the following strategies and objectives, you will reconnect with the elegant and fundamental hormonal processes that allow us to wake up every day and express our full humanity. Here is how everything is supposed to work per our genetic hardwiring: A couple of hours after the sun sets, hardwired circadian mechanisms prompt the pineal gland, located near the center of the brain, to flood the bloodstream with the all-powerful sleep hormone melatonin, which is responsible for sleepiness and also a variety of important defense and repair mechanisms. This is a process known as *dim light melatonin onset* (DLMO). Melatonin binds to receptors in various areas of the body to make you feel increasingly sluggish and drowsy. Your brain waves relax and blood pressure, heart rate, respiration rate, and body temperature drop. In concert with a melatonin spike, dopamine levels drop in the retina to make your eyes feel heavy, and the inhibitory neurotransmitters GABA and adenosine rise in the brain. This reduces nerve activity, memory processing, and reactions to physical stimuli. In fact, the way caffeine keeps you awake is by blocking adenosine processing.

After a good night's sleep where you cycle optimally through the various important stages, including sufficient REM sleep as well as deep sleep, you should gracefully transition into a wakeful state upon sunrise. Over the course of the night, deep sleep is emphasized early on, while REM sleep predominates as you get closer to sunrise. For this reason, it's much easier to awaken from REM sleep than from a deep-sleep cycle. Surely you can reference the difference between popping up in the morning with no trouble versus being roused from a deep sleep in the middle of the night and taking awhile to clear your head and become alert? This is also why staying up late and trying to sleep later into the morning to break even does not work, and why it's so important to honor a consistent bedtime—you cannot recapture the deep-sleep window of opportunity.

When morning sunlight hits your retina and receptors in skin cells throughout your body, the signal travels through the optic nerve to other regions of the brain, including the pineal gland. The light cue prompts melatonin levels to fall and serotonin and cortisol to spike within 30 minutes of waking. Adenosine levels decrease steadily as you sleep, and are low when you awaken, increasing alertness. The adenosine-cortisol-serotonin effect is most effective closest to dawn, another reason to try to rise with the light of day.

If you are chronically sleep deprived, you may as well forget about escaping carbohydrate dependency and becoming fat- and keto-adapted. Instead, your late nights in front of a screen light will spike the prominent stress hormone cortisol, spike the prominent appetite hormone ghrelin, and inhibit fat metabolism. The cortisol spike will give you a second wind of energy and alertness, and the ghrelin spike will prompt you to grab some quick energy carbohydrates. You'll be able to power through your emails late into the night, but abusing precious fight-or-flight resources in the process. You indeed feel alert and focused in front of the screen, because when you blast the suprachiasmatic nucleus (SCN) in your hypothalamus with light, it triggers the same wonderful hormonal and neural functions that make you feel alert and peppy at sunrise. If you make a habit of triggering SCN activity at night—liquidating your circadian assets—your body will have more and more trouble feeling bright and shiny in the morning.

I realize that evenings are often the best or only opportunity to relax, socialize with close friends and loved ones, and unwind from the stresses of the day with some digital entertainment. Honoring the overall objective to live awesome, I don't want to cramp your style and order you to shut it down at 2100 hours sharp every night. Instead, let's see if we can create a foundation of excellent sleep habits, an ideal sleeping environment, and an appropriate emphasis on sleep as the key to healthy immune, cognitive, and metabolic function.

If you work odd hours or have other challenges such as first responder work, honor the spirit of these objectives and do the best you can. If you are making a solid effort to meet these objectives and still experience sleep difficulty, consider seeking help from a sleep center accredited by the American Academy of Sleep Medicine (www.sleep education.com), a functional medicine specialist, or a health coach. If you have a condition like sleep apnea you are unaware of, you will struggle unnecessarily in your sleep sanctuary. If you are under the care of a physician and taking sleep medication like millions of others, try to garner support for the goal of eliminating medication through lifestyle modifications.

ENTRAIN YOUR CIRCADIAN RHYTHM IN THE MORNING

Establish a consistent pattern of awakening near sunrise and immediately exposing your eyeballs to direct sunlight. This will trigger the desirable spike in serotonin and cortisol and drop in melatonin and adenosine. Even an overcast day will give you enough blue light exposure to suppress melatonin and spike the energizing hormones.

Since serotonin is a precursor to melatonin, your morning sun exposure helps program serotonin to start converting into melatonin some 12 hours after awakening via DLMO. Temperature therapy can also be a good morning wakeup call, where you get a hormetic hormonal boost from either a cold plunge, a hot shower or sauna, or a morning exercise session. Unlike the chronic overproduction of cortisol due to overtraining or overly stressful lifestyle patterns, the morning cortisol spike is a desirable genetic mechanism that prepares you for the energy demands of a busy day.

Realize the distinction between trying to awaken at the same time each day versus awakening at or near sunrise over the course of the year. This is more precise than the general recommendation to get 7 to 8 hours of sleep per night, because you require more sleep during the shorter, colder winter days and can function well with less sleep during the longer, warmer summer days. In *Lights Out: Sleep, Sugar, and Survival*, the authors estimate that 8 hours is a good goal for most people in the summer, but you may need up to 9.5 hours per night in the winter. Obviously, the variation between winter and summer sleep patterns is connected to how far you live from the equator.

Get as much sun exposure as you can during everyday life, especially for vitamin D production as mentioned earlier. When you awaken, do some form of physical movement to get blood, oxygen, and energizing circadian hormonal processes flowing. Elevate your body temperature with a moderate workout, hot shower, or sauna session to increase alertness. A strenuous workout is okay if you are up for it, but realize your body is better suited for athletic peak performance in the late afternoon.

On the other side of the circadian coin, establishing a consistent bedtime is imperative—again, with a bit of leeway based on the seasons. Realize that the initial hours emphasize deep sleep, while the lighter REM sleep is emphasized as you approach morning. If you stay up past your bedtime and then try to sleep in to compensate, you'll still be deficient in deep sleep. Your best bet is to adhere to that consistent sunrise awakening, and aim for an afternoon nap, if necessary. A nap will automatically emphasize whatever type of sleep you're deficient in.

Do the best you can to minimize food intake after dark without adversely affecting important social opportunities. Heed the previously discussed recommendations to limit digestive function to a maximum time window of 12 hours. At the least, try not to consume any calories in the final hour before bedtime, particularly alcohol and sugar, which can spike stress hormones and interfere with melatonin release.

MINIMIZE ARTIFICIAL LIGHT AND DIGITAL STIMULATION AFTER DARK

When the sun sets, spring into action by making a concerted effort to tone down your overall light exposure and digital stimulation. Install the free software program f.lux (justgetflux.com—available for both Apple and PC operating systems). F.lux adjusts the "color temperature" of your screen after sunset to make it less intense and more aligned with the ambient light. Be sure to enable the Night Shift feature on Apple phones, pads, and computers, or Night Mode on your Android phone, to generate a similar softening effect at nighttime. Use the popular blue light-blocking eyewear with yellow or orange lenses, especially in the final hour before bedtime. Favor candlelight, firelight, Himalayan salt lamps, orange-colored insect light bulbs, or the newly hip old-school tungsten bulbs with the orange filament visible inside. If you must use a screen for work or entertainment, try to get most of it done earlier in the evening.

Reserve the final 2 hours before bedtime for mellow activities: a neighborhood stroll, board games, drawing, leisure reading, chatting with loved ones, or writing in your gratitude journal. Implement a calming ritual such as a candlelight bubble bath before bed. No matter what, cease screen use in the final hour before bedtime. If you lie down to go to sleep and experience ruminating thoughts, write them down on a bedside notepad to free your mind for a peaceful sleep.

ESTABLISH A SLEEP SANCTUARY

Maintain an incredibly tidy and minimalist bedroom, reserved for sleep, intimacy, and other restful activities like pleasure reading and meditation. Absolutely no screens, piles of mail, stacks of magazines, partially completed home improvement projects, or any such clutter allowed. Absolutely no mini-work areas! Google "minimalist bedroom design" imagery to get some inspiration to achieve a sanctuary feel. It's essential to create both a physical and psychological separation between your bedroom and other areas of your house where you do work or consume entertainment. Maintain a temperature of between 60 and 68°F (16 and 20°C) to facilitate the slowing of assorted metabolic functions that help your body get into and stay in sleep mode. For this same reason, you don't want to do a workout or sauna in the evening hours.

It's extremely important to achieve total darkness for maximum sleep efficiency. Use blackout blinds or drapery, and cover even tiny LCD screens and power indicator lights with electrical tape. Even minor light influences can significantly disrupt your attempt to cycle gracefully throughout all phases of sleep. Blindfolds are helpful, but it's not only your eyes that are sensitive to light; skin cells all over your body have very sensitive light receptors. One study revealed that flashing a single beam of light on the back of the knee was enough to disrupt melatonin production. Taking a quick glance at your smartphone screen to see what time you stirred in the middle of the night can be surprisingly harmful beyond suppressing melatonin. Dr. Nerina Ramlakhan, sleep therapist and author of *Tired but Wired* asserts that checking the time can "send you into a whirl of calculations and worry about how much sleep you will or won't be getting." Strongly consider charging your devices in the hallway, or at least out of arm's reach.

Don't be one of the 80 percent of Americans who check their phones upon awakening (per a 2013 *Adweek* report), or worse yet when you stir at some point during the night. Numerous studies reveal that once you activate the shallow, reactionary brain function in the frontal cortex with a smartphone engagement—especially first thing in the morning when you are locking habit patterns into place—it's difficult to transition into high-level strategic problem-solving mode.

NAP WHEN YOU NEED TO

Napping is a cultural centerpiece in countries across the globe, but has been widely disregarded and even disparaged by many economic powerhouse nations. Developing a habit of taking a quick nap, whether to actually sleep or just rest your brain from high-demand cognitive tasks, can give you a significant productivity boost that you may not even realize you need and deserve. Realize that an early-afternoon energy lull is a natural element of the human circadian rhythm, and thus a good opportunity to recharge the batteries for sustained productivity, mood, and energy levels until bedtime. Heighten your awareness of that time in the afternoon when you experience a dip in energy and cognitive function, and develop the discipline to go down for a nap.

As with the sleep sanctuary tips, creating a supportive environment is essential. First, separate yourself from your work environment, just as you separate your bedroom from the action areas of your home. If you don't happen to have a napping pod in your executive suite at work, you can hopefully find a go-to park bench or quiet, shady parking spot to unplug for a while. Get a total darkening blindfold and a smartphone app with mellow nature sounds or white noise to habituate your brain to nap time. The common excuse of being unskilled or poorly adapted to napping is simply an indication that you require more repetition and/or a better environment.

Experts recommend a minimum naptime of 20 minutes to refresh your sodium-potassium pumps so you can pop up feeling alert and energized. If you are deficient in evening sleep, you may require a nap of up to 90 minutes in length. You'll know because of something called the *homeostatic sleep drive*, or *sleep pressure*. Sleep pressure is linked directly to slow-wave sleep—the deepest, most restorative type of sleep. It builds naturally throughout the day to peak at bedtime, but if you are deficient in deep sleep (generally from going to bed too late), sleep pressure will become unbearable by afternoon. You may have experienced the phenomenon of unwittingly falling asleep in a boring meeting or on the subway and feeling surprisingly refreshed after just a few minutes. Do whatever you can to implement a habit of 20-minute naps anytime you experience a significant afternoon dip, and allow for longer naps when you run behind on evening sleep.

The widely held notion that napping can disrupt evening sleep is unfounded by science. Dr. Sara Mednick, sleep expert, Harvard-trained psychologist currently at UC Riverside, suggests that a quality afternoon nap can even help insomniacs do better because they aren't in overtired zombie mode when trying to fall asleep. Even if you happen to awaken feeling groggy, this is merely an indication that you plunged into slow-wave sleep to correct deficiencies. It might feel unpleasant to shake off a drug-like stupor and return to emails, but you will clear in a few minutes and experience hours of heightened productivity with no downside. If you plan correctly, you can actually nap strategically to reap specific benefits. Dr. Mednick explains that morning naps will contain proportionately more REM sleep than afternoon naps, which will contain more slow-wave sleep. For that reason, morning naps will be better for recharging creative thinking skills and solidifying emotional memories, while afternoon naps are great for physical and hormonal restoration.

HEAVENLY HEMP
YOGURT AND SOUR
CREAM [PAGE 202]

HERBES DE PROVENCE
SCRAMBLE [PAGE 203]

SHAKSHUKA [PAGE 254]

MORNING LONGEVITY
SMOOTHIE
[PAGE 277–278]

HOMEMADE PROTEIN
BARS [PAGE 287]

FRIED EGGS OVER SEASONED GROUND BEEF [PAGE 201]

MATT'S MIGHTY BACON AND CHEESE SCOTCH EGGS [PAGE 205]

BACON-WRAPPED
CHICKEN TENDERS
[PAGE 281]

SMOKED SALMON
OVER SPINACH WITH
HERBED COCONUT
YOGURT [PAGE 208]

ELLE'S 2-IN-1 BEEF
SHORT RIBS [PAGE 218]

ZAM ZAM VEGGIE
STIR-FRY [PAGE 231]

BROCCOLI-BACON
SOUP [PAGE 257]

LIVER BURGER BLEND
[PAGE 241] WITH BAKED
CAULIFLOWER [PAGE 256]

LEMON-TURMERIC
CHICKEN THIGHS
[PAGE 222] WITH SWEET
AND SAVORY CURLY
KALE WITH BALSAMIC
REDUCTION [PAGE 264]

DUDES PRESTO PESTO
SCALLOPS [PAGE 212]

CHINESE DUMPLING
SOUP [PAGE 248]

SEAFOOD BOWLS
[PAGE 224]

CREAMY CABBAGE AND
STEAK BOWL [PAGE 215]

BRAISED GARLIC PORK
SHOULDER [PAGE 213]

**DARK CHOCOLATE AND
SEA SALT SQUARES**
[PAGE 285]

KETO CHEESECAKE
[PAGE 288]

**KETO CHOCOLATE
MOUSSE À LA JORGE
MUCHO** [PAGE 282]

RECOVERY

When you embrace the idea that the more hours you work or exercise, the more hours you need to devote to rest and recovery, you have progressed beyond the flawed additive model of energy expenditure and are poised for a breakthrough. However, you also must face what might be the ultimate conundrum of hectic modern life, since there are only 168 hours in a week from which to pull. Alas, we are in a renaissance era where peak performers in every arena are modeling a more balanced approach and trying to avoid recovery debt.

Olympic and professional athletes, who have long realized that they have precious little energy for anything besides training and lying around, are now going deeper into cutting-edge practices designed to enhance recovery. Many peak performance experts, entrepreneurial leaders, and celebrities are touting the benefits of napping, meditation retreats, and mindful disconnecting from technology. While the thought leaders are setting a great example, many mere mortals seem to feel stuck with too much to do with too little time. I recall getting taken to task years ago by a reader of my book *The Primal Blueprint*, relating to my enthusiastic promotion of afternoon naps and evening cold plunges in my swimming pool. The message was something along the lines of, "Great for you, Mark, but as a single mom, I literally don't have time to nap, and there ain't no pool

in my backyard." It was an occasion for reflection, and I have strived to convey the message that we must do the best we can with the circumstances we face.

That said, I'm not one to support excuses and rationalizations when it comes to health. Taking that first step to disengage the subconscious and recognize when you are inhaling food to cope with stress, getting repeatedly distracted at work, or overtraining to avoid dealing with relationship dysfunction can be extremely difficult, but it's an urgent priority in order to give yourself a fighting chance at living awesome. This way, if you engage in behaviors that are not aligned with your long-term health, you are acknowledging them as choices with repercussions. Consequently, you'll have an easier time gracefully returning to healthy habits without the drama, denial, or self-pity that keeps you stuck in destructive subconscious behavior patterns. Furthermore, when you listen to your intuition and make good decisions—saying no to more entertainment options and yes to more sleep, or skipping that extra workout that's for your ego instead of your body—you build momentum with your good decisions. When you face each day with an energized body and refreshed brain, you are better able to stick to best laid plans and not succumb to the temptations and distractions that get you when you're exhausted and your guard is down.

CONDUCT REBOUND WORKOUTS

Joel Jamieson, noted strength and conditioning coach, and trainer of world-champion MMA fighters in Washington (8WeeksOut.com—as in eight weeks out from a title bout), promotes a system called Rebound Training that validates, through the tracking of heart rate variability, the concept that doing some distinct forms of exercise can boost parasympathetic activity and actually speed recovery time in comparison with total rest. This is an exciting new concept for fitness enthusiasts who have long believed that hard work in the gym or on the road is best paired with parking yourself on the couch and stuffing your face.

A Rebound Workout features extensive breathing, dynamic stretching, foam rolling, and mobility exercises to get blood and oxygen flowing without stressing the body; doing only the raise portion of a deadlift, then dropping the weight to prevent muscle damage; and doing 10-second sprints on the stationary bike, followed by a 60-second recovery period where you make a devoted effort to lower your heart rate quickly. The deadlifts and the sprints both stimulate sympathetic fight-or-flight nervous system activity, but without the muscle strain of doing a high-impact workout. Since the sympathetic nervous system stimulation is so brief, followed by long recovery, you teach your body to rebound by calling the parasympathetic into dominance during the recovery interval. What's more, when you hone the ability to quickly drop your heart rate during the recovery

period, you can implement this skill any time you feel stressed in daily life to instantly calm yourself.

Rebound Workouts are ideal for those days when you are fatigued from a recent breakthrough workout, or otherwise in high-stress, low-energy mode from hectic daily life; days you don't feel like going to the gym! The benchmark for a successful Rebound Workout is feeling better after the workout than before you started. Note that feeling tired or beat up from hard workouts or hectic work days is different than having symptoms of a respiratory illness. In the latter case, you are better off staying in bed than doing any form of exercise. When you are fighting a cold, the most I would ever recommend is a short walk.

AVOID THE DREADED COGNITIVE MIDDLE GEAR

A recovery-debt lifestyle will not only trash you physically, but can also severely compromise cognitive function. The problem here is unlike your sore throat or distressed stomach, your recovery-deficient brain has a difficult time perceiving that it's not performing to its potential.

When you are in recovery debt, you can easily get stuck in what author, speaker, and performance scientist James Hewitt calls the "cognitive middle gear." You may be under the illusion that you are busy and productive, but you're actually engaged in a string of medium-demand cognitive tasks that are a far cry from true peak performance. In an article on JamesHewitt.net titled "The Attention Paradox," Hewitt details the "interweaving tasks" of a hypothetical office worker's day, with each quip validated by a footnote to actual research (we reach for our phones an average of 150 times per day, etc.). My favorite excerpt comes during a morning of conference room meetings where the worker "switches between checking his smartphone and replying to e-mails, while pretending to write notes on his laptop."

Yep, this is the kind of stuff we engage in when we've been working too hard, training too hard, and sleeping and chilling too little. Popular podcaster and author of the *4-Hour* books, Tim Ferriss describes the middle gear mode as "indiscriminate constant action." With his obsession with time optimization and systems efficiency in all areas of life, Ferriss strongly impresses what a disgraceful waste of life it is when you are repeatedly drawn into this mode:

"If you consistently feel the counterproductive need for volume and doing lots of *stuff*, put these on a Post-it Note:
• Being busy is a form of laziness—lazy thinking and indiscriminate action.
• Being busy is most often used as a guise for avoiding the few critically important but uncomfortable actions.

Remember, *what* you do is more important than *how* you do everything else, and doing something well does not make it important."

Even as I pride myself as a self-starting, self-disciplined, self-made entrepreneur, I must admit that this stuff hits home. I can recall many a compromised workday where overstimulation got the better of me, caused my guard to drop, and resulted in an afternoon spent with too many computer windows open, too few words written, too much puttering around, and too little to show for it. Conversely, I have found that when my evening sleep habits are excellent, and when I discipline myself to take short breaks whenever I experience myself slipping cognitively—7 minutes on the slackline or a 20-minute nap in the sun—I am vastly more productive at work. I get more done in less time, with fewer mistakes, and greater enjoyment.

The objective here is to pay careful attention to those times when you slip into the cognitive middle gear, and then take immediate corrective action. In today's world of hyperconnectivity and overstimulation, your corrective action will often be to power down and pay attention at the meeting, or close the YouTube window and get the spreadsheet finished. At other times when you've been cranking away for a sustained period, your best choice is to take a nap, get some exercise, have a healthy meal, and return to peak cognitive tasks with renewed focus and intensity.

DISCONNECTING

While we routinely use digital entertainment to disengage from the pressure and intensity of peak cognitive demands during the workday, this is more diversion than true recovery. Your brain requires regular downtime to zone out and engage in low-stimulation activities and environments. Part of the reason we feel fried at the end of a busy day is because our brains have been hyperstimulated without sufficient downtime. We routinely strive to do something that is literally impossible: multitasking. MIT neuroscience professor Earl Miller asserts that the human brain can only process one information stream at a time. What's actually happening when we are driving and talking on the phone is that we are rapidly redirecting our attention back and forth between the distinct tasks to create an illusion of multitasking.

While you may feel satisfied when you work through your email inbox during a conference call, a Stanford University study found that media multitaskers were unable to pay attention, control memory, and switch from one task to another as well as those who focused on one task at a time. Other studies have shown that multitasking compromises learning and impairs memory recall. Your attention span, creativity, and intellectual ability decline. Your stress levels increase, and you'll get that familiar feeling of being "fried." So, while there is obvious value in social interaction and indulging in the many digital entertainment and education options available, taking time for solitary, single-

tasking activities each day is becoming more and more essential to maintain a balance amidst the hyperstimulation of modern life.

Nothing fits the bill here better than spending time experiencing nature. When you spend time outdoors, in open space with expansive scenery, listening to natural sounds like chirping birds and whistling wind, and engaging your other senses with the smells and textures of nature, you are giving a much-needed respite to your amygdala. This is the primitive, reactive part of your brain that is hypervigilant to the nonstop intense, unnatural, and overwhelming stimulation brought by hyperconnectivity and noisy, crowded urban living.

Rachel and Stephen Kaplan, environmental psychology professors at the University of Michigan, explain that humans engage attention in two disparate ways: directed attention and fascination. The *attention restoration theory* suggests that the inherent fascination with nature helps us recover from the "impulsivity, distractibility and irritability" caused by our daily overdose of directed attention. The attention restoration theory supports the popular practice of forest therapy in Japan, where there are officially designated forest therapy sites, free medical checkups in park areas, and health-care plans with a forest therapy component.

Studies support that merely spending time in a wooded area triggers a powerful hormonal and cellular response. In one Japanese study, salivary cortisol dropped an average of 13.4 percent when subjects simply looked at a forest setting for 20 minutes. Pulse rate, blood pressure, and activity on the sympathetic (fight or flight) nervous system decreased as well. Even more remarkable is the significant—and lasting—impact on so-called "natural killer" cells (NK cells), powerful lymphocytes known to fight off infection and attack cancer growth. A longer 3-day trip in the forest with daily walks resulted in a 50-percent rise in NK activity as well as an increase in the number of NK cells. What's perhaps most surprising is this: Subjects who participated in this series of forest-bathing trips showed immune NK benefits that lasted more than a month.

Other studies show that merely gazing at a large body of water like the ocean prompts a reduction of stress hormones and a sensation of calmness. Michael Merzenich, a neuroscience professor at University of California, San Francisco, explains, "Our attraction to the ocean may derive from its lack of physical markers. On land, we are constantly mapping our environment in our minds so we can pick out dangers (snake!) amid landmarks (tree, bush, rock). Looking over a calm sea is akin to closing our eyes."

It seems nothing compares to communing with nature for recharging your batteries. Swedish environmental psychologist Terry Hartig has performed numerous lab and field experiments demonstrating how restorative natural environments help people recover from "normal psychological wear and tear." In one study, where subjects were deliberately fatigued by cognitive challenges, a group who walked in nature recovered better than groups who engaged in quiet reading or listening to music. The nature group performed better on a follow-up cognitive test, and reported more positive emotions and less anger than the control groups.

Amazingly, research confirms that if you can't pop over to the ocean or into the forest during a busy day at work, merely looking at a photograph of natural imagery, or having a partial view of nature from an office or hospital room window, can improve mental disposition and speed healing from illness in comparison to a bland industrial imagery. Forward-thinking architects, interior designers, and city planners are leveraging this research with innovative ideas such as earthen roofs, structural materials fabricated to look like tree branches, or business parks, residential developments, and golf courses built in harmony with the surrounding environment.

In addition to prioritizing plain old sleeping and napping, make a concerted effort to give your brain some authentic downtime by spending time in nature without a device or agenda. You will return to the real world with restored attention and enthusiasm for peak cognitive tasks. If you can't get to actual nature, surround yourself with proxies, such as a mini-fountain on your desk, artwork evoking nature, and print or digital imagery of nature. Gaze at that screensaver for a few extra seconds before moving your mouse!

THE 21-DAY BIOLOGICAL CLOCK RESET

After a comprehensive education about the four pillars of *Keto for Life*, especially learning the "why's" that will help you cultivate the powerful weapon of intrinsic motivation, it's time to take action by committing to an intensive and reparative 21-Day Biological Clock Reset. When you commit wholeheartedly to this brief journey, you will effectively reset your biological clock and also create new habits that will feel natural and easy to maintain for a long time into the future.

The 21-Day Biological Clock Reset features daily challenges from each of the Four Pillars of *Keto for Life*. The journey, while short in duration, is designed to be highly focused and tough! This is the only way to escape from the powerful pull of ingrained habits and cultural forces pushing you into distraction, carbohydrate dependency, and burnout. I am giving you all the tools you need to succeed, and I respectfully ask that you make the same level of commitment in return. Be sure to pick a convenient time to start, where your overall level of life stress is low, and you can spend a total of around an hour each day doing the challenges and accompanying journal exercises.

In particular, I want you to take the journaling assignments seriously. It's simply not enough to read the material, complete the assigned tasks, and move on with your busy life. It's easy to exhibit heightened awareness and resolve on the day you're doing a challenge, and then drift back into destructive subconscious behavior patterns over time. Implementing new healthy habits requires mindfulness, repetition, and endurance. When you generate a detailed written account of your experiences during the fast-paced Reset, you strengthen the immediate impact of the challenges, and also create a valuable resource to consult with frequently over time. What's more, on numerous occasions, the journal assignment is the central element of the challenge. So, before you begin, get yourself a simple spiral notebook and commit to packing it full of honest and authentic insights that are totally private and uncensored.

While it's not realistic to operate in the intense 21-Day Reset mode indefinitely (unless you're a fitness professional or Instagram model, I suppose), you will be exposed to a variety of healthy lifestyle practices that you can pick and choose from to integrate into your daily routine. For example, productivity experts are big into morning routines these days. Whether it's just making your bed, sitting cross-legged on a cushion and conducting a 20-minute meditation, or jumping into a tub of near-freezing water, there is tremendous value in starting each day proactively with a methodical routine.

Since choosing "all of the above" is unlikely during time-stressed mornings, you will pick your absolute favorite stuff from everything you tried during the Reset and design a doable routine to carry forward into the future. In fact, on a few oc-casions during the Reset, you will see a challenge labeled as "carry forward," which entails you will honor the recommendation on the remaining days of the challenge. By designing challenges that are sustainable for a lifetime, the 21-Day Biological Clock Reset approach differs from a boot camp experience. It's distressingly common to plunge into a crazy, unsustainable diet or exercise regimen for 21 days and then spit back out into real life, exhausted, and doomed for a regression from even your original starting point.

My hope is that you will experience so much enjoyment and benefit from the Reset that you will be inspired to repeat it once a year. Not only will it help you correct course when busy life chips away at some of your peak performance habits, it will also poise you for random amazing breakthroughs that occur when good people keep doing good things. Time and again in my own life and with friends, family, and my readers, these magical occasions have occurred. An entrepreneur's business takes off after she stuck to her values and bigger vision through tough times. Good fortune lands in the lap of those who live in gratitude. An athlete who remains patient with the training process and resists the temptation of instant ego gratification is rewarded with a victory at a future competition.

PROOF OF GETTING YOUNGER

Yes, you really can lower your biological age in just a few weeks! This can be validated by improvements in both blood test results and fitness assessments such as the 1-mile run or pushup test. To obtain concrete proof of your progress, perform the fitness assessments out of the gate, then repeat them regularly over time. If you currently have specific health challenges, or just techie inclinations, also consider running some blood panels at the outset of your 21-Day Reset. When you repeat the panels after even just 3 weeks, you can expect significant positive changes in the major metabolic and inflammatory risk markers. Here are some general guidelines for how to improve your blood work, and also to request important tests that are often outside the scope of routine screenings:

Fasting glucose: Stay below 100. If you have a red flag here, buy an inexpensive portable glucose meter and track it daily. You'll see how eating keto can help you move from prediabetic to healthy in a short time.

Fasting insulin: Definitely a special request, but a valuable indicator of how well your overall dietary strategy promotes longevity. Dr. Peter Attia believes the single best longevity predictor is a theoretical "insulin area under the curve" value. This means you produce an *optimally minimal* amount of insulin to nourish and repair your cells over your lifetime, and avoid the wildly excessive insulin production that occurs as a consequence of high carbohydrate eating patterns. It's critical to get your fasting insulin below 8 immediately. Strive to get below 3.

Hemoglobin A1C (HbA1C): This is estimated average glucose over a time period of several weeks, in contrast to the snapshot value generated by a fasting glucose reading. It's critical to get below 6.0 immediately. Strive to get below 5.3.

High-sensitivity C-reactive protein (hsCRP): This is a popular marker of systemic inflammation. Stay below 1.0.

Homocysteine: Another popular inflammation marker. Stay under 12.

Testosterone: The ultimate antiaging tracker for males. Strive to maintain serum testosterone into the high normal of the healthy range of 200 to 1,000. Testing for free testosterone (the amount circulating in the bloodstream) is perhaps even more important, but again is a special request. Free T scales vary among labs, so strive to land in the medium-to-high normal range.

Thyroid panels: Request a broader spectrum that includes T3, reverse T3, TSH, free T3, and free T4, and strive to land in the normal ranges.

Triglycerides-to-HDL ratio: Experts like Dr. Cate Shanahan and Dr. Ron Sinha believe this is the single most valuable heart disease risk tracker. It's critical to get below 3.5:1 immediately, and to get triglycerides under 100 and HDL over 40. Strive to reach an ideal of 1:1 or better.

Vitamin D: While the "normal" range starts at 30 ng/ml, vitamin D advocates recommend that everyone strives to get vitamin D well above 50 at a minimum, and up to 75 as an ideal. This is primarily achieved through exposing large skin surface areas to direct sunlight at the times of day and year of peak solar intensity in your area. Achieving a slight tan indicates that you are making vitamin D effectively.

KETO STARTING LINE

We are making the critical assumption that you are already fat- and keto-adapted at the start of this Reset. This means you have completely eradicated all grains, sugars, sweetened beverages, and refined industrial seed oils, and emphasize nutrient-dense ancestral foods. This means you can fast comfortably from 8 p.m. to 12 noon the following day, and do so routinely. Consequently, you will eat in a keto-friendly pattern throughout the Reset. You will tackle numerous challenges that launch from this higher baseline, such as integrating longevity superfoods and supplements into your routine, consuming your first calories at 12 noon or later every day during Week 3, and improving your mealtime and shopping behaviors. If you are not yet fat- and keto-adapted, please complete the process described earlier (and more thoroughly in *The Keto Reset Diet*) of ditching unhealthy modern foods and fine-tuning with morning fasting before starting the 21-Day Biological Clock Reset.

DAILY MEAL PLAN

To assist you in staying aligned with keto with minimal hassle during the Reset, a suggested menu is presented each day. You may benefit from following meal plans to the letter, especially with so much going on during the 21 days. If you are already confident in your meal-planning abilities and have a good rhythm of favorite meals and eating times, you can use the suggestions for inspiration and customize your experience. Be sure to make a proper effort to integrate the suggested longevity superfoods and supplements into the mix, especially if you haven't been featuring these foods to date.

CALENDAR AND LOGISTICS

Day 1 is envisioned as a Monday, so that some of the more time-consuming or weekend-appropriate challenges land on days 6 and 7, 13 and 14, and 20 and 21. If your work days off are nonweekend, modify your start time accordingly. If other logistical difficulties arise during your 21-day journey, go ahead and swap out challenges on different days, or postpone challenges for a future date beyond the 21-day sequence. If you must postpone a challenge, make a firm commitment to complete it by a specific future date so you don't diminish your overall experience.

WEEK ONE

This week is about getting focused, organized, and quantified. You'll do some macronutrient tracking, fitness assessments, journaling, get logistics dialed in for matters relating to each of the pillars, and clean up any loose ends—such as the final purge on Day 1! Here we go, time to reset your biological clock!

DAY 1

DIET: Final Toxic Food Purge

Assuming you have already done a great job discarding all grains, sugars, and refined oils from your home, you are going to look deeper for any lingering foods that are offensive or borderline offensive and toss them. Beyond that, you are going to tighten up your consumption options when dining out in restaurants or ordering food on the go. Look more closely at labels to be sure you aren't ingesting any industrial oils. Canola and other industrial seed oils are still found in most restaurant kitchens, buffet offerings, and packaged and frozen meals. Even the finest restaurants commonly cook their foods with inexpensive industrial oils, or a blend of olive oil and offensive oils. Get into the practice of asking your server or store manager specific questions about their cooking practices, and insist that your meal be cooked in butter or otherwise free of toxic oils.

It's also essential to make a dietary transformation in your mind, which will take willpower and decision fatigue off the table and help you operate in simple, clean, stress-free absolutes. Make the bold declaration that the big three most offensive foods are no longer options and that you simply refuse to eat them; you are physically incapable of opening your mouth and ingesting foods from the banned list. The next time the dessert cart is wheeled over, or someone offers you a fresh baked cookie from the bake sale, you can decline automatically before you even process the information presented to you as a choice.

To get a little more clarity on your assignment, let's review a list of foods containing the offensive ingredients:

Grains include bread and other wheat products (biscuits, chips, crackers, muffins, pancakes, pasta, waffles); corn, rice, hot and cold cereals, and puffed snacks (popcorn, rice cakes, Cheetos); cooking grains (barley, millet, rye, etc.).

Sugars include sweets and treats (except dark chocolate with 80% or higher cacao and other approved high-fat substitutes); sweetened beverages (fruit and vegetable juices, sports drinks, soft drinks, sweetened teas, sweetened nut milks, powdered mixes, cocktail mixes); baking ingredients like flours and sweeteners (except replacements such as almond flour and stevia); condiments and sauces (except Primal Kitchen products, mate!); and nonfat and low-fat dairy products (e.g., fruity yogurt, low-fat milk, frozen yogurt).

Refined industrial seed oils include canola, soybean, corn oil and the like; buttery spreads and sprays; and oils found in processed, packaged and frozen foods, fast foods, and restaurant meals.

MOVEMENT AND PHYSICAL FITNESS:
Fitness Assessments

Establish baseline aerobic and strength values by conducting a maximum aerobic function (MAF) test in your favorite cardiovascular activity, and a maximum effort single set for each of the Primal Essential Movements. If you wish, you can also conduct measurements of your waist-to-height ratio and waist-to-hip ratio to track improvements in body composition over time.

MAF test: You will need a wireless heart rate monitor or exercise equipment with accurate readouts for heart rate as well as measured effort. Choose a fixed course such as 8 laps around a running track, or pedaling 4 miles on a stationary bike. Commence the test, keeping as close as possible to your "180 minus age" heart rate throughout, and record your result. You will repeat the test at the end of the 21-Day Reset, and repeat every few weeks in the future to track aerobic progress and monitor over-stress/overtraining issues. Journal these details: Date, heart rate, course description, and result.

PEM assessment: Conduct a single set of max-effort repetitions for each of the four Primal Essential Movements: pushups, pull-ups, squats, and planks. Take a 5-minute break between each max-effort exercise to ensure you are rested for the ensuing exercise. If you can't do a pull-up or unassisted squat, skip these exercises, because it's impossible to gauge how much assistance you provided. Journal the date and the reps or time achieved for each exercise.

Body composition assessments: A simple clothing tape measure can provide extremely valuable data as to your metabolic health and optimal body composition. According to Dr. Phil Maffetone, your waist circumference should be less than half your height in inches. If you exceed this ratio you are in the category he calls "overfat," even if you maintain a seemingly healthy weight. Dr. Ron Sinha's recommendations are for a female waist of less than 35 inches, and male less than 31 inches. He also recommends a waist-to-hip ratio of less than .95 for men and .85 for women. Journal the date and your measurements, and repeat over time. Remember how you can correct the four metabolic syndrome blood markers in 21 days? Well, waist circumference is the often-referenced fifth marker. If you are outside the recommended ranges, it may take longer than 21 days to correct, but you can make steady progress over time—especially when you are slingshot from an awesome 21-Day Biological Clock Reset!

MENTAL FLEXIBILITY: 21-Day Reset Journal

As you learned in the beginning of this section, journaling will dramatically strengthen the impact of your 21-Day Reset. Note that this general journaling recommendation is distinct from tomorrow's assignment to keep a gratitude journal. Any kind of blank notebook or pad will do here, but handwriting is preferred to typing notes digitally.

REST AND RECOVERY: Sleep Sanctuary

Speaking of purges, after you are done in your pantry and fridge, take the operation to your bedroom and create a sanctuary. Get rid of any clutter, messiness, and superfluous nonsleep-related items. No television or other screens, no stacks of paperwork or mail. Declutter until your hideaway starts to resemble the designer bedrooms you can search for on Google. Try to achieve total darkness in the room at night (this may be impossible upon sunrise, which is okay), using black tape to obscure tiny light emissions from LCD screens and plug-in appliances and gadgets, and perhaps add blackout curtain liners. See if you can manage a charging station outside of the bedroom, or at least out of bedside arm's reach.

DAY 1 MEALS

BREAKFAST
- Bigass omelet with vegetables, cheese, avocado, bacon, salsa

LUNCH
- Fasting or light snack such as dark chocolate, hard-boiled eggs, nuts and nut butter, sardines, smoked salmon, uncured salami and cheese or vegetables with nut butter

DINNER
- *Keto for Life* entrée, such as Braised Garlic Pork Shoulder (page 213), Broccoli Ranch Chicken (page 214), Creamy Cabbage and Steak Bowl (page 215), or Dudes Presto Pesto Scallops (page 212)

DAY 2

DIET: Healthy Food Shopping #1
Try to up your game a notch by purchasing the absolute highest quality foods you can obtain in each category. Look deeper into your own community for better options, such as a local butcher, fresh fish market, natural foods market, co-op, farmers' market, CSA (community supported agriculture) membership, and even local feed stores, for pastured eggs from local farmers. Realize that locally grown produce and animal products are ranked

higher than even USDA Certified Organic. Besides the sustainability factor, local foods are typically fresher and more nutritious than foods that may have been picked too early, artificially ripened, and transported to you from distant origins. Local products are typically from small farmers who may not be USDA certified, but are less inclined to use industrial chemicals and processing methods.

For whatever your area lacks, utilize the Internet to get unique or premium products shipped to your door. ThriveMarket.com membership offers all manner of healthy food products at discount. VitalChoice.com and USWellnessMeats.com deliver an assortment of premium quality, wild-caught fish and grass-fed/sustainably raised land animals. WildIdeaBuffalo.com delivers grass-fed buffalo meat. LoneMountainWagyu.com delivers rare pure bred Japanese-style wagyu beef. Alter Eco, Theo, and Tazo have their affordable bean-to-bar, high-cacao-percentage dark chocolate on Amazon.com, while premium handcrafted bean-to-bar dark chocolate is available direct from Lillie BelleFarms.com, CoracaoConfections.com, and CreoChocolate.com. Consider all your routine purchases and go-to meals to see if there is any room for improvement. I can recall numerous occasions over the years where I further scrutinized some of my repeat Internet, supermarket, or big-box store purchases, or asked more questions about my favorite restaurant meals, and made extremely beneficial switches to healthier options. For example, I stopped drinking wine for a stretch because I experienced sleep disturbances and digestive distress. It turns out I was most likely reacting to the chemical additives and hidden sugar content found in most commercial wines. When I was introduced to sugar-free, chemical-free, irrigation-free European brands imported by DryFarmWines.com, my symptoms vanished entirely and I could enjoy wine again. With dark chocolate, I learned to look for the "bean-to-bar" and "Fair Trade" designations on the label to avoid buying products of questionable origin. The ingredients in your discount dark chocolate bars are likely sourced from farms and countries with inequitable farmer compensation and child labor. By monitoring safe and sustainable seafood recommendations at SeafoodWatch.org, I continually modify my fish consumption habits. Do the best you can with your resources and budget considerations, but today is about elevating your awareness and finding better options.

Browse the recipe section of this book and others and jot down some basic favorites that you can prepare in the days ahead to make the transition away from grain-based meals as comfortable as possible.

MOVEMENT AND PHYSICAL FITNESS:
JFW—Strategy and Commitments

Get out your journal and make a big-picture assessment of your daily activity patterns, identify problem areas, and list some specific ways that you can increase the amount of walking you do in everyday life. Can you take the stairs at the office every day for the next 21 days? Can you park at the farthest spot in the lot every time you go shopping for the next 21 days? Pay particular attention to breaking up periods of prolonged stillness with brief walks. Make a specific commitment such as walking to the mailbox, or around the office courtyard every single morning before lunch. Choose either a morning stroll to start your day, or an evening stroll to end your day, and commit to doing it every single day. Even if it's only 5 minutes, it's time to make JFW a lifestyle priority and a long-term habit.

MENTAL FLEXIBILITY: Gratitude Journaling

You can make entries within your 21-Day Reset journal, or get a separate gratitude journal that you will maintain over the long term. There are numerous gratitude-specific journals on the market that range in price, or just use another spiral notebook. Whatever you do, start writing something down every single day to cultivate an attitude of gratitude. If you're resistant to the idea, make things entry-level simple by just writing a few things you are grateful for each day; you don't even need to use complete sentences. Repeat this exercise every day for the next 21 days and make it a habit. Again, 5 minutes of thoughtfulness and journaling is great, but if you've got only 5 seconds one day, at least write something down!

REST AND RECOVERY:

Mellow Evenings—Logistics

Acquire some new eyewear and light bulbs to help minimize artificial light and digital stimulation after dark. Get a pair of yellow- or orange-colored lenses with a UV-protected designation. The UV coating will ensure you are shielded from most of the harmful effects of blue light exposure emitted by screens and white light bulbs. UVX blue light blocking glasses are $10 on Amazon and are rated higher than many premium fashion brands and block out almost all the artificial blue light from screens and light.

Also, acquire some alternatives to harsh flourescent or LED lighting that blast you with melatonin-disrupting blue light. Alternatives that are gaining popularity include the vintage Edison bulbs with orange filament, orange-colored bug bulbs from home supply stores, Himalayan salt lamps, and good old-fashioned candle and firelight. Finally, be sure that you install light protection software onto all of your devices. Download and install the free program f.lux onto desktops and laptops, and make sure Night Shift is enabled on Apple devices, or Night Mode on Android devices.

DAY 2 MEALS

BREAKFAST

- Bone broth with egg yolks

LUNCH

- Bigass salad with assorted vegetables, nuts and seeds, healthy protein source, and healthy oil dressing. Search YouTube for "Mark Sisson BASS" (Bigass Steak Salad)

DINNER

- *Keto for Life* side dish, such as Baked Cauliflower (page 256), Broccoli-Bacon Soup (page 257), Curried Creamed Spinach (page 259), or Spiced Braised Cabbage (page 263), or entrée from today's shopping experience

DAY 3

DIET: Longevity Superfoods and Supplements

Today you will focus on consuming the longevity superfoods and supplements detailed in Pillar #1 and presented in today's meal suggestions. If you have not integrated any of the suggested longevity supplements yet, do some Internet research or visit a quality health food store and consider a purchase today of items such as collagen protein, melatonin (especially if you are a frequent jet traveler), omega-3 fish oil, MCT oil, organ meats capsules from AncestralSupplements.com (especially if you are deficient in organ meat meals), probiotics and prebiotics (especially if you are deficient in eating these foods), and vitamin D (especially if you are deficient in sun exposure). The category of ketone supplements is worth exploring, especially if you are a serious athlete looking for a performance and recovery boost, and a vastly superior option to the mainstream sugary powders, bars, and gels. Visit PerfectKeto.com to learn more.

MOVEMENT AND PHYSICAL FITNESS: Work Breaks

Today you will execute the recommendations to take frequent breaks from prolonged periods of stillness at work or at home: 5 minutes every hour, 10 minutes every 2 hours, and a minimum 20-minute break at midday. In total, you'll take four breaks of 5 minutes, two breaks of 10 minutes, and a lengthy midday break.

Journal the time of day and the activities you engaged in during the breaks, using the template below. Mix it up and try one of the office exercise routines mentioned, ascend and descend a few flights of stairs, or take a walk in fresh air and sunlight.

20-minute midday break	
Time of day:	Activity:
5-minute breaks	
Time of day:	Activity:
Time of day:	Activity:
Time of day:	Activity:
Time of day:	Activity:

10-minute breaks	
Time of day:	Activity:
Time of day:	Activity:

MENTAL FLEXIBILITY:
Batch Email Communication

You must hit this one hard early into the 21-Day Reset, for it may be one of the most beneficial changes you can make to improve work productivity and minimize cognitive stress of a typical day. It's difficult to issue a specific challenge here due to individual variation in job responsibilities and email obligations. Try to honor the spirit of the challenge by compressing your engagement with email into distinct time periods, personalized to the realities of your workday. It might be possible for many of us to devote 30 to 60 minutes at the start of the day, disengage for hours of produc-

tive work, and engage for another time block at the end of the day. Even if the nature of your work compels you to jump onto email every hour, you can still honor the spirit of the batching objective by turning it off between formal sessions.

Outside of your job responsibilities, commit to limiting your personal email use to one or two distinct periods during the day and disengage otherwise. Close apps, close windows, turn off notifications, and don't tempt yourself in any way. Consider deleting the email app from your mobile device so you have the built-in limitation of needing your workstation. Journal the details of your exercise using the following template:

Batching email—Time period #1:	
Batching email—Time period #2:	
Batching email—Time period #3:	
Notes:	

REST AND RECOVERY: Say "No!"

Time to exercise the esteemed ability to say "no" to getting distracted, overstimulated, or spread too thin. Journal 3 to 5 behavior patterns or obliga-

tions in your life that create stress and fatigue—stuff you really should say no to, but can't seem to pull the trigger. Then, take action today in the name of simplifying, decluttering, and achieving stress-rest balance in life. This could be everything from a personal no to a Netflix habit that's been keeping you up past your bedtime, to resigning from a wine club treasurer role that's become too stressful and time-consuming. See if you can identify and execute both big nos and little nos in today's challenge. When you flex your power in diverse areas, it will help strengthen your overall resolve to filter, prioritize both at work and at play, and never overextend yourself. Complete the day's journal exercise by describing the action you took with each item that you listed at the start of the day.

DAY 3 MEALS

BREAKFAST

• Morning Longevity Smoothie (page 277)

LUNCH

• Salad made with sauerkraut, kimchi, or tempeh

DINNER

• *Keto for Life* organ meat entrée (pages 232 to 244), such as liver, tongue, heart, or kidney

DAY 4

DIET: Food Journal and Macronutrient Calculations #1

The exercise of food journaling and calculating macros can help increase your general awareness of eating habits and appreciation of food,

allow you to dial in a keto eating strategy, and also achieve a fairly accurate caloric intake deficit for precise fat-reduction goals. Many folks complain about the tedious nature of writing down everything that goes in their mouth, but also relate how they eat more slowly, with more appreciation, and less mindless snacking. That said, journaling and calculating macros should come with a warning to respect the difference between heightened awareness and unhealthy obsessions. If you have a history or high risk of disordered eating, consider skipping this challenge or consulting with a professional prior.

The food journaling challenge entails writing down everything you eat and drink for both today and tomorrow. Carry around a small notepad, as well as measuring tools (a cup with ¼ marks, tablespoon, and even a kitchen scale if you want to be hardcore) to obtain accurate quantities. Reading labels will also help with your reporting. With your day's journal complete, you can visit an online macronutrient calculator such as MyFitnessPal .com, input your information (searching for your particular foods and portion sizes in their database), and generate a macronutrient report. The smartphone app Senza allows you to keep track of macros on the go at each meal.

Review your report with particular attention to the carbohydrate contribution of various foods. During the Reset, it's essential to stay below 50 grams of gross carbohydrates each day (don't count leafy greens or avocados). With protein, it's okay to maintain an average of 0.7 grams per pound (or 1.54 grams per kilo) of lean body mass per day over time, with more fluctuation allowed on a daily basis.

MOVEMENT AND PHYSICAL FITNESS:
Aerobic Workout #1

Use a heart rate monitor to ensure you exercise at your "180 minus age" heart rate in beats per minute for the duration of the session. Make the session slightly longer than your typical workout time. Most fitness enthusiasts are shocked at the disparity between a true aerobic intensity and the black hole intensity that many drift into when operating according to perceived exertion. Get used to slowing down, staying comfortable, and enabling maximum fat oxidation with minimum glucose burning and stress hormone production.

MENTAL FLEXIBILITY: Pivoting Exercise

Get out your journal and describe three areas or issues in your life where you feel "stuck" in some way. For each, describe a new empowering belief and a specific pivoting action (or two) that you can take today to progress in a new direction. For example, maybe you feel stuck in an unfulfilling job and are staying due to economic pressures or a fear about trying something new. You can form a new belief that you have other promising career opportunities, and then take some initial steps to pursue a new career. For example, enrolling in a professional training course or making an appointment with a consultant to obtain expert guidance and formulate a plan of action.

If you are resistant to doing this exercise, or can't seem to build enthusiasm and confidence for the proposed pivots, play the WhaT WiTCH game (asking yourself repeatedly What's the Worst That Can Happen? for problems you are ruminating over). Hopefully, you will gain some perspective that it's okay to quit, it's okay to fail, and everything you do can serve as a learning experience to propel you forward in life.

REST AND RECOVERY:
Calming Bedtime Ritual

Create a calming bedtime ritual that you can repeat each evening. This could be a bubble bath, foam rolling or stretching session, a brief meditation, or a stroll around the block with the dog, or a stint of reading by the fire or in bed with a headlamp. The goal is to create a behavioral cue that prompts a graceful and deliberate transition out of high-stimulation mode into sleep mode. My friend Mia is devoted to doing a jigsaw puzzle on her iPad right before going to sleep. Completion of the puzzle represents the final objective of the day for her brain, and permission to cease thinking about the problems and challenges of the day and go to sleep. The puzzle-to-pillow plan!

Granted, using technology right before bed departs from the screen curfew recommendation, but with blue-light blocking glasses and a dark room, the exercise works for her. Our brains respond extremely well to ritual and environmental cues that trigger an associated behavior, so things like leaving your phone behind to charge in the hallway, putting on your pajamas after the bath or shower, or switching from regular lamps to a reading headlamp will all trigger your brain to transition into sleep mode.

DAY 4 MEALS

BREAKFAST
• Bigass omelet with vegetables, cheese, avocado, bacon, salsa

LUNCH
• Fasting or light snack

DINNER
• *Keto for Life* entrée (pages 210 to 231)

DAY 5

DIET: Relaxed Eating Experience
Today you will pay special attention to creating a quiet, calm, distraction-free eating environment, and consuming your food at a leisurely pace. Don't use any screens, and don't even read a newspaper or magazine. Instead, just concentrate on savoring each bite of food and perhaps some mellow conversation. Strive to chew every single bite 20 times. While this suggestion is widely disregarded, the salivary enzymes in the mouth make a great contribution to efficient digestion when they are given the chance to go to work.

Remember, the parasympathetic nervous system is nicknamed "rest and digest," while the sympathetic is the "fight or flight." Even a routine news broadcast playing in the background at the dinner table can prompt fight-or-flight stimulation. Even worse is eating at your desk or while driving. I like to say that I never eat a single bite of anything that I don't absolutely love the taste of, so let's package that idea with never eating a single bite of food in a high-stimulation environment. Stress is antithetical to eating, period.

Creating a habit of distraction-free meals can improve digestion, strengthen family and friendship bonds, and give your brain a necessary break from hyperconnectivity and nonstop cognitive stimulation. Enjoy some relaxing meals today and take note of any heightened sensations of hunger, satiety, and taste that you experience when you are focused on food. If you happen to have a television in the kitchen, remove it as part of this day's challenge.

MOVEMENT AND PHYSICAL FITNESS: Morning Movement Routine
Choose from the offerings in Pillar #2 (page 88) and custom-design a first-thing-in-the-morning routine to get the blood and oxygen flowing and brain focused for a productive day. It can last as little as 5 minutes, but you may find more benefit from taking at least 12 minutes to get a productive movement session that promotes flexibility, injury prevention, and mindfulness. The yoga sun salutation (page 100) is a great starting point, even if you have minimal experience with flexibility/mobility exercises.

MENTAL FLEXIBILITY: Varying Your Routine

There are many positive attributes of daily routines and rituals. You learned how an energizing morning routine builds focus and discipline throughout the day, and how bedtime routines can facilitate a smooth transition into sleep. There is also great value in shaking things up once in a while to expand your comfort zones and explore new possibilities.

Make today as different as possible, from the moment you wake up until you go to sleep. Try out a brand-new morning movement routine. Take a cold shower instead of a hot one. Eat something different (or fast) instead of the usual breakfast. Take a different route or mode of transportation to work. Introduce yourself to a few people you've never spoken to at work or around town. Try a different workout at the gym, or a different route on your daily outdoor workout. Watch a new television show while doing a different rolling routine. Journal your experience by listing and commenting on each different thing that you did today. Even if you don't make any amazing new discoveries to alter your existing daily routine, completing this challenge will improve your mental flexibility and your ability to adapt to all manner of life changes.

REST AND RECOVERY:
Circadian Alignment Morning—
Carry Forward Challenge

Awaken near sunrise and immediately expose yourself to direct sunlight by taking a walk outside or conducting a movement routine such as sun salutation or a custom-designed flexibility/mobility sequence. I know it's a big ask to have you repeat a challenge every single day for the duration of the course, but I'd like you to do it for this simple act with an extremely minimal time requirement. Hopefully by Day 21 you'll be so enamored with the experience that you'll get outside for a few minutes going forward for the rest of your life.

DAY 5 MEALS

BREAKFAST
- Fasting or bigass omelet

LUNCH
- Fasting or bigass salad or leftover entrée

DINNER
- *Keto for Life* organ meat entrée (pages 232 to 244), such as liver, tongue, heart, or kidney

DAY 6

DIET: Hara Hachi Bun Me—
Carry Forward Challenge

This is an ancient Confucian practice of eating until you are 80 percent full. It's very popular among the longevity all-stars in Okinawa, and caloric efficiency is a major recurring theme among longevity populations. Today, at each meal you will highlight *hara hachi bun me* and make a concerted effort to eat slowly and mindfully until you're satisfied—instead of the "full" that we have been socialized to pursue at meals. You will honor this challenge at all ensuing meals during the Reset, and envision this practice as a lifelong practice.

Since you are trying to unwind subconscious programming that started in childhood with praise for cleaning your plate, make a conscious and dramatic effort to leave a few bites behind, turn down second helpings, and toss small portions that you might typically be inclined to save. Please maintain a heightened awareness of this 80 percent concept at every meal for at least a month, and hopefully it will become your permanent default pattern at meal times.

MOVEMENT AND PHYSICAL FITNESS:
Sprint Workout #1

Honor the high-intensity repeat training (HIRT) strategy with an explosive, short-duration sprint workout, whether running, or low- or no-impact options. Honor the guidelines detailed in Pillar #2 by keeping work efforts between 10 and 20 seconds, taking luxurious rest intervals, and doing between 4 and 10 repetitions. Be sure to complete the warm-up and preparatory drills beforehand, entailing 5 to 10 minutes of low-intensity cardio, a dynamic stretching sequence, and some wind sprints. If you are a novice, completing the wind sprints as described in the text can suffice for your first sprint workout. Strive to add a bit more work on your second sprint workout on Day 18, and to make continued progress in the future. Do not overdo it out of the gate and get injured or discouraged. Journal the specifics of your session so you can monitor progress or revise as desired over time. Remember, as you get fitter, strive to improve your speed instead of adding more time or more reps.

MOVEMENT AND PHYSICAL FITNESS:
Evening Stroll

As part of your wind down and departure from screen use in the final hour or two before bedtime, get some fresh air and bring a dog along if you are lucky enough to have a companion. If you're feeling hesitant due to cold weather, realize that getting a bit chilly before bed will help facilitate a good night's sleep, since the lowering of body temperature is one of the key hormonal processes involved.

MENTAL FLEXIBILITY: Grand Play Outing

Play falls into the Mental Flexibility category for this challenge because many people seem to be so busy with core daily responsibilities and hyperconnectivity that they don't even ponder the importance of play. Hard-core fitness enthusiasts admit that they would rather conduct a quantifiable workout than depart for something wild and wacky. Instead, cultivate the mental flexibility to feel comfortable taking both mini-play breaks and occasional grand play outings. Take advantage of the weekend and conduct an exciting outdoor physical challenge—something that's definitely not part of your regular routine and pushes you a bit out of your comfort zone. Journal your experience and include some ideas for future adventures.

REST AND RECOVERY: Mellow
Evenings—Action

Time to put policy into action and experience a dark, calm, quiet mellow evening. Try out your new shades and different light sources (hopefully they arrived by Amazon Prime by now?), and be sure to finish your screen use 2 hours before bedtime. I know this is super tough, but commit to the evening screen curfew whereby the final 2 hours before bedtime are darker, quieter, mellower, and free from digital stimulation. If you insist on watching a screen in the final 2 hours before bed, opt for a passive engagement with a television program rather than active engagement with email or online shopping.

As bedtime approaches, implement the calming bedtime ritual that you dialed in on Day 4. In the morning, journal your entire experience, including any improvements in your sleep quality and overall enjoyment of a calm, dark, mellow evening after a busy day.

DAY 6 MEALS

BREAKFAST

- Morning Longevity Smoothie (page 277), perhaps with additional fresh or frozen fruit

LUNCH

- Bigass salad, perhaps with sweet potato

DINNER

- *Keto for Life* entrée (pages 210 to 231)

DAY 7

DIET: Bootcamp-Style Cooking Session #1

Katie French, author of *Paleo Cooking Bootcamp*, promotes a highly focused cooking session of a couple hours on the weekend that generates an assortment of ready-made prepared meals and snacks designed to last throughout a busy week. This "intentional cooking" experience starts with creating an itemized grocery list for the meals you have slated for your bootcamp cooking binge, then an efficient sequencing through the food preparation, cooking, and cooling stages of the various recipes. Today, get acquainted with bootcamp cooking by creating a strategic shopping list, then spending a focused period of time prepping and storing meals for use during the week ahead. Here are some ideas of foods and meals you can prepare in advance and store for use during the week:

- Chop vegetables for salad or a stir-fry and store in mason jars or glass food storage containers
- Fry up jumbo portions of ground beef or burgers
- Oven-bake a whole chicken or turkey
- Bake or fry jumbo amount of salmon and chop up for salad centerpiece
- Tuna salad recipes from this book or elsewhere
- Slow cooker or Instant Pot stew or bone broth
- Slow cooker or Instant Pot pork shoulder or other large meat cut
- Classic Egg Casserole (page 200) or other egg casserole dish

- Homemade salad dressings, sauces, and marinades
- Snacks and treats using dark chocolate and/or coconut products, especially if you have kids or teens. Check out *Keto Cooking for Cool Dudes* for inspiration.

If you enjoy the experience and want some expert guidance for maximum skill development, visit paleocookingbootcamp.com.

MOVEMENT AND PHYSICAL FITNESS:
Create a Dynamic Workplace

Remember, the primary objective is to create *variation* in your office workday. Creating a stand-up desk option is an excellent first step, but don't feel intimidated that you have to switch to standing up all day. The best strategy is to stand for as long as comfortably possible, then return to sitting, then rinse and repeat all day. Your feet crave variation and sensory stimulation, so search Amazon for a pebble mat or a wobble board/ergonomic balance board that stretches calves, hones balance skills, and allows for posture variation. If you have more leeway at work, try sitting on a bosu ball and using a low coffee table for a desk.

MENTAL FLEXIBILITY: Changing Self-Perceptions About Aging

Take some quiet time with journal in hand to write down three ways that you have a negative self-perception about aging. Perhaps you've uttered a throwaway comment in recent days about your diminishing cognitive or physical skills? Have you bowed out of any recreation opportunities or physical challenges due to a belief that you're too old?

For each negative self-belief, write a rebuttal where you describe a potential new perspective, followed by an action you can take to validate your new belief. For example, you stopped going to lunchtime pickup basketball and told your buddies you were getting too old. You can rebut this by saying that you can accept a gradual decline in skills, but still attend and give your best effort. Maybe you've watched your kids from the sidelines, playing on the park slides or kicking the soccer ball around, or driven the boat while they had their fun wakeboarding or waterskiing. You can then commit to participating at the next recreational opportunity. Please take this exercise seriously and reflect deeply for areas where negative self-perceptions have creeped into your belief systems and daily behaviors. Remember, changing negative self-perceptions about aging delivers a similar longevity return on investment as quitting smoking!

REST AND RECOVERY: Take a Nap

Hey, Day 7 is supposed to be a Sunday, so no excuses! If you're not a napper, time to start building your skills. Create a quiet, dark area and commit to a minimum 20-minute napping period, or longer if desired. If you can't fall asleep, don't worry. Just relax, close your eyes, attempt to clear your mind, and focus on taking deep, diaphragmatic breaths. Try using a nature sounds app to create an auditory cue for naptime that will strengthen with repetition. If you are already a professional napper, you'll knock off one of your easier challenges.

DAY 7 MEALS

BREAKFAST
- Bone broth with egg yolks

WEEK TWO

The diet challenge to kick off the week is to refrain from snacking, even on nutritious, keto-friendly foods, and carry it forward for the rest of the Reset. As innocent as it seems, snacking can significantly compromise your fat-reduction efforts. "Any food you consume prompts an insulin response and shuts off internal fat-burning, even if it's low or no carbohydrate," explains Dr. Cate Shanahan. While your Week Three challenge will escalate to fasting until noon and eating within keto guidelines daily, go into intermediate degree of difficulty this week by obtaining all of your calories during meals.

DAY 8

DIET: No Snacking—*Carry Forward Challenge*
Snacking may compromise your fat-reduction goals more than you realize. When you consume any sort of food, even a quick, high-fat snack, you shut off ketone production and fat metabolism and trigger an insulin response. Today's no-snacking challenge will also give your digestive system much needed

LUNCH
- Fasting or light snack

DINNER
- Bootcamp bounty!

rest between meals. Please carry this challenge forward for the duration of the Reset, and envision it as a lifelong habit. As you say goodbye to the absentminded grazing between meals, you should experience a heightened awareness and appreciation of food when you enjoy a proper meal.

MOVEMENT AND PHYSICAL FITNESS:
Cooper 1-Mile Run Fitness Assessment

Make sure you feel 100 percent rested and motivated to deliver a peak performance effort, free from soreness, immune disturbances, or lingering fatigue from previous workouts. Otherwise, choose a different day for your test. Find a standard 400-meter running track or a dead flat pedestrian trail with accurate distance markers or your own GPS technology. Warm up thoroughly with very slow jogging, followed by dynamic stretching and technique drills, then a few wind sprints.

For best results, it's essential to maintain a consistent pace throughout your timed mile. It follows that your successive quarter-mile efforts should be very close in time (e.g., 2 minutes per 400-meter lap) and feel something like: easy, steady, vigorous, and then hard! *Note*: Four laps of a standard track total 1,600 meters, while a mile is 1,609 meters. So add a short stretch on your final lap to obtain an accurate mile time.

At age 50, males must break 10 minutes, and females break 12 minutes, to qualify for the "good" category. Males under 8 minutes and females under 9 minutes are in the outstanding category. Dudes who can't break 12 minutes and gals who can't break 13 minutes have a serious risk marker for disease and decline. Trust that improvement can happen quickly if you increase daily movement and conduct more comfortably paced, longer-duration aerobic workouts. Journal your results and repeat the test every couple of months to track your progress.

MENTAL FLEXIBILITY: Declutter Level 1

Start with your clothing, or with your office paperwork stacks if you prefer. Strive for a minimalist outcome and the clarity and efficiency it brings. If you haven't worn something or used something in a year, you can assume that tossing it won't cause you much pain. Realize that with bank and credit card statements, books, magazines, owner's manuals, CDs, and DVDs, most everything you are worried about tossing can be easily reacquired digitally if necessary. In fact, it's possible to maintain a nearly all-digital office/personal work space if you just evolve from some outdated processes. Journal your experience and even take before-and-after pictures to celebrate your hard work.

REST AND RECOVERY: Self-Care Challenge

The oxymoronic title might help you realize how ridiculous it is to be too busy to indulge in regular self-care. It's hard to top getting a full-body massage for self-care, so make that, or something similar, happen today. Enjoy yourself and commit to making it a monthly habit, perhaps by scheduling future appointments with your practitioner. Yes, bodywork is another hit to your budget, but plenty of science validates the benefits of massage to boost general health, immune function, and disease prevention. What better investment is there than to invest in yourself? Hey, if massage is not your thing, taking off early from work for an afternoon of fishing can count for this challenge, or getting a manicure/pedicure. Write a few notes in your journal about the experience, and how you can make regular self-care a habit.

DAY 8 MEALS

BREAKFAST

- Fasting with water, tea, or coffee

LUNCH

- Salad made with sauerkraut, kimchi, or tempeh

DINNER

- *Keto for Life* entrée (pages 210 to 231)

DAY 9

DIET: Fasted Morning

Wait to consume your first calories until you experience true sensations of hunger. Achieving a 16-hour fast (e.g., 8 p.m. to 12 noon) gives you a high score in metabolic flexibility, but don't force the issue today (don't worry, things will get tougher later in the Reset!). The idea today is to track your natural ability to feel energetic and focused without food, and see if you can progress over time.

Evening meal finish time:	
Morning meal start time:	
Fasted hours:	

MOVEMENT AND PHYSICAL FITNESS:
Strength Workout #1

Conduct a brief, high-intensity strength training session consisting of the Primal Essential Movements (page 112), a Maximum Overload workout (page 114), or a custom-designed workout consisting of sweeping, full-body, functional movements. Be sure that you take sufficient rest between efforts to preserve explosiveness throughout the workout and prevent the cumulative fatigue that compromises workout quality and delays recovery. Record workout details in your journal so you can track your progress and make modifications as desired.

MENTAL FLEXIBILITY:
Reprogramming Rumination

Identify three life circumstances or decisions that are eating at you right now. Perhaps it's a FOMO or FOKU (fear of keeping up) issue, a past altercation that you are rehashing ad nauseam, or a future uncertainty keeping you up at night. Describe each issue in detail, your thoughts about them, and how the thoughts are having a negative impact on your life. Immediately after you enter your information, commence Dr. Elisha Goldstein's four-step reprogramming exercise as follows: First, make a concerted effort to relax by taking deep, diaphragmatic breaths. Next, retrain your attention into a relaxed state of present awareness. Counting your deep breaths is the best retraining strategy. Third, forgive yourself for ruminating. Perhaps you can say the mantra, "There I go ruminating again!" aloud in a lighthearted manner. Fourth, resolve to repeat this retraining and reprogramming exercise any time you fall into rumination for the rest of your life. Finish your journaling by describing how the exercise helped calm you or perhaps redirected your negative thoughts into more empowering thoughts.

REST AND RECOVERY:
Prolonged Work Break

Take a minimum of 20 minutes in the middle of your workday to walk outdoors into sunlight, fresh air, and open space. Leave all connectivity behind, clear your mind from the stresses of a busy day, and focus on appreciating your natural environment. Can you hear birds chirping or discern which direction the wind is blowing? Remove your sunglasses and focus your eyes on a distant object, then a nearer object, then a different distant object, and continue the sequence 10 times or more. This will help rejuvenate eye muscles fatigued from prolonged screen focus. Perform some dynamic stretches such as lunge walks, and some counterbalancing exercises such as arm circles or gentle trunk twists. This will help mobilize muscles that are tense and tight from prolonged hunching over desks, at your steering wheel, or when typing out text messages. By the time you return to your desk, you should feel completely refreshed and focused for many more hours of productivity.

DAY 9 MEALS

LUNCH

- Bigass salad

DINNER

- *Keto for Life* side dish (pages 255 to 264)

DAY 10

DIET: Prepare Fresh Meals

Prepare all of your meals yourself today, using fresh ingredients and whole foods only. Avoid anything that has been prepared in advance, processed, packaged, or frozen. While there are more and more acceptable options for busy people to source high-quality take-out food, take some extra time today to connect with the entire experience of shopping for raw materials and preparing your meals from scratch. Take it as far as you can by striving to consume only locally sourced products. Journal your thoughts about your experience, including whether or not you experienced greater satisfaction from being hands-on from start to finish.

MOVEMENT AND PHYSICAL FITNESS:
Self-Myofascial Release Session

Perform a devoted session of at least 10 minutes' duration, honoring the instructions to work from the center of the body out to the extremities. The foam roller is the tool of choice, but try to integrate some ball work with a lacrosse, golf, or therapy ball. Remember to respect the difference between mild to significant discomfort that you breathe through to release trigger points, and the sharper, more localized pain that suggests you are working on the wrong areas, using poor technique.

MENTAL FLEXIBILITY:
Stimulating Brain Challenge

Pursue a creative intellectual challenge away from your core daily responsibilities, whether it's taking the first step toward a grand project (e.g., music or language lessons), or doing something for fun today, such as writing some poetry or initiating a landscaping project in the yard. As with physical play, your brain craves departures from intense focus on highly specialized career pursuits. Enjoying some creative intellectual challenges will help you return to your core daily responsibilities feeling refreshed, energized, and perhaps with a helpful new perspective for problem solving.

REST AND RECOVERY: Device-Free Evening

After the sun sets this evening, disengage as much as possible from any screen use and entertain yourself in other ways. Go ahead and keep your phone nearby, but resolve to use it for emergencies only. With your newly acquired free time, perhaps you can take an evening stroll, or read magazines, the newspaper, or a good book. Nurture family or partnership connection with relaxed conversation, board games, or hobbies like making recipes or doing an art project together. In the process, you'll counter the disturbing statistic that double-income couples with kids converse for only 35 minutes per *week*. Horrors to imagine the stats of parents conversing with teenagers beyond daily logistics! Self-care is always an option, such as a stretching and foam rolling session, an extra-long bath, or going to sleep an hour early. Tomorrow

morning, journal your thoughts about the evening experience. Hopefully the enjoyment of a screen-free evening will have you repeating the exercise whenever possible.

DAY 10 MEALS

BREAKFAST
- Full-fat yogurt with nuts, cinnamon, and cacao nibs

LUNCH
- Bigass salad

DINNER
- *Keto for Life* organ meat entrée (pages 232 to 244)

DAY 11

DIET: Two Meals a Day—
Carry Forward Challenge

With all this talk about fasting, digestive circadian rhythm, escaping carbohydrate dependency, and becoming metabolically flexible, it follows that you should never require more than two meals a day to achieve total dietary satisfaction and optimal metabolic function. Today you will execute this exercise and also leverage your Day 8 challenge of no snacking. If you're feeling up to a further challenge today, strive to consume just one meal, or perhaps one proper meal and a small snack. Let's call this a carry-forward challenge, so you eat a maximum of two proper meals a day for the rest of the Reset, and make this a sensible goal for the rest of your life!

The ultimate goal of this exercise is to transition out of the flawed and dated mentality that three meals a day is necessary or even healthy. As you learned, chronic overfeeding and carbohydrate dependency promotes oxidation, inflammation, lifelong accumulation of excess body fat, and increased cancer risk from overstimulation of growth factors. It's far healthier to routinely depart from regimented meals, both intuitively and deliberately, to boost mitochondrial biogenesis and upregulate fat- and ketone-burning.

MOVEMENT AND PHYSICAL FITNESS:
Office Exercises

Get busy in your cubicle with some quick and challenging exercises that promote balance, flexibility, and functional strength. Suggestions from the text include deep squats, desk dips, one-legged balancing, and balletic karate kicks. Journal the details (describing the exercise and the number of reps or duration) and try some variations so you can dial in a short template routine to repeat nearly every day.

MENTAL FLEXIBILITY: Destroy Self-Limiting Beliefs and Pursue Your Dream Life

Get out your journal and play this "what if?" game: How you would spend your time if you had ten million bucks—complete financial freedom? Would you really quit work tomorrow and play golf every day, or lounge on the beach in Hawaii with a cocktail? Might these knee-jerk answers actually get old after seven days, or seven weeks? Instead, take some time to reflect on what type of work, hobbies, and daily behavior patterns would give you the best blend of happiness via instant gratification, as well as the long-term fulfillment that comes from making a positive contribution to society by pursuing the highest expression of your talents.

Describe your ideal lifestyle in as much detail as possible. Next, list the self-limiting beliefs, excuses, and dysfunctional behavior patterns that are holding you back, and the specific actions and empowering beliefs that you can replace them with. Finally, take some form of action today toward your vision for a more purposeful life. Ideally, it will be something outrageous to make a dramatic impact. This could be merely verbalizing your dreams for the first time to a supportive friend or family member, or creating some sort of display in your house for a constant visual reminder. It could be a logistics step, such as registering for the innovative online career growth courses from Seth Godin (altMBA) or Marie Forleo (B-School), or the Primal Health Coach certification, or even purchasing a ten-pack of yoga classes. Outrageous can even happen inside your own mind, as you resolve to reject subconscious programming that you're not good enough, and start to believe in the dreams you are writing about.

REST AND RECOVERY: Cognitive Middle Gear Challenge

Getting stuck in the cognitive middle gear means being busy but lacking prioritization, discipline, and true productivity. Today, you will heighten your awareness of being stuck in the cognitive middle gear and apply some distinct strategies to prevent it. First, journal three to five behavior patterns that are promoting recovery debt instead of balance. Perhaps it's excess artificial light and digital stimulation after dark, an overly ambitious exercise program that's causing fatigue, a lack of focus in the office, or insufficient breaks from prolonged periods of stillness.

For each of the items on your list, offer a specific solution. For example, implementing dark, mellow evenings, establishing do-not-disturb time periods in your office, or executing the recommended work breaks from the Day 3 challenge.

Finally, during today's workday and time at home, heighten your awareness of every time you get distracted, fatigued, or pulled away from a priority task. To drive the point home, make a quick journal entry describing these cognitive middle gear occasions. Perhaps someone stopped by your office, taking you off the spreadsheet and into low-priority conversation. Maybe you clicked on YouTube all by yourself, getting drawn into basketball highlights in the middle of replying to an important email. Creating a written record of your behavior patterns might scare you straight into a more disciplined workday, especially if you happen to fall into the pattern of being too busy to take frequent breaks.

DAY 11 MEALS

BREAKFAST
- Fasting with water, tea, or coffee

LUNCH
- Fasting or light snack

DINNER
- *Keto for Life* entrée (pages 210 to 231)

DAY 12

DIET: Time-Restricted Feeding— *Carry Forward Challenge*

Today you will limit your digestive function to a maximum of 12 hours and carry this challenge forward for the rest of the Reset. This is envisioned as a lifelong habit, where you stay mindful to limit your digestive function to a maximum of 12 hours per day. You are probably already doing a great job eating your meals in a compressed time window of perhaps much less than 12 hours, and will definitely lock into fasting until 12 noon for all of next week. However, don't forget the distinctive feature of Time-Restricted Feeding (TRF) that the ingestion of any xenobiotic substance starts your digestive clock, even if it is noncaloric. For example, coffee, herbal tea, water with lemon juice, or swallowing a vitamin pill all wake up the digestive system first thing in the morning. If you welcome the day at 6 a.m. with some hot tea, and enjoy a few squares of dark chocolate at 9 p.m., it's time to tighten up your TRF game!

MOVEMENT AND PHYSICAL FITNESS:
Morning Flexibility/Mobility Sequence

Time to test out the suggestions from Pillar #2 and see what gives you the most enjoyment and bene-fits. On Day 20, you will custom-design a morning longevity routine, integrating your favorite flexibil-ity/mobility stuff with other movement and mind-fulness endeavors you've tried during the daily challenges. For today, complete the basic morn-ing sequence exercises of hamstrings + kickouts and the frog kicks, then consider adding advanced moves like scissors, bridges, alternating bird dog, and full Matty's.

MENTAL FLEXIBILITY: Defining Your Social and Intimate Circles

Bust out your increasingly interesting and robust 21-Day Reset journal and write down the members of your intimate circle and your larger social circle. Note that those in your intimate circle don't have to occupy a repeat position in your social circle. Add an asterisk next to people who you envision occupying one of the circles, but with whom you currently have a weakened connection. Reach out today in each case to strengthen these con-nections, such as making plans for lunch or other social occasion, or catching up by phone if you are far away.

Answer a few questions in your journal as fol-lows: How does the size of each circle feel to you? Remember there are no strict rules here, but the guidelines mentioned in the text may be helpful: an intimate circle of 12 or less, and social circle of 50 or less. Are email, texting, and social media compromising the time and energy you have to devote to live interpersonal relationships? What changes in behavior can you make accordingly (e.g., join a community group, throw a party or schedule a reunion, establish limits for your social media interactions)?

REST AND RECOVERY:
Early-to-Bed Challenge

Congratulations on a strong couple of weeks of hard work and devotion to lifestyle transforma-tion. Coupled with your routine daily respon-sibilities, you must be tired come Friday night, eh? Tonight's assignment is to move your typical lights-out bedtime up by 1 hour. Journal your ex-perience in the morning, paying close attention to if you feel more alert and energized. I must admit that I don't execute this challenge very often, but I always feel fantastic when I get to bed a bit early.

DAY 12 MEALS

BREAKFAST

- Fasting or hard-boiled egg bowl with walnuts, sun-dried tomatoes, avocado, and mayonnaise (made with avocado oil)

LUNCH

- Fasting or hard-boiled egg bowl

DINNER

- Sushi or *Keto for Life* international entrée such as French Bistro Layered Salmon and Avocado Tartare (page 249), Quick Italian Chicken with Basil and Avocado Dressing (page 250), or Thai Omega Balls (page 252)

DAY 13

DIET: Celebration Dinner

Invite friends over, pick one of the delicious entrées from this book or another keto book, and prepare your menu from start to finish. Take time to shop for the healthiest ingredients, enjoy the preparation efforts with family or friends, and have a great celebration. If you have keto-enthusiast friends, you can suggest a potluck gathering. Journal the food you shopped for and prepared and overall thoughts about the occasion.

MOVEMENT AND PHYSICAL FITNESS:
Yoga Sun Salutation

Perform the sequence exactly as described in Pillar #2 (page 100), and the two additional advanced moves if desired. First thing in the morning is an ideal time to salute the sun, and right before bed can also be a great way to unwind and facilitate sleep. Remember to synchronize your breathing with the movements: Inhale to stretch or assume a pose, exhale to compress or release the pose. Since the sun salutation is today's Movement and Physical Fitness challenge, commit to doing it three separate times: morning, midday, and night. Hopefully, you will be inclined to integrate this

simple but powerful practice into your everyday routine.

MENTAL FLEXIBILITY:
Relationship Expiration Dates?

Time to address toxic relationships by either severing ties or addressing lingering rifts and resentments with direct conversation. Spend some time in reflection and identify relationships where you really need to take some form of action, but have been avoiding the inevitable. If it's time to let go, dispense your message in as few words as possible without unnecessary emotion, rationalization, or defensiveness. Whatever the person says, refrain from an emotional reaction no matter what. If you have been avoiding a talk with a relationship that you wish to repair, apologize for the pain that the rift has caused (you don't have to accept blame), and state your desire to reconnect in a healthy manner.

REST AND RECOVERY: Nature Experience

Recall the amazing research about forest therapy in Japan (page 148), where merely spending time in nature quickly lowers blood pressure and stress hormones. Of course, therapeutic benefits arise from connecting with nature in general, so if you have a desert or beach instead of a forest, this will become your go-to experience. Plan an extended outing, accessing the best your local environment has to offer. If you can only manage to walk in a nearby park, that's better than skipping the challenge. However, since it's the weekend and all, strive for a more ambitious outing such as a hike in nearby mountains or a stand-up paddling session at a lake or on the ocean. Journal your experience and list some ways that you can make time in nature a regular part of your lifestyle.

DAY 13 MEALS

BREAKFAST

- Fasting or Morning Longevity Smoothie (page 277)

LUNCH

- Fasting or salad made with sauerkraut, kimchi, or tempeh

DINNER

- Sushi or *Keto for Life* international entrée such as Breton Butter Scallops with Garlic and Bacon (page 246), Thai Minced Pork Salad (page 251), or Shakshuka (page 254)

DAY 14

DIET: Bootcamp-Style Cooking Session #2

Go for it again, hopefully elevating your game from the Day 7 challenge. First, list the meals you would like to prepare for the week ahead, then create a grocery list, then source the best ingredients, and finally execute a highly focused, 2-hour cooking session. Repeat what worked the best in the first session and try out some new stuff to continually grow your database of go-to meals. If you have kids, involve them in the cooking process for a family bonding experience and a powerful life

lesson of becoming totally connected to the joy of home meal preparation. Journal details about your preparation order and other logistics so you can continually refine your bootcamp skills.

MOVEMENT AND PHYSICAL FITNESS:
Aerobic Workout #2—Overdistance
Today you will extend beyond your usual workout duration with what I like to call a "Breakthrough Workout." This is a session that is challenging enough to stimulate a fitness improvement. In this case, it is the duration of the workout that provides the breakthrough stimulus, because you will again maintain a heart rate of "180 minus age" heart beats per minute, or below, for the duration of the session. Journal the details, including workout type, route, duration, and whether you were able to maintain aerobic heart rates the entire time.

MENTAL FLEXIBILITY:
Reference Group Evaluation
The reference group that you select and nurture has a powerful influence on your attitude, behavior patterns, and path through life. Do you think you're the aggregate of the people you hang out with most? Can you see how happiness, obesity, and everything in between is contagious up to three degrees? In your journal, describe five ways that your reference group is affecting you in a positive manner and five ways that your reference group may be affecting you in a negative manner.

Make one entry to describe the influence of your intimate circle and another to describe the influence of your larger social circle. Sometimes those at a significant distance have a surprising influence, either positive or negative. Perhaps this exercise will illuminate relationships that deserve a strengthened connection. Writing some specific examples might help you with ongoing efforts to nurture healthy circles and take action on expiration dates, or at least create some healthy distance if negative energy gets too close to you.

REST AND RECOVERY:
Parasympathetic Stimulation
Have your partner give you a full body massage, with long powerful strokes that move significant blood (always toward the heart) and stimulate lymphatic function. If you don't have access to massage, conduct an ambitious self-myofascial release session, lasting at least 10 minutes. Work through your sore muscles and pressure points, but also spend some time rolling through the abdominal cavity area, which can be especially effective at stimulating parasympathetic activity. After your self-care massage or rolling, conduct a sun salutation sequence or other intentional breathing exercise. Pay close attention and see if you can notice a calming effect that indicates you have transitioned from sympathetic dominance during a hectic day into parasympathetic activity.

DAY 14 MEALS

BREAKFAST
- Fasting or bigass omelet

LUNCH
- Fasting or bigass salad

DINNER
- Sushi or *Keto for Life* entrée (pages 210 to 231)

WEEK THREE

This week you will focus on fasting until at least 12 noon each day, which will help you break through to a higher level of metabolic flexibility quickly. Noon is your minimum objective, but feel free to leverage your momentum and try to extend your first meal out further on certain days if you like. You'll tackle this very challenge on Day 17. You'll wrap up the Reset this week by repeating some of the workouts and assessments you did earlier, with superior results expected. Good luck!

DAY 15

DIET: Fasting Until Noon, New Recipes
Fast until 12 noon, then expand your repertoire today with some foods and meals you've never tried before. Spend some time perusing cookbooks or Internet videos for ideas. If you've enjoyed your foray into organ meats, boldly venture further into this world with some new selections. Write down numerous ideas that you can try out in the future.

MOVEMENT AND PHYSICAL FITNESS:
Strength Workout #2

Implement the high-intensity repeat training strategy with another explosive, short duration workout of PEMs, Maximum Overload, or a custom workout featuring sweeping full-body, functional movements. As a fun add-on component to this day's challenge, see if you can integrate mini-strength sessions (aka Maffetone's "slow weights") every single day for the duration of the challenge. This can be a single set of pull-ups, deep squats, or stretch cords as you pass by the apparatus in your home or yard, such that you accumulate 2, 3, or 5 sets over the course of an entire day.

These sneaky sessions obviously don't count as official workouts, but over time they add up to thousands of pounds of additional physical work and fitness stimulation. Getting into this simple habit of lifting heavy things in life will stimulate breakthroughs in your formal sessions, because you will be launching your formal efforts from a much higher platform than an active couch potato.

MENTAL FLEXIBILITY: Being the Best Partner You Can Be

Time to roll up your sleeves and address the make-or-break longevity factor that is your intimate partnership. Nurturing a loving partnership is the essence of living long and living awesome, while living with dysfunction and toxicity promotes accelerated aging and disease. Unlike the simple and linear mechanics of a diet overhaul, your relationship status can often swing wildly across the continuum from lousy to lovely in the blink of an eye. No matter how strained and stressful things are right now, realize that if you are able to change the way you operate in a relationship, the relationship transforms by definition. Commit to being the best you can be without expectation or demand for reciprocation. Open your heart and do it for the betterment of yourself, the partnership, and for all humanity!

First, journal the top three relationship issues that you are struggling with right now. This exercise is personal and confidential, so express your true feelings, even if they carry some anger and blame. At the same time, journal your top three positive relationship attributes. It will be very helpful to smile and acknowledge these in the background as you wade in and deal with difficult issues.

With your three struggles, write some lifestyle circumstances that may be contributing factors. These can include job pressures, hectic daily schedules, difficulties with children or other family members, health challenges, and so on. Next, write down three to five ways that you can change your approach to improve your relationship. This can include alleviating life stress (e.g., working fewer hours) as well as changing relationship interactions directly (e.g., scheduling a weekly date night without the kids). Tomorrow your challenge is to put some suggestions from relationship experts into action. *Note:* If you are not currently in an intimate partnership, complete the exercises with an eye toward your ideal partnership.

REST AND RECOVERY: Partner in Crime

The 21-Day Biological Clock Reset is designed to be a personal exercise, with your personal journal intended to make you highly accountable to yourself. Today, you'll mix it up a bit by enrolling a willing friend or family member in your challenge of bringing more rest, recovery, and downtime into your life. Describe a few of the challenges that you have completed in this section to date, and invite him or her to take part in one of their choosing today. Ideally, you will play the role of mentor here, exposing your partner to some exciting new concepts and helping him or her create a sleep sanctuary or take frequent breaks at work. If today's engagement is a success, perhaps your partner will join you for further challenges, and become inspired to do their own 21-Day Biological Clock Reset?

DAY 15 MEALS

BREAKFAST

- No calories before noon this entire week, but you can certainly enjoy a morning coffee or tea

LUNCH

- Bigass salad

DINNER

- *Keto for Life* organ meat entrée (pages 232 to 244)

DAY 16

DIET: Fasting Until Noon, Food Journal and Macronutrient Calculations #2

Take a second opportunity to journal your food intake and run the numbers through an app or online macronutrient calculator. Take note of any potential problem areas, such as getting a high percentage of your 50-gram carb allotment from the incidental amounts present in high-fat dairy products, nuts, or dark chocolate. It's possible to overdo keto-friendly foods and exceed keto guidelines. Remember that one of the most profound benefits of keto is appetite regulation, so make sure you pay attention to hunger and satiety signals in concert with adhering to keto macros.

MOVEMENT AND PHYSICAL FITNESS: Fasted Workout

If you possess a good-to-great level of metabolic flexibility, try conducting a challenging workout in a fasted state, and continuing to fast for 1, 2, or 4 hours after the workout. Make this either an overdistance aerobic session (longer duration than usual), or a brief, explosive, high-intensity session. The objective here is to upregulate ketone manufacturing, fat-burning, and also autophagy—the natural cellular detoxification process that occurs when your cells are starved of energy. Pairing a challenging workout with fasting is an advanced strategy, but if you can pull it off, it's a great way to obtain accelerated fat reduction and mitochondrial benefits. Journal the particulars, such as how many hours you fasted before the workout, the nature of the workout, and how many hours you fasted after the workout. Repeat the challenge in the future to track improvements in metabolic flexibility.

MENTAL FLEXIBILITY: Relationships— Mars and Venus Work

Males, time to indulge your partner in a Venus talk, followed by some additional caretaking. Invite her to share, listen intently without interrupting or dispensing advice, and end with a hug and a positive affirmation for her. Follow up the conversation with a meal, massage, evening stroll, a longer two-way conversation, or perhaps some brain- and hormone-optimizing sexual activity. Journal your experience with particular attention to how these dynamics might be different than typical patterns, and how you can make Venus talks in particular a daily occurrence.

Females, express everything today as a preference, and refrain from using a complaining tone of voice. Remain open and receptive to assistance and moral support from your partner. This will nurture your female side, which can easily get depleted by hectic, competitive modern life. Heed the expert advice from Dr. John Gray and see if relationship tension can be alleviated in the bedroom. Journal your experience with particular attention to how your communication feels different than usual, and how you can replace nitpicking with preference talk every day.

REST AND RECOVERY: Meditation Challenge

We haven't talked much about meditation, but it's been in the background of discussions about mindfulness, gratitude, and morning routines. Today you will try a brief and simple meditation session and see how it goes. Sit or lie down in a comfortable position. Close your eyes halfway, so you remain present and not sleepy. Commence 20 deep, diaphragmatic breaths, taking care to expand your chest and abdomen to inhale, then relax everything to exhale. Keep a running count of your breaths 1 through 20 and attempt to think of nothing else during your exercise. If random thoughts appear in your head, acknowledge them calmly, release them, and return to your breath count. It's surprisingly difficult to make it to 20 without getting totally derailed. Keep at it, knowing that 5 minutes is plenty to start out with. Again, repetition and endurance will get you into a good meditation groove. The wildly popular Headspace app can give you further guidance if you want to escalate your commitment comfortably over time.

DAY 16 MEALS

LUNCH
- Bigass salad or leftover entrée

DINNER
- *Keto for Life* side dish (pages 255 to 264)

DAY 17

DIET: Extended Fast

When the clock strikes 12 noon, see how much longer you can last feeling comfortable, alert, and energized. At a certain point, hunger sensations will kick in, at which time you can test the edges of your metabolic flexibility and work through it for a little longer. Your first sensation might be a lively stomach, caused in part by a spike of the prominent hunger hormone ghrelin. The ghrelin spike only lasts for about 20 minutes, and will almost always subside as your system realizes you ain't getting food right away and have to turbocharge fat- and ketone-burning instead. During the interim, before you finally sit down to a meal, get up and move, for this will boost fat metabolism and brain oxygenation. Occasionally extending the time before your first meal by 30, 60, or 90 minutes after you first get hungry is a great way to drop excess body fat and boost the cellular repair and renewal processes that are the essence of longevity.

Record the times of the previous evening's meal and the first meal the following day, and any other comments about the experience.

MOVEMENT AND PHYSICAL FITNESS:
Formal Movement Class

Complete a class with a guided instructor in the activity of your choice: yoga, Pilates, tai chi, or one of the popular modern adaptations of these established classics. If you are a complete novice and feeling intimidated about joining a group activity, do some prequalifying to ensure you are taking an appropriate class and the instructor is aware of your concerns. It's not uncommon for newbies to encounter overenthusiastic instructors who extend beyond sensible effort, resulting in muscle soreness, or worse, injury. Take it easy, start slow, have fun, and try different stuff over time.

MENTAL FLEXIBILITY: Declutter Level 2

Leverage the initial work you did on Day 8 by either finishing what you started or decluttering one or two more areas of your life today. How's your vehicle looking, your fridge, your kitchen pantry? Looking at clutter enters your subconscious awareness, triggers a stress hormone spike, and causes you to move away from the stimulus. By contrast, when you take action to declutter, you build tremendous momentum toward a more organized, less stressful life in general. Journal your experience today and create a list of additional areas of life you can potentially declutter in the future.

REST AND RECOVERY:
Four Daily Intentions Exercise

Start your day by reciting Dr. Deepak Chopra's Four Daily Intentions aloud, then writing them onto an index card and/or sticky note. Refer to them frequently, display them prominently, and commit to living in alignment with them throughout the day. Notice when you behave in conflict with them and correct course immediately. Realize the power of a simple gesture such as saying, "I'm sorry," to access your loving, compassionate heart.

Deepak Chopra's Four Daily Intentions:

- *Joyful, energetic body:* No toxic substances or people allowed
- *Loving, compassionate heart:* Accept others as they are; that's what we all want
- *Reflective, quiet, alert mind:* Be chill and intuitive instead of eternally peppy
- *Lightness of being:* Appreciate the present, stop ruminating!

DAY 17 MEALS

LUNCH

- Fasting or light snack

DINNER

- Celebratory dinner! Perhaps a night out for some sushi?

DAY 18

DIET: Fasting Until Noon, Healthy Food Shopping #2

Review your purchases from Day 2 and discover what worked and what didn't. Do any necessary restocking today. Do some comparison shopping, including trying new brands or new stores to continually strive for the best. Finally, carefully organize your notes and create a working shopping list that you can continually revise and update.

MOVEMENT AND PHYSICAL FITNESS: Sprint Workout #2

Time for a second sprint session, but please make sure you are 100-percent rested and motivated for a peak performance effort. If not, table this challenge until next week! Remember the necessary sequence of warm-up, prep drills, wind sprints, and work efforts lasting 10 to 20 seconds, totaling 4 to 10 reps, and with luxurious rest intervals. Journal your results and reference them frequently. As you get more competent, strive mostly to improve your speed and explosiveness rather than increase the duration or volume of your sprints.

MENTAL FLEXIBILITY: Mini–Play Sessions

Focus on little things that add up to a playful day and a playful lifestyle. Organize a wastebasket hoops challenge in the conference room. Take an extra 5 minutes to fool around in the yard with the kids or the dog when you arrive home. See if you can keep your balance walking on a curb in the parking lot, or get some small beanbags and practice juggling for a few minutes here and there throughout the day. Journal the mini–play sessions you engaged in today and your thoughts about them.

REST AND RECOVERY: Taking Chill Time

Sit and do nothing for 5 minutes on two separate occasions today. Ideally, get outdoors and gaze at nature scenery. If you can't get outside, sit in your car or even a chair at home or work. Relax and allow your mind to daydream. If you want to meditate, go ahead and complete your 20 breath counts. Otherwise, just try to achieve a quiet mind and allow thoughts to float into and out of your consciousness.

If you catch yourself ruminating, say aloud, "There I go ruminating again," and redirect your attention to your breathing. Strive to take 5 minutes of chill time any time you have been performing a peak cognitive task for more than 40 minutes straight, or any time you have been sitting for a couple hours straight, or any time you feel frazzled from overstimulation. If this exercise seems inane to you, realize there is tremendous power in being able to dial your brain activation up or down, and also to redirect away from rumination into present awareness.

DAY 18 MEALS

LUNCH
- Bigass salad or leftover entrée

DINNER
- *Keto for Life* organ meat entrée (pages 232 to 244)

DAY 19

DIET: Carb Refeed Day
Once in a while it's acceptable to depart from strict keto guidelines and enjoy foods that you are restricting in the name of keto. With your sprint workout performed yesterday, today is a good opportunity to experiment with increased carb intake (along with cold exposure) as a recovery strategy. Since you are in the midst of a rigorous reset, you'll skip the treats today and instead favor colorful, nutrient-dense carbohydrates like sweet potatoes and fresh fruits, or perhaps extra servings of dark chocolate or nut butter.

Granted, your long-term pursuit of living awesome will possibly include celebratory treats now and then. On these occasions, be sure to choose the finest handmade offerings instead of chemical-laden processed junk food. There is a big difference between enjoying a chocolate chip cookie fresh out of the oven and made from scratch by grandma, versus the edible foodlike substance called a chocolate chip cookie found on convenience store shelves. Many keto enthusiasts have fun making less objectionable versions of popular treats like cheesecake or brownies, and you can find numerous ideas in books or Internet videos. Keto-friendly treats should certainly not be a centerpiece of your keto experience, but when you are in the mood for some dietary diversions, be sure to respect your overall commitment to healthy eating.

MOVEMENT AND PHYSICAL FITNESS:
Cold Exposure
Dabble in the wonderful world of cold exposure by ending your morning or evening shower with 2 minutes of the coldest temperature water. Cold exposure is the quintessential hormetic stressor. Even a brief exposure will increase blood circulation and oxygen delivery and spike norepinephrine—the prominent mood-elevating and -focusing hormone—for up to an hour afterward. If you can

create a more elaborate experience, such as jumping in a nearby cold ocean or lake at the appropriate times of year, finding a health club with a cold plunge (rare, but worth joining the club!), or even going all-in and purchasing a 15 cubic foot chest freezer for your backyard, go for it!

Leaders in the field of cold exposure have amassed an amazing body of evidence about the health and hormonal benefits. (Visit Dr. Rhonda Patrick's FoundMyFitness.com to download a free 22-page pdf report on the scientific benefits of cold exposure). Dr. Jack Kruse (jackkruse.com) says cold exposure helps you access "ancient pathways" associated with fat burning, cellular repair, and antiaging. Former NASA research scientist Ray Cronise claims cold exposure (cold showers, sleeping without sheets, and walking outdoors underdressed) helped him lose 27 pounds in 6 weeks. There are also major psychological benefits: If you can muster the discipline and focus to overcome that initial aversion to cold and execute a daily regimen, this resolve will carry over into other areas of life—batching email, minimizing light after dark, doing the sun salutation every morning, and so on.

MENTAL FLEXIBILITY: Create and Maintain a To-Do List

Stay proactive and focused all day long through disciplined use of the all-powerful weapon that is a prioritized to-do list. Honoring a to-do list will help you combat the major mental stressors of today that are hyperconnectivity, distractibility, and multitasking. Start this morning by creating a written to-do list, with the objectives categorized logically (personal, work, family) and items listed in order of importance. If you already maintain a functional to-do list, see if you can up your game a bit today by spending some extra time reviewing and prioritizing the items on your list and plotting the most efficient strategies to get stuff done (e.g., running errands in a particular order).

Remember, habit modification requires repetition and endurance, so create a strategy to carry items over into the next day, and the next week, maintaining a disciplined order of priority. Set aside a few minutes every single morning to curate the to-do list before you get going with work. A digital to-do list might make carryover easier, but go with your personal preference. Realize a common flaw among well-meaning to-do list enthusiasts is to not spend the necessary time creating, editing, and referring to the to-do list throughout the day—especially when things get hectic. Alas, this is when you need prioritization more than any other time, so get some great habits going today.

REST AND RECOVERY: Rebound Workout

On the heels of your sprint workout yesterday, this is a great opportunity to learn the art of recovery workouts. Instead of sitting on the couch and eating chips, get to the gym or suitable fitness area at home and try out some of the Rebound Training protocols recommended by Joel Jamieson at 8WeeksOut.com. Start with some deep, diaphragmatic breathing exercises while lying flat on the ground. Inhale forcefully through your nostrils, inflating your abdomen to ensure the diaphragm muscles are expanded completely. Exhale in a relaxed manner by allowing the chest and abdomen to deflate naturally. Complete 20 breath cycles, then proceed to a basic foam rolling session. Start at the trunk and roll away from the body, giving your thighs and calves some good work. Then proceed along the length of your back (go lighter on your lower back) and finish with a bit of rolling through the abdomen.

Next, commence a few of the dynamic stretches as described in Pillar #2: Deep squats, knee-to-chests, pull quads, open hips, mini-lunges, and leg swings. Then, do a handful of brief, intense work efforts with extended recovery time. This will trigger a brief fight-or-flight reaction followed by a strong parasympathetic compensatory response. Choose some positive-only deadlifts (lift bar and drop to ground) or some tempo intervals of a 10-second bicycle sprint, followed by a 60-second recovery. Finally, complete a cooldown of 5 to 10 minutes of very easy cardio at a heart rate of 10 to 30 beats below 180 minus age. Journal your experience, including workout particulars, so you have a protocol to follow next time.

DAY 19 MEALS

LUNCH

- Bigass salad or *Keto for Life* breakfast suggestion (pages 197 to 209) such as hard-boiled egg bowl or yogurt bowl

DINNER

- *Keto for Life* entrée (pages 210 to 231)

DAY 20

DIET: Food Journal and Macronutrient Calculations #3

Repeat your exercise from Days 4 and 16 and input the data into your favorite app or online calculator. Have some fun and try to guess your meals' macros prior to generating the total. Over time, you'll want to build your eyeball estimation skills in order to stay aligned with keto without having to constantly quantify everything. Along those lines, spend 10 extra minutes interacting with your app or online calculator to research and/or input some of your favorite meals into your custom database. For example, you will obtain a general macronutrient profile for an omelet in any calculator, but if you routinely make yours with 4 eggs, chopped mushrooms, onions, and tomatoes, melted cheese, and half an avocado, input your creation so you can input it again with one click and also commit it to memory.

MOVEMENT AND PHYSICAL FITNESS:
Custom-Design a Morning Longevity Routine

Time to pick and choose from the favorite things you have been exposed to during the 21-Day Biological Clock Reset. The goal here is to design a realistic and sustainable morning sequence that you can repeat every single day until it becomes ingrained as habit. If you are typically pressed for time in the morning and only have 7 minutes to allocate, that's fine. When you can develop the discipline and focus to immediately awaken and jump into a sun salutation sequence, some balancing or mobility exercises, or even a cold tub or shower, you set the stage for a highly focused, productive, proactive life. Journal your step-by-step sequence and tweak it over the next several days beyond the course completion until you get it right. Over time, feel free to make both minor tweaks and major overhauls, but you should always have *something* specific in place as a morning routine.

MENTAL FLEXIBILITY: Pivoting Follow-Up
Get out your journal and answer the following questions honestly. How do the issues you discussed on the Day 4 pivoting challenge look today? Have you made some progress out of "stuck" mode? What new beliefs and actions worked for you? If you have not made progress, what's holding you back? Are you afraid to quit, or to take a risk? Do you need to play the WhaT WiTCH game again?

After journaling the status of your previous issues, take some time to consider if any new issues have arisen that might require a pivot, and list them accordingly. Expand your focus beyond the three major life issues you were asked to cover on Day 4 and consider even minor and mundane daily behavior patterns that might require a pivot. For example, you keep getting to work late because your kid's not ready for carpool on time; it's somehow been 10 days since you've been to the gym; you keep snacking on junk food at work. Getting good at making small pivots toward better health, balance, and productivity add up over time. Jour-

nal a few ideas right now and resolve to make the pivots happen in the days ahead.

REST AND RECOVERY: Weekend Disconnect
In the spirit of the weekend, strive to unplug for an entire day from technology. Schedule a major outing in nature with family or friends, or at least an evening at home filled with socializing, board or card games, or reading instead of screen engagement. Disconnect from all social media for a 24-hour period and keep text and email use to a bare minimum of essential communication only.

DAY 20 MEALS

LUNCH
- Bigass salad or *Keto for Life* breakfast suggestion (pages 197 to 209)

DINNER
- *Keto for Life* entrée (pages 210 to 231), international entrée (pages 245 to 254), organ meat entrée (pages 232 to 244), or sushi

DAY 21

DIET: Journal Exercise and Future Plans
Reread the description of each daily Diet challenge, then do some free-form journaling about your experiences over the past three weeks. Describe some of your favorite activities and foods, and some of the stuff that was difficult or unpleasant. List some ways that you intend to modify your

dietary habits in the future, based on your positive experiences with the daily challenges. List some "needs to improve" areas, and revisit them three weeks after this daily exercise to provide a written update. By repeating today's journal exercise every three weeks in the months ahead, hopefully your needs-to-improve list will get smaller and eventually vanish.

MOVEMENT AND PHYSICAL FITNESS:
Repeat MAF And PEM Assessments

Remember to conduct these tests only on days when you feel 100-percent rested and motivated to perform. If you have been working hard with fitness endeavors during the Reset, you may require additional recovery days before conducting these tests.

Do the MAF test first so you are fresh, then the PEM exercises. Allow for complete recovery between each PEM effort—3 to 5 minutes should suffice. You should expect some improvement on each test since your baseline assessments, but keep in mind that three weeks is not long enough to achieve miracles. If your values are similar or slightly worse, don't worry about it. If your values are significantly worse, you are likely fatigued from a challenging three weeks that you perhaps weren't fully prepared for, overstressed in life, or

not fully recovered on the day of the test. Journal your results in an identical manner to the previous tests, and keep good records over time for repeat tests.

MENTAL FLEXIBILITY:
Gratitude Journal Recap

Relax and take some time to carefully read every entry in the journal you started at the outset of the challenge. Write a summary journal entry describing your experience of gratitude journaling each day, and also about your gratitude for completing the 21-Day Biological Clock Reset!

REST AND RECOVERY: Do It!

That's right, rest, recover, and take some downtime to complete your final "challenge." Congratulations on completing the Reset!

DAY 21 MEALS

LUNCH

- Bigass salad or *Keto for Life* breakfast suggestion

DINNER

- *Keto for Life* entrée (pages 210 to 231), international entrée (pages 245 to 254), organ meat entrée (pages 232 to 244), or sushi

DAY 22 AND BEYOND—LONGEVITY ONE DAY AT A TIME

You did it! I hope that you feel energized and ready to tackle anything that life has to throw at you. You can feel confident in the fact that these longevity strategies will serve you well by extending not only your lifespan but also your healthspan. You have to make the commitment. Don't let busy life get in the way, because when you slack on longevity practices, you are less resilient and less able to combat chronic stress. Here is a quick recap of the challenges that came with the suggestion to implement immediately and permanently:

DIET

1. **Ditch grains, sugars, and refined seed oils:** Establish a zero-tolerance policy and eliminate these nutrient-deficient foods from your consciousness and your range of choices. When sweets, treats, and grain foods occasionally enter your life, make them a special-occasion celebration and recalibrate immediately back to baseline.

2. **Live in the keto zone:** Emphasize colorful, nutrient-dense plant and animal foods of the highest possible quality in each food category. Focus on the longevity superfoods and supplements to go after that final 20 percent of longevity potential. Make fasting and Time Restricted Feeding the central element of your dietary strategy.

3. **Two meals maximum, no snacking, 80 percent full:** It's not just what you eat, it's also how you enjoy food as one of the great pleasures of life. Make mealtimes special occasions in a relaxed environment, refrain from snacking, and honor *hara hachi bun me*.

MOVEMENT AND PHYSICAL FITNESS

1. **Create morning routine (Day 20):** Dial in your favorite sequence and do it every single day without fail. You can make adjustments over time, but the emphasis here is on a regimented series of movements that becomes automatic and habitual. Include some exposure to direct sun to entrain circadian rhythm.

2. **JFW:** Walking forms the centerpiece of your movement and physical fitness pillar. Find assorted ways to move more in everyday life, especially to break up prolonged periods of stillness and energize your brain and fat metabolism.

3. **Aerobic emphasis:** The vast majority of your cardiovascular exercise must be conducted at or below "180 minus age" heart rate, otherwise you will drift toward breakdown, burnout, and carbohydrate dependency.

4. **Go hard and go home:** Perform brief, explosive strength and sprint workouts, which deliver a profound antiaging hormonal response. You'll

avoid pain, suffering, and the sad and steady demise that happens when you let yourself go. A little goes a long way—don't overdo it!

MENTAL FLEXIBILITY

1. **Gratitude journal:** You don't have to make an entry every day, but keep a journal at your bedside. Note that in times of struggle, when you are least likely to write in a gratitude journal, that's often when you receive the most benefit by doing so.

2. **Batch emails:** Email is the most offensive source of distraction and cognitive stress. Establish a batching strategy that works for you and close the window down so you're not tempted—the world can wait!

3. **Declutter:** Stuff is overrated, and carries a hidden cost at the cellular level. Downsizing brings joy to yourself and others!

4. **Stop ruminating!:** Call it out, then redirect thoughts into a relaxed state of present awareness, for the rest of your life.

5. **Hone relationship skills:** For the sake of humanity, be the best you can be with your partner. Males: Never speak with a negative emotional charge—take cave time instead. Females: State everything as a preference instead of a complaint—don't nitpick.

6. **Intimate and social circles:** Deemphasize digital relationships, prioritize live interpersonal connections, nurture winning reference groups, take action with expiration dates.

REST AND RECOVERY

1. **Sleep sanctuary:** Create a tidy, cool, totally dark environment, free from screens, clutter, or work-related items.

2. **Screen curfew:** Make a general commitment to emphasize screen use earlier in evening, and implement calming rituals later in the evening.

3. **Cognitive middle gear:** Heighten your awareness when you get busy yet unproductive. Take a movement break, or nap, or just some chill time, and come back refreshed and focused.

4. **Self-care:** You deserve it, and you're never too busy.

KETO
FOR LIFE
RECIPES

decided to make this recipe project a collaborative effort among numerous prominent authors, coaches, chefs, and keto experts. The goal here was to present a diverse selection of dishes, both gourmet and quick and easy, in numerous creative categories, including beverages, side dishes, snacks and treats, and much more. Meet the great group of experts who helped make this recipe collection something special.

The Cool Dudes: The Cool Dudes are Brad Kearns, my longtime coauthor and publishing sidekick, and Brian McAndrew, my longtime videographer and audio engineer who makes me look good on podcasts and YouTube. These dudes love to eat healthy, but aren't inclined to sweat over complex gourmet meals. So, they created a whole book full of quick, fun, easy keto recipes called *Keto Cooking for Cool Dudes*.

Keris Marsden and Matt Whitmore: This dynamic duo from London, in the running for the world's fittest, healthiest, most motivating couple, wrote the bestselling books, *The Paleo Primer* and *The Paleo Primer: A Second Helping*. They offer a complete package of lifestyle programming, creative recipes, and fitness coaching at FitterFood.com.

Dr. Cate Shanahan: Dr. Shanahan's book *Deep Nutrition* is a true masterwork and has been a major catalyst for the ancestral health movement over the past decade. The book describes her "Four Pillars of World Cuisine" as fresh foods, meat on the bone, organ meats, and fermented foods. That's what longevity is all about! Dr. Cate is a great resource for recipes because she has had to be extra creative to inspire NBA Hall-of-Famers like Steve Nash and Kobe Bryant in overhauling their diets when she served as the nutritional consultant and travel meal planner for the Los Angeles Lakers.

William Shewfelt: A dynamic young leader in the carnivore diet movement, William's website (PrimalBody.co) helps you drop body fat with a focused, no-nonsense approach that is beautiful in its simplicity and convenience. While carnivore was initially dismissed as a potentially dangerous gimmick, it is getting more scientific support and user success stories each day. Listen to William and award-winning documentary filmmaker Chris Bell cover carnivore on the *Better, Stronger, Faster* podcast, and other carnivore experts like Dr. Paul Saladino (*Fundamental Health* podcast) and Dr. Shawn Baker (*Human Performance Outliers* podcast, with cohost Zach Bitter). You will be intrigued, to say the least.

Devyn Sisson: My daughter wrote and published one of the more creative and unusual cookbooks you will find, titled *Kitchen Intuition*. The subtitle says it all: *Cook with Your Hands. Laugh with Your Belly. Trust Your Intuition.* See if you can honor her penchant for creativity and flair in the kitchen by straying from the script any time you feel like it with the recipes in this book. Maybe you'll discover some interesting revisions that you can share with the Keto Reset Facebook Group!

Sarah Steffens: Sarah is a personal chef, nutrition coach, and recipe consultant to The Whole30 Program. She delivers a positive message about mindful eating and great recipe ideas at SavorandFancy.com. Sarah maintains a thriving business, preparing nutritious paleo-, keto-, and Whole30-friendly meals to private clients, so her creations are kitchen-tested by real people and constantly revised and perfected. The multitalented Sarah also took the recipe photos for *Keto Cooking for Cool Dudes*.

Dr. Lindsay Taylor and Layla McGowan: My co-authors on the *Keto Reset Instant Pot Cookbook,* they also wrote *Keto Passport*, which features the best traditional dishes from every corner of the globe, modified to be keto friendly. You'll enjoy the international-style recipes they inspired. Lindsay presides over the lively Keto Reset Facebook Group, so go jump into the mix and say hello. Also check out Lindsay's diverse creations for busy families on Instagram @theusefuldish. Layla blends her culinary passion with devoted practice of both yoga and extreme powerlifting. Follow this Renaissance woman on Instagram @strong.and.wellfed.

Tania Teschke: Author of the award-winning masterpiece on French food, wine, and culture, *The Bordeaux Kitchen,* she is an expert in organ meats and other nutrient-dense dishes in traditional French cuisine. She has studied with French chefs, traditional home cooks, and an award-winning Basque butcher, and holds a diploma in wine science from the University of Bordeaux. Tania has lived abroad with her family for many years, immersing herself into the best of French and European culinary culture. She has been on a personal journey of health and healing for many years, and applies this tremendous base of knowledge and experience to her message. Tania also helped increase my interest and competency in wine pairing.

DON'T STRESS THE MACROS!

Macronutrient calculations are provided for each recipe to help you stay aligned with your keto goals. We can call these recipes, "keto friendly," but I suggest you avoid worrying about hitting specific macronutrient percentages at a specific meal or even on a specific day. While the recommended keto macros of 65 to 75 percent fat, 15 to 25 percent protein, and 5 to 10 percent carbohydrate are reasonable calculations from a day of satisfying keto meals, targeting macros to make a perfect pie chart can potentially deemphasize the centerpiece keto element of burning stored body fat.

When you are metabolically flexible, you don't need to consume extra fat in the name of meeting macro targets, or for the inaccurate assumption that it leads to higher ketone production. Your dietary fat intake should be sufficient to achieve satiety, simple as that. Consequently, if you minimize fat intake to drop excess body fat, your carbohydrate and protein percentages may rise higher than the keto boilerplate on these days of heightened caloric efficiency. That's not only okay, but it likely provides a more valuable keto experience than if you load up on extra fat in an effort to hit the 65 to 75 percent guideline every single day. Remember, the greatest cellular, immune, cognitive, and metabolic benefits of keto come when it's driven by fasting, not high fat intake.

REST AND DIGEST

While the recipe lineup includes quick and easy preparations to balance the elaborate gourmet meals, it's important to remember that meal preparation and eating should never be a rush job. Longevity cultures maintain time-intensive rituals around procuring, preparing, and sharing food with family and friends. In France, shopping for fresh food daily at the town-square outdoor market has been a centerpiece of their small-town culture and community connection for centuries.

I have long made it a practice of simply avoiding eating if I don't have the time or the peace of mind to sit down and properly enjoy a meal at a leisurely pace. This happens on days of back-to-back meetings, grueling trade shows where I'm on my feet socializing and talking for hours, and any day of airplane travel. Realize that eating food is aligned with parasympathetic "rest and digest" function; best results with digestion and nutrient assimilation come when you are relaxed. Trying to wolf down food at times when you are "sympathetic dominant," such as during jet travel, can often result in gas, bloating, and other digestive distress, and possibly energy crashes later on (even if you ate a keto-aligned meal).

It follows that optimizing your keto experience and your pursuit of metabolic flexibility entails 1) making mealtimes a sacred experience of relaxation and pleasure, 2) making stored body fat the go-to resource for your energy needs, and 3) doing the best you can to source the highest quality foods. Emphasize locally grown produce and animal products, or find certified organic, grass-fed, pasture-raised, and the like. While it's not always possible or affordable to find the very best, at least put some standards in place. For example, agree to avoid cheap feedlot animal products, nonorganic dairy products (which likely contain hormones, pesticides, and antibiotics), GMO products, high-glycemic fruit transported from distant origins in the wintertime, fast-food restaurants, and most stuff in a package or wrapper.

Pay attention to details and elevate your foodie game whenever possible. Some experts recommend using only organic spices (to avoid concentrated doses of pesticides in prepared spice preparations) and rotating them out of the pantry every six months—not six *years*, but six months (since they can oxidize in the bottle over time)! Avoid industrial iodized salt, which has been bleached, stripped of nutrients, and is often laden with fillers and impurities. Instead, use ancient sea salt or Himalayan pink salt. Always use freshly ground pepper, and try to do the same for herbs and spices whenever possible.

With condiments like mayonnaise and salad dressing, be sure to avoid products made with refined industrial seed oils, and find cleaner options, such as the increasingly popular avocado oil–based products. Keep your spirits high in the kitchen by constantly rotating in fresh recipes and never stressing about perfection. Nurture your curiosity and pride of accomplishment so that eating awesome becomes a huge part of your life. We hope you enjoy these healthy, colorful, diverse offerings.

KETO BREAKFASTS

CHEESE AND SCALLION BAKE

If you're sick of fried or scrambled eggs for breakfast, baked egg recipes are sure to reinspire you. Also, you can make large portions and save leftovers for easy reheating during a busy week. This dish is a great choice for your cooking boot camp effort on Days 7 and 14 of the 21-Day Biological Clock Reset.

PREP TIME: 10 MINUTES
COOKING TIME:
35 TO 40 MINUTES

MAKES 3 SERVINGS

6	large eggs
2⅔	cups (600 g) low-fat cottage cheese
1	teaspoon garlic powder
1	teaspoon dried Italian seasoning
	Sea salt and ground black pepper
	Olive oil to coat baking dish
	3 scallions, chopped

1. Preheat the oven to 350°F (180°C).

2. In a blender, combine the eggs, cottage cheese, and garlic powder and blend for several seconds. Season with the herbs and sea salt and pepper to taste and set aside.

3. Grease an 8 x 12-inch ovenproof pan or a flan or quiche dish with olive oil or line it with parchment paper.

4. Scatter the scallions into the dish and pour the egg/cottage cheese mixture over the scallions. Bake until golden and cooked through, 35 to 40 minutes. Serve hot.

MACRONUTRIENTS PER SERVING
CALORIES: 263
FAT: 13 G
CARBOHYDRATE: 7 G
PROTEIN: 30 G

CHICKEN BREAKFAST HASH

When you just don't feel like eggs for breakfast, try this easy-to-prepare dish with a high satiety factor. Rosemary is known to help with memory, so you won't forget how tasty this was!

PREP TIME: 10 MINUTES
COOKING TIME:
10 MINUTES

MAKES 1 SERVING

- 2 slices uncured sugar-free bacon, chopped
- 4 ounces (113.40 g) boneless, skinless chicken thighs, diced
- 1 teaspoon garlic powder
- ½ teaspoon dried rosemary
- ¼ teaspoon sea salt
- ⅛ teaspoon ground black pepper
- 1 scallion, minced
- ½ avocado, diced

1. In a skillet, combine the bacon, chicken, garlic powder, rosemary, sea salt, and pepper. Cook over medium heat until the chicken is cooked through and the bacon begins to get crispy, 8 to 10 minutes. Add half of the scallion and toss together in the skillet.

2. Serve with the avocado and remaining minced scallion.

MACRONUTRIENTS PER SERVING

CALORIES: 403

FAT: 28 G

CARBOHYDRATE: 10 G

PROTEIN: 31 G

CLASSIC EGG CASSEROLE

This is a great way to make a delicious, filling keto breakfast for a group of people. Feel free to add grated cheese and bacon if you don't have picky or vegetarian-leaning eaters in the group.

PREP TIME: 10 MINUTES
COOKING TIME:
30 MINUTES

MAKES 4 SERVINGS

12 large eggs

¼ cup (59.15 ml) heavy whipping cream

2 cups chopped vegetables (broccoli, asparagus, Brussels sprouts, spinach, mushrooms, onions, tomatoes, bell peppers)

1 teaspoon sea salt

1–2 pinches ground black pepper, garlic powder, or mixed spices as desired

Optional: 1 cup (113 g) grated cheese and 2 slices of cooked sugar-free bacon

1. Preheat the oven to 350°F (180°C).

2. Crack the eggs into an 8 x 12-inch baking dish and whisk in the cream, vegetables, sea salt, and spices.

3. Add the cheese and the bacon, if using, with 5 minutes remaining in the cooking time.

4. Bake until semi-firm and a table knife inserted in the custard comes out clean, about 30 minutes. If it's too watery inside, cook for 5 more minutes and repeat the knife test. The bake will continue to cook a bit when it's out of the oven, so you can err a bit on the early removal side.

MACRONUTRIENTS PER SERVING (WITHOUT CHEESE AND BACON)	MACRONUTRIENTS PER SERVING (WITH CHEESE AND BACON)
CALORIES: 306	CALORIES: 410
FAT: 21 G	FAT: 23 G
CARBOHYDRATE: 5 G	CARBOHYDRATE: 6 G
PROTEIN: 19 G	PROTEIN: 22 G

FRIED EGGS OVER SEASONED GROUND BEEF

It doesn't get easier than a ground beef scramble, a new staple you'll be enjoying if you haven't been already. Keep your dried herbs and spices close to the stove for quick cooking and you'll find you've got this whole keto thing down.

PREP TIME: 5 MINUTES
COOKING TIME: 10 TO 12 MINUTES
MAKES 1 SERVING

- 1 tablespoon (14.17 g) salted butter
- 4 ounces (113.40 g) ground beef
- 1 teaspoon dried oregano
- 1 teaspoon garlic powder
- ¼ teaspoon smoked paprika
- ½ teaspoon sea salt
- ¼ teaspoon ground black pepper
- 1 scallion, minced
- 2 large eggs

MACRONUTRIENTS PER SERVING
CALORIES: 479
FAT: 36 G
CARBOHYDRATE: 4 G
PROTEIN: 35 G

1. In a large skillet, melt the butter over medium heat. Add the ground beef and mince it with a wooden spoon until the meat is cooked through, 8 to 10 minutes.

2. Drain the fat from the skillet. Stir in the oregano, garlic powder, smoked paprika, ¼ teaspoon of the sea salt, ⅛ teaspoon of the pepper, and half the minced scallion. Slide the seasoned beef onto a plate and cover to keep warm.

3. Return the skillet (still coated with the fat from the beef) to medium-high heat. Crack the eggs into the skillet and season with the remaining ¼ teaspoon sea salt and ⅛ teaspoon pepper. Cook until done, flipping after about 30 seconds.

4. Slide the eggs over the ground beef on the plate and garnish with the remaining minced scallion.

HEAVENLY HEMP YOGURT AND SOUR CREAM

This entry from Dr. Cate Shanahan, author of the 2020 release *The Fatburn Fix*, demonstrates her efforts to steer her elite NBA players away from high-carb staples like oatmeal into the incredible nutrient density and diverse tastes and textures of this preparation. Designed as a breakfast option, Dr. Cate says it tastes so good she enjoys it for dessert. The yogurt she recommends is whole-milk Organic Valley Grassmilk (with cream on top) because she finds it the healthiest and best tasting.

PREP TIME: 5 MINUTES

MAKES 1 SERVING

- 1 tablespoon sour cream
- 1 cup (225 g) plain whole-milk yogurt
- 1 tablespoon hemp hearts
- 1 tablespoon cacao nibs
- 2 tablespoons unsweetened large coconut flakes
- 8 whole sprouted almonds (or 2 tablespoons slivered almonds)
- 2 teaspoons wheat germ
- Pinch of sea salt
- ½-inch piece candied ginger, minced into tiny bits
- ⅛ teaspoon ground cinnamon (optional)

1. In a bowl, stir the sour cream into the yogurt just a few times to distribute the sour cream.

2. For best results, sprinkle the remaining ingredients over the top of the yogurt mixture in the order shown in the list of ingredients.

MACRONUTRIENTS PER SERVING
CALORIES: 455
FAT: 28 G
CARBOHYDRATE: 28 G
PROTEIN: 19 G

HERBES DE PROVENCE SCRAMBLE

Herbes de Provence is unexpected in a scramble and gives this dish a sophisticated twist. Make this to impress someone special!

PREP TIME: 10 MINUTES

COOKING TIME:
10 MINUTES

MAKES 1 SERVING

4   large eggs

¼   teaspoon sea salt

⅛   teaspoon ground black pepper

1   teaspoon herbes de Provence

1   tablespoon (14.17 g) salted butter

1   ounce (28.35 g) haricots verts, chopped

1   ounce (28.35 g) cherry tomatoes, halved

½   avocado, diced

1   ounce (28.35 g) feta cheese, cubed (optional)

MACRONUTRIENTS PER SERVING (INCLUDES FETA)

CALORIES: 642

FAT: 55 G

CARBOHYDRATE: 11 G

PROTEIN: 32 G

1. In a small bowl, whisk together the eggs, sea salt, pepper, and herbes de Provence.

2. In a skillet, melt half of the butter over medium heat. Add the green beans and sauté until soft, 5 to 7 minutes. Remove the beans and set aside.

3. In the same skillet, melt the remaining butter over medium heat. Tilt and swirl the pan so the butter coats the entire bottom. Add the egg mixture. Use a spatula to gently toss the eggs until they are nearly cooked through.

4. Return the green beans to the pan, add the tomatoes and avocado, and gently scramble until the eggs are cooked through. If desired, sprinkle half of the feta over the eggs to melt.

5. Slide the eggs onto a plate. Sprinkle with the remaining feta (if using). Serve immediately.

LEMON-TURMERIC SCRAMBLE WITH RADISHES

The combination of cottage cheese, turmeric, and radish is rare, but works so perfectly. This scramble is creamy with just the right crunch. The turmeric and black pepper in this dish work as anti-inflammatory agents, so you'll be glad you tried this.

PREP TIME: 10 MINUTES
COOKING TIME: 5 TO 7 MINUTES
MAKES 1 SERVING

4   large eggs

¼   teaspoon sea salt

⅛   teaspoon ground black pepper

½   teaspoon ground turmeric

1   tablespoon (14.17 g) salted butter

1   scallion, minced

¼   cup (25 g) minced radishes

⅔   cup (108 g) low-fat cottage cheese (optional)

1. In a small bowl, whisk together the eggs, sea salt, pepper, and turmeric.

2. In a medium skillet, melt the butter over medium heat. Add half of the minced scallion and sauté until soft, about 1 minute. Add the egg mixture. Use a spatula to gently toss the eggs until they are cooked through to your liking.

3. Slide the eggs onto a plate and garnish with the minced radishes and remaining scallion. Serve hot, with cottage cheese if desired.

MACRONUTRIENTS PER SERVING (INCLUDES COTTAGE CHEESE)

CALORIES: 426

FAT: 21 G

CARBOHYDRATE: 8 G

PROTEIN: 45 G

MATT'S MIGHTY BACON AND CHEESE SCOTCH EGGS

Matt Whitmore is a fitness beast; you should have seen him teaching one high-energy workout session after another at our PrimalCon retreats. He burns a ton of daily calories and relies on nutrient-dense preparations like these eggs to keep him performing and recovering at his best.

PREP TIME: 25 MINUTES
COOKING TIME: 30 TO 35 MINUTES

MAKES 10 SCOTCH EGGS

12	large eggs
1¾	pounds (800 g) fresh pork sausage, casings removed
6	slices bacon, chopped
3–4	scallions, chopped
1	cup (125 g) grated cheddar cheese
½	cup (48 g) almond flour

MACRONUTRIENTS PER SCOTCH EGG

CALORIES: 502

FAT: 41 G

CARBOHYDRATE: 2 G

PROTEIN: 23 G

1. Preheat the oven to 350°F (180°C).

2. Bring a large pot of water to a boil. Place 10 of the eggs in the boiling water, return to a boil, and set a timer for 4 minutes. Immediately drain and cool the eggs under cold water. Once cool, peel the cooked eggs.

3. Meanwhile, in a large bowl, combine the sausage meat, bacon, scallions, and cheddar, using your hands.

4. In a small bowl, beat the 2 remaining eggs. Scatter the almond flour on a plate.

5. Shape the meat mixture around each hard-boiled egg (being careful not to layer it too thick). Dip each coated egg into the beaten eggs, then roll each egg in the almond flour.

6. Transfer the eggs to an 8 x 12-inch baking pan. Bake until the sausage coating is cooked through, about 30 minutes. Serve warm.

PEACHES AND CREAM YOGURT

Dr. Cate loves this dish for dessert, but it also makes a great breakfast or quickly prepared lunch. On her inclusion of wheat germ in the recipe: "I know wheat is sacrilegious, but this stuff has tons of vitamin E, and most folks never get enough E." The Bakto Flavors flavoring she recommends is made with natural essences and extracts. Dr. Cate prefers using sprouted and salted almonds in this recipe, but raw or dry roasted are also good alternatives.

PREP TIME: 5 MINUTES

MAKES I SERVING

1 cup (225 g) whole-milk plain Greek yogurt

1 tablespoon sour cream

2 tablespoons hemp hearts

1 tablespoon toasted wheat germ

4–8 drops Bakto Flavors Natural Peach Flavor, to taste

12 almonds

In a serving bowl, stir together all the ingredients and enjoy.

MACRONUTRIENTS PER SERVING
CALORIES: 408
FAT: 24 G
CARBOHYDRATE: 19 G
PROTEIN: 32 G

PORK SAUSAGE AND GRAVY

Who would have thought you could make the world's best breakfast gravy without dairy and flour? Well, you can! Creamy almond butter does miracles in a pork-based gravy. Experiment with canned coconut milk, too, and this will be even more decadent.

PREP TIME: 5 MINUTES
COOKING TIME: 10 TO 12 MINUTES
MAKES 4 SERVINGS

- 1 pound (453.59 g) ground pork
- 1 teaspoon fennel seeds
- 1 teaspoon dried oregano
- 1 teaspoon smoked paprika
- 1 teaspoon garlic powder
- ¼ teaspoon sea salt
- ⅛ teaspoon ground black pepper
- ½ cup (118.29 ml) unsweetened almond milk
- 2 tablespoons smooth almond butter
- 1 scallion, minced
- 2 cups (60 g) baby spinach

1. In a large skillet, combine the pork, fennel, oregano, smoked paprika, garlic powder, sea salt, and pepper. Cook over medium heat, mincing the meat with a wooden spoon, until the meat is cooked through, 8 to 10 minutes.

2. Without draining the excess grease, add the almond milk and almond butter to the skillet, stirring well. Gently stir in the scallion and baby spinach until the spinach is wilted.

3. Serve warm in a bowl.

MACRONUTRIENTS PER SERVING

CALORIES: 365

FAT: 29 G

CARBOHYDRATE: 3 G

PROTEIN: 22 G

SMOKED SALMON OVER SPINACH WITH HERBED COCONUT YOGURT

It's fancy pants, for sure, but simple to make. Use a high-quality smoked salmon, maybe one with added spices like black pepper and mustard. This recipe is great for breakfast and can also be served in small sizes as a party snack.

PREP TIME: 10 MINUTES
COOKING TIME: 3 TO 5 MINUTES

MAKES 1 SERVING

1 tablespoon (14.17 g) salted butter

2 cups (60 g) baby spinach

½ cup (112 g) plain coconut yogurt

1 scallion, minced

Grated zest of ¼ lemon

1 teaspoon dried dill

¼ teaspoon sea salt

⅛ teaspoon ground black pepper

4 ounces (113.40 g) smoked salmon, torn into pieces

Chopped fresh parsley (optional)

1. In a medium skillet, melt the butter over medium heat. Add the spinach and sauté, stirring with a spatula, until the spinach is wilted, about 3 minutes. Press the spinach with the spatula and tilt the pan to drain excess water from the spinach.

2. In a small bowl, toss together the coconut yogurt with the scallion, lemon zest, dill, sea salt, and pepper.

3. Slide the wilted spinach onto a plate and top it with torn pieces of smoked salmon. Garnish with the herbed coconut yogurt and the parsley (if using).

MACRONUTRIENTS PER SERVING

CALORIES: 343

FAT: 18 G

CARBOHYDRATE: 19 G

PROTEIN: 28 G

TURKEY BREAKFAST WRAPS

What, you thought wraps were off limits? Time to get creative and use deli sliced turkey as your tortilla. Where it says filling "options," know that you can put them all in there together. Good stuff, literally!

PREP TIME: 5 MINUTES

MAKES 1 SERVING

4   slices deli turkey

FILLING OPTIONS

½   avocado, mashed

2   ounces (56.70 g) smoked salmon and/or 2 hard-boiled eggs, sliced

     Handful of watercress or arugula

Add your chosen filling to the center of each turkey slice, wrap, and enjoy.

MACRONUTRIENTS PER SERVING (WITH SALMON)
CALORIES: 210
FAT: 11 G
CARBOHYDRATE: 7 G
PROTEIN: 24 G

MACRONUTRIENTS PER SERVING (WITH HARD-BOILED EGGS)
CALORIES: 366
FAT: 22 G
CARBOHYDRATE: 9 G
PROTEIN: 36 G

KETO ENTRÉES

ALMOND BUTTER CHICKEN SALAD

Almond butter makes a delicious creamy sauce for this chicken salad. It takes just a few minutes to prepare and will satisfy hunger without any of those old, but now unfamiliar, crashes that excess carbs bring. Use creamy or crunchy almond butter and toss in some toasted sesame oil and a few canned water chestnuts to jazz it up even more.

PREP TIME: 10 MINUTES

MAKES 1 SERVING

2   tablespoons raw almond butter

1   scallion, minced

1   teaspoon sea salt

½   teaspoon ground black pepper

12   ounces (340.19 g) water-packed canned chicken

½   cup (71 g) diced celery

1. In a large bowl, combine the almond butter, scallion, sea salt, and pepper. Add the chicken and celery and toss to coat.

2. Serve in a bowl.

MACRONUTRIENTS PER SERVING
CALORIES: 400
FAT: 20 G
CARBOHYDRATE: 7 G
PROTEIN: 53 G

DUDES PRESTO PESTO SCALLOPS

The Cool Dudes report that this is one of the fastest, easiest gourmet meals you can ever imagine. The exquisite end product is great as an appetizer on a toothpick or as a fancy main course.

PREP TIME: 20 MINUTES
COOKING TIME:
5 MINUTES

MAKES 2 SERVINGS

- 1 bunch fresh basil, leaves picked
- ½ cup (71 g) pine nuts
- 1 tablespoon fresh lemon juice
- ⅓ cup (78.86 ml) extra-virgin olive oil or avocado oil
- 2 ounces (56.70 g) firm aged cheese, grated
- ½ onion, peeled
- 1 pound (453.59 g) sea scallops
- 1 tablespoon (14.17 g) salted butter

MACRONUTRIENTS PER SERVING
CALORIES: 595
FAT: 34 G
CARBOHYDRATE: 7 G
PROTEIN: 58 G

1. In a blender, combine the basil leaves, pine nuts, lemon juice, olive oil, cheese, and onion and puree to blend. Transfer to a bowl.

2. Rinse the scallops in warm water and pat them dry thoroughly with a paper towel. This helps them sear rather than steam.

3. In a large cast-iron skillet, heat the butter over medium-high heat. Swirl the butter evenly in the pan. Carefully arrange the scallops in the skillet so one of their flat surfaces is directly touching the pan. Sear for 1½ minutes. Carefully flip the scallops and cook the other side for 1½ more minutes. They should have a golden crust and be translucent in the center.

4. Drain the scallops in a sieve, then transfer them to the pesto bowl. Toss to coat the scallops well, then serve.

BRAISED GARLIC PORK SHOULDER

Do yourself a favor and make this braised pork as soon as possible! Juicy, tender pork is one of life's greatest gifts (maybe that's an exaggeration, or maybe not!) and can be enjoyed as a main dish or added to salads and scrambles. There are three cooking options to choose from: stovetop, slow cooker, or Instant Pot.

PREP TIME: 15 MINUTES
COOKING TIME:
50 MINUTES
(STOVETOP)

MAKES 6 SERVINGS

3 pounds (1.35 kg) bone-in pork shoulder

4 cups (946.35 ml) chicken stock

7 cloves garlic, minced

1 tablespoon dried oregano

1 tablespoon sea salt

1 teaspoon ground black pepper

½ cup (58 g) sliced radishes

½ cup (30 g) chopped fresh cilantro

MACRONUTRIENTS PER SERVING
CALORIES: 208
FAT: 16 G
CARBOHYDRATE: 3 G
PROTEIN: 17 G

1. *For stovetop:* Heat a large soup pot or Dutch oven over medium-high heat. Once the pot is hot, add the pork shoulder and allow it to brown slightly, flipping once or twice after about 2 minutes per side.

2. Add the chicken stock, garlic, oregano, sea salt, and pepper. Cover, reduce the heat to low, and cook, stirring occasionally, until the liquid has evaporated, about 45 minutes.

3. *For a slow cooker:* Brown the meat as described above, then transfer to a slow cooker. Add the chicken stock, garlic, oregano, sea salt, and pepper. Cover and cook on High for 1 hour and then Low for 7 to 9 hours, until the meat flakes right off the bone.

4. *For an Instant Pot:* Brown the meat on the stovetop or in the Instant Pot as directed. Add the chicken stock, garlic, oregano, sea salt, and pepper. Secure the lid and set the steam release valve to Sealing. Set the cook time to 60 minutes on High pressure. Allow the steam to release naturally for 30 minutes before unlocking the lid.

5. Serve in a shallow bowl, and garnish with the radishes and cilantro.

BROCCOLI RANCH CHICKEN

Broccoli and ranch dressing have been a winning formula since the beginning of time. They work again in this skillet chicken dish. Feel free to use frozen broccoli to save on time, and experiment with various cheeses to put your own spin on a classic favorite.

PREP TIME: 10 MINUTES
COOKING TIME:
20 MINUTES

MAKES 4 SERVINGS

1   tablespoon (14.17 g) salted butter

1   medium onion, diced

1   teaspoon garlic powder

2   teaspoons sea salt

1   teaspoon ground black pepper

1   pound (455 g) boneless, skinless chicken thighs, chopped

1   pound (453.59 g) broccoli, chopped

½   cup (118.29 ml) ranch dressing

1   cup (113 g) shredded extra-sharp cheddar cheese

1. In a large skillet, melt the butter over medium heat. Add the onion, garlic powder, sea salt, and pepper and cook until the onion is soft, about 5 minutes.

2. Add the chicken and broccoli, cover, and cook until the chicken is cooked through and the broccoli is tender, 10 to 15 minutes.

3. Drain off any excess liquid. Add the ranch dressing and cheddar and allow the cheese to melt. Serve hot.

MACRONUTRIENTS PER SERVING
CALORIES: 480
FAT: 34 G
CARBOHYDRATE: 11 G
PROTEIN: 36 G

CREAMY CABBAGE AND STEAK BOWL

If you like easy cooking with big rewards, you'll love this recipe with bold flavors and textures. If you have time, let the steak marinate for 30 minutes before cooking.

PREP TIME: 30 MINUTES
COOKING TIME:
8 MINUTES

MAKES 1 SERVING

6	ounces (170.10 g) flank steak
½	teaspoon garlic powder
½	teaspoon sea salt
⅛	teaspoon ground black pepper
1	tablespoon (14.17 g) salted butter
4	cups (400 g) shredded cabbage
1	scallion, minced
2	tablespoons mayonnaise made with avocado oil
½	avocado, diced

1. Rub the steak with the garlic powder, sea salt, and pepper. If you have time, let the steak sit for 30 minutes at room temperature.

2. In a large skillet, melt half of the butter over medium-high heat. Add the steak and sear for 2 minutes on each side. Remove from the skillet. Let rest at room temperature for 5 minutes before slicing into strips on a cutting board.

3. Meanwhile, add the remaining butter, the cabbage, and the scallion to the skillet and toss with a spatula until wilted, about 3 minutes. Gently stir in the mayonnaise.

4. Spoon the cabbage mixture into a bowl and top with the sliced flank steak and diced avocado.

MACRONUTRIENTS PER SERVING

CALORIES: 780

FAT: 61 G

CARBOHYDRATE: 24 G

PROTEIN: 42 G

CURRY TUNA SALAD OVER ARUGULA

When you're craving the heat, try this tuna salad with some hot sauce. It's a cinch to prepare and will warm you up, even on a cold day. Eat it out of a bowl or serve it inside a low-carb tortilla.

PREP TIME: 15 MINUTES

MAKES 1 SERVING

½   avocado, diced

½   cup (71 g) diced celery

½   cup (58 g) sliced radishes

¼   cup (35 g) chopped dill pickles

¼   cup (45 g) pitted chopped green olives

¼   cup (15 g) chopped fresh cilantro

1   tablespoon diced jalapeño

2   tablespoons mayonnaise made with avocado oil

1   teaspoon curry powder

¼   teaspoon sea salt

⅛   teaspoon ground black pepper

1   can (5 ounces/142 g) water-packed tuna, drained and flaked

2   cups (40 g) arugula

In a large bowl, combine all ingredients except the tuna and arugula. Gently fold in the tuna. Serve over the arugula in a bowl.

MACRONUTRIENTS PER SERVING
CALORIES: 506
FAT: 40 G
CARBOHYDRATE: 13 G
PROTEIN: 34 G

DR. CATE'S OPEN SESAME: MAGICALLY GOOD CANNED TUNA DINNER

Here's a clever way to prepare good ol' tuna and work this meal into your regular rotation, especially when you're on the road. Dr. Cate says this dish "keeps many of my players, and patients, out of drive-throughs." For the greens in this recipe, Dr. Cate suggests spinach, spring mix, arugula, shredded cabbage, shredded Brussels sprouts, and/or finely chopped kale. For extra color, she suggests adding a small shredded carrot.

PREP TIME: 5 MINUTES

MAKES 1 SERVING

- 2 tablespoons toasted sesame oil
- 1 tablespoon olive oil or avocado oil
- 1½ teaspoons Dijon mustard
- 1½ teaspoons rice vinegar, apple cider vinegar, or distilled white vinegar
- 1½ teaspoons traditionally brewed soy sauce (such as Kikkoman)
- 1 can (12 ounces/340 g) water-packed tuna, drained and flaked
- 4 cups your favorite greens (spinach, spring mix, arugula, shredded cabbage, Brussels sprouts, or kale)

  Sea salt

  Squirt of fresh lemon juice (optional)

1. In a large bowl, whisk together the sesame oil, olive oil, mustard, vinegar, and soy sauce.

2. Add the tuna to the bowl and stir thoroughly to distribute the dressing evenly over every shred of tuna. Add the greens and mix carefully to get a little bit of tuna over every leaf. Sprinkle with sea salt to taste. Add a few squirts of lemon juice, if desired.

MACRONUTRIENTS PER SERVING
CALORIES: 591
FAT: 42 G
CARBOHYDRATE: 15 G
PROTEIN: 39 G

ELLE'S 2-IN-1 BEEF SHORT RIBS

This recipe comes from *Paleo Thyroid Solution* author and longtime Primal Blueprint podcast host Elle Russ. These ribs are made in the Instant Pot and they are, of course, delectable!

PREP TIME: 5 MINUTES
COOKING TIME: 1 HOUR
MAKES 2 SERVINGS

FOR THE SEASONING (CHOICE A)

- 3 tablespoons (42.52 g) pastured unsalted butter, at room temperature
- 1 tablespoon ground cumin
- 1 tablespoon sweet paprika
- 1 tablespoon smoked natural sea salt

FOR THE SEASONING (CHOICE B)

- 3 tablespoons avocado oil
- 1 tablespoon truffle salt
- 1 teaspoon fresh or dried rosemary, chopped

FOR THE RIBS

- 4 beef short ribs
- 1 cup (240 ml) water or chicken or beef broth or stock (or ½ cup/118.29 ml water and ½ cup/118.29 ml red wine)

1. Make the seasoning: In a small bowl, mix the choice of seasonings. Rub the mixture all over the ribs.

2. Prepare the ribs: Set the Instant Pot to Sauté on the "normal" setting. Add the ribs and brown them on all sides, 3 to 5 minutes. Remove the ribs from the pot and press Cancel.

3. Add the liquid and deglaze the pot. Place the metal steam rack/trivet in the pot. Place the ribs on top of the rack, secure the lid, and set the steam release valve to Sealing. Set the pressure cook time to 45 minutes.

4. When the times is up, allow the pressure to release naturally for 10 minutes, then carefully switch the steam release valve to Venting. When fully released, open the lid. Use tongs to transfer the short ribs to a serving plate and enjoy immediately.

Variations for Seasoning A
- Serve the ribs lightly brushed with healthy BBQ sauce.
- Cut leftover meat into pieces and use in a taco recipe for a decadent meal.

Variations for Seasoning B
- Serve the ribs with some truffle butter melted over the meat or melted in a side bowl for extra flavor.
- Cut the meat into cubes and use in a paleo, grain-free pasta dish or over mashed cauliflower.

MACRONUTRIENTS PER SERVING (SEASONING A)
CALORIES: 389
FAT: 31 G
CARBOHYDRATE: 3 G
PROTEIN: 24 G

MACRONUTRIENTS PER SERVING (SEASONING B)
CALORIES: 423
FAT: 34 G
CARBOHYDRATE: 3 G
PROTEIN: 23 G

GINGER-SESAME POACHED EGG SOUP

Dr. Cate says, "this simple, soothing soup is easy to pull together for a light lunch or dinner side, and pleases the tough crowd I work with." The eggs in this recipe are poached in the broth. Add any greens you may have on hand to this soup.

PREP TIME: 10 MINUTES
COOKING TIME:
15 MINUTES

MAKES 4 SERVINGS

---

1   tablespoon toasted sesame oil

5   slices (¼-inch/6 mm thick) fresh ginger (or 1 teaspoon ground ginger)

2   cloves garlic, minced or thinly sliced

6   cups (1.4 liters) chicken stock, homemade or store-bought

2   tablespoons non-MSG soy sauce or coconut aminos

12 ounces (340.19 g) cabbage, sliced or shredded

4   large eggs

    Several scallions, thinly sliced, for garnish

1. In a wide pot, heat the sesame oil over medium-high heat until shimmering. Add the ginger and garlic and cook, stirring constantly, until the garlic is just golden brown around the edges, about 1 minute.

2. Add the stock and soy sauce and bring to a boil. Add the cabbage to the boiling soup, stir to combine, and bring back to a boil. Reduce the heat to maintain a simmer.

3. One at a time, crack an egg into a small ramekin or bowl and carefully lower each raw egg into the soup. (This will help ensure the yolks do not break.) Keep the eggs as far apart from one another as possible using a wooden spoon. Simmer undisturbed until the whites are set but the yolks are still runny, 3 to 4 minutes.

4. Serve in a bowl and garnish with scallions. Store leftovers in an airtight glass container in the refrigerator for up to 4 days.

MACRONUTRIENTS PER SERVING

CALORIES: 217

FAT: 8 G

CARBOHYDRATE: 7 G

PROTEIN: 15 G

GREEN CHILI CHICKEN

This slow-cooked chicken can be made in a pinch and enjoyed over a few days. Thigh meat is juicy and tender and keeps you feeling satisfied from its higher fat content.

PREP TIME: 5 MINUTES
COOKING TIME: 5 TO 6 HOURS

MAKES 8 SERVINGS

- 1 tablespoon (14.17 g) salted butter
- 2 pounds (910 g) boneless, skinless chicken thighs
- 1 tablespoon sea salt
- 7 cloves garlic, minced
- 1 tablespoon dried oregano
- 1 can (4 ounces/113 g) diced green chiles, undrained
- ½ cup (30 g) chopped fresh cilantro, for garnish

1. Place all the ingredients except the cilantro in a slow cooker. Cover and cook on Low for 5 to 6 hours.

2. Serve in shallow bowls and garnish with the cilantro.

MACRONUTRIENTS PER SERVING
CALORIES: 222
FAT: 11 G
CARBOHYDRATE: 2 G
PROTEIN: 28 G

LAMB BURGERS

Ground lamb with a little spice is one of the most satisfying meat dishes on the planet. Because they are not widely consumed in the United States, lamb products can be more sustainable and nutritionally superior to mass-produced feedlot beef products. All lamb from New Zealand is 100 percent grass-fed, while American lamb is almost always grass-fed (some is grain-finished).

PREP TIME: 15 MINUTES
COOKING TIME:
15 MINUTES

MAKES 4 SERVINGS

1 pound (453.59 g) ground lamb

1 onion, finely chopped

1 tablespoon chopped fresh mint leaves

1 tablespoon healthy mustard (free from refined sugars or seed oils)

1 teaspoon dried oregano

½ teaspoon red pepper flakes

   Sea salt

1 teaspoon coconut oil, butter, or ghee

1. In a bowl, mash up the lamb. Add the onion, mint, mustard, oregano, pepper flakes, and a sprinkling of sea salt. Mix together well by hand. Form the mixture into 4 patties.

2. In a skillet, heat the cooking oil over medium-high heat. Add the burgers and cook on both sides for 4 minutes each for medium-rare or 5 minutes on each side for medium.

MACRONUTRIENTS PER SERVING

CALORIES: 346

FAT: 28 G

CARBOHYDRATE: 3 G

PROTEIN: 19 G

LEMON-TURMERIC CHICKEN THIGHS

This recipe never fails to impress and it is really so simple to prepare! Slice your lemons thin and allow them to caramelize as they cook on top of the chicken. You may be tempted to remove them after cooking, but eat them up! Their flavor mellows once cooked and they can even taste sweet.

PREP TIME: 10 MINUTES
COOKING TIME:
45 MINUTES

MAKES 4 SERVINGS

4   bone-in, skin-on chicken thighs (about 1.5 pounds/680.39 g), patted dry

2   tablespoons (28.35 g) salted butter, at room temperature

2   teaspoons sea salt

1   teaspoon ground black pepper

1   teaspoon garlic powder

1   tablespoon ground turmeric

4   thin lemon slices, seeds removed

½   cup (30 g) chopped fresh cilantro (optional)

1. Preheat the oven to 400°F (200°C).

2. Place the chicken thighs in a cast-iron skillet. Rub each thigh with butter so that each thigh is coated evenly. Sprinkle the sea salt, pepper, garlic powder, and turmeric evenly over each thigh. Top each with a lemon slice.

3. Bake until the internal temperature of the chicken reaches 165°F (74°C), about 45 minutes.

4. Serve garnished with cilantro (if using).

MACRONUTRIENTS PER SERVING
CALORIES: 172
FAT: 14 G
CARBOHYDRATE: 2 G
PROTEIN: 9 G

QUICK CHOPPED PASTRAMI SALAD

You can serve this salad cold or, if you have a few extra minutes, sauté it all up in a skillet. You won't be missing the bread from your old pastrami sandwich after you've tried this.

PREP TIME: 10 MINUTES

MAKES 1 SERVING

- 6 ounces (170.10 g) sliced pastrami, chopped
- 1 cup (100 g) shredded cabbage
- 2 tablespoons mayonnaise made with avocado oil
- 1 tablespoon yellow mustard
- ¼ teaspoon sea salt
- ¼ teaspoon ground black pepper

In a large bowl, combine all the ingredients and toss together.

MACRONUTRIENTS PER SERVING

CALORIES: 351

FAT: 29 G

CARBOHYDRATE: 9 G

PROTEIN: 19 G

SEAFOOD BOWLS

If you are falling off your best intentions to prepare gourmet keto meals, sometimes a "bowl" recipe can take the pressure off. It's also fun once in a while to throw everything together and just dig in without the complexity of a main and a bunch of different sides.

PREP TIME: 20 MINUTES

MAKES 1 SERVING

1   large avocado, halved, pitted, flesh scooped out, and skins retained for serving

Grated zest and juice of 1 lime

1   scallion, minced

½   teaspoon red pepper flakes

Handful of chopped fresh cilantro

Sea salt and ground black pepper

¼   cucumber, diced

1   stalk celery, sliced

¼   pound (113.40 g) cooked peeled and deveined jumbo shrimp

Pinch of smoked paprika, for garnish

Mixed greens or iceberg lettuce, for serving

1. Place the avocado flesh in a large bowl. Add the lime zest and juice and mash with a fork into a creamy consistency. Add the scallion, pepper flakes, and cilantro and mix into a kind of guacamole mixture. Season with sea salt and black pepper to taste.

2. Fold the cucumber, celery, and shrimp (dice if you prefer smaller bites) into the guacamole mixture. Serve in the avocado shells, garnished with a sprinkling of smoked paprika, alongside salad greens.

MACRONUTRIENTS PER SERVING

CALORIES: 454

FAT: 32 G

CARBOHYDRATE: 27 G

PROTEIN: 38 G

SPICY SESAME CHICKEN

Simple, spicy, and habit forming! If you are inclined to try the repeating meals strategy to align with keto out of the gate, this is a good one to keep in the rotation.

PREP TIME: 5 MINUTES
COOKING TIME: 1 HOUR
30 MINUTES

MAKES 6 SERVINGS

1 whole chicken (about 1.5 pounds/680 g)

2 tablespoons toasted sesame oil

1 teaspoon garlic powder

1 teaspoon ground ginger

1 teaspoon onion powder

1 teaspoon red pepper flakes

Sea salt

Optional: fresh cilantro, sliced fresh chiles, and lime wedges, for serving

Mixed greens, for serving

MACRONUTRIENTS PER SERVING
CALORIES: 292
FAT: 22 G
CARBOHYDRATE: 2 G
PROTEIN: 22 G

1. Preheat the oven to 350°F (180°C).

2. Place the chicken in a small roasting pan. In a small bowl, mix together the sesame oil, garlic powder, ground ginger, onion powder, pepper flakes, and sea salt to taste. Fully coat the chicken with the mixture.

3. Bake the chicken until it reaches 180°F (82°C), about 1 hour 30 minutes. Baste the chicken in the juices after the first hour of cooking.

4. If desired, serve the chicken topped with cilantro, chiles, and lime wedges for squeezing. Serve with the mixed greens.

TROUT AND ASPARAGUS QUICHE

Tell me you're not excited by merely reading the title! Try something you've never encountered before. Besides, the combo really works.

PREP TIME: 15 MINUTES
COOKING TIME: 45 TO
50 MINUTES

MAKES 4 SERVINGS

1	tablespoon butter, avocado oil, or coconut oil
¼	pound (113.40 g) asparagus, chopped
2	trout fillets (3 ounces/85 g) cooked
6	large eggs
⅔	cup (150 ml) whole milk
1	teaspoon chopped fresh parsley
2	tablespoons grated cheddar cheese
	Sea salt and ground black pepper
2	tablespoons chopped fresh chives

1. Preheat the oven to 350°F (180°C). Line an 8 x 8-inch baking pan with parchment paper (or grease the pan with oil or butter).

2. In a skillet, heat the butter over medium heat. Add the asparagus and cook until just before it softens, about 5 minutes. Don't overcook!

3. Flake the cooked trout into the baking pan, then add the asparagus.

4. In a food processor, combine the eggs, milk, parsley, and cheese. Season with sea salt and pepper to taste, then stir in the chives. Pour the mixture over the trout and asparagus.

5. Bake until golden on top and cooked through, 45 to 50 minutes. Let cool before slicing and serving.

MACRONUTRIENTS PER SERVING

CALORIES: 230

FAT: 12 G

CARBOHYDRATE: 4 G

PROTEIN: 22 G

TUNA SALAD WITH PUMPKIN SEEDS

Sometimes the classics are what we want most. This tuna salad with red onion, dill pickle, and mustard is just that. It's doctored up with pumpkin seeds, rich in fiber, magnesium, and antioxidants. The splash of apple cider vinegar offers a host of health benefits, and adds some excitement to the taste.

PREP TIME: 10 MINUTES

MAKES 1 SERVING

- 1 can (5 ounces/142 g) water-packed tuna, drained and flaked
- 2 tablespoons mayonnaise made with avocado oil
- Juice of ½ lemon
- 1 tablespoon extra-virgin olive oil
- 1 teaspoon yellow mustard
- 1 teaspoon apple cider vinegar
- 2 tablespoons hulled pumpkin seeds
- 1 tablespoon minced dill pickle
- 1 teaspoon minced red onion
- ¼ teaspoon dried dill
- ½ teaspoon sea salt
- 2 cups (60 g) baby spinach

In a bowl, toss together all the ingredients.

MACRONUTRIENTS PER SERVING
CALORIES: 569
FAT: 49 G
CARBOHYDRATE: 5 G
PROTEIN: 38 G

TUNA SALAD WITH WALNUTS

This tuna salad will become your go-to when you need a quick meal with your favorite staple ingredients. High-quality tuna and mayonnaise make all the difference, so keep those handy as you whip up this simple classic. The added avocado and walnuts enhance the salad's satiating powers.

PREP TIME: 10 MINUTES

MAKES 1 SERVING

2   tablespoons mayonnaise made with avocado oil

2   cups (60 g) baby spinach, chopped

½   cup (71 g) diced celery

½   avocado, diced

2   tablespoons chopped walnuts

1   scallion, minced

¼   teaspoon sea salt

⅛   teaspoon ground black pepper

1   can (5 ounces/142 g) water-packed tuna, drained and flaked

In a large bowl, toss together all the ingredients except the tuna. Gently stir in the tuna. Serve in a bowl.

MACRONUTRIENTS PER SERVING

CALORIES: 537

FAT: 43 G

CARBOHYDRATE: 13 G

PROTEIN: 36 G

TURKEY BOWL

Remember what I said about bowls! Grab a big one for this preparation and make enough for leftovers. Know there is a difference in quality with turkey, so get the premium, freshly sliced stuff. Forget the prepackaged stuff as it almost always has additives, save for a few committed brands that are hard to find. Read labels—avoid chemicals!

PREP TIME: 5 MINUTES

MAKES 1 SERVING

2 tablespoons extra-virgin olive oil

Juice of ½ lemon

1 teaspoon Italian seasoning

Pinch each of sea salt and ground black pepper

4 ounces (113.40 g) deli turkey, chopped

2 cups (60 g) baby spinach

½ avocado, diced

1. In a bowl, whisk together the olive oil, lemon juice, Italian seasoning, sea salt, and pepper until well combined. Toss in the turkey and mix well with the sauce.

2. Add the desired serving size of avocado and spinach and enjoy. Save the meat sauce mixture for leftovers, adding fresh avocado and spinach when you're ready to eat.

MACRONUTRIENTS PER SERVING
CALORIES: 492
FAT: 41 G
CARBOHYDRATE: 12 G
PROTEIN: 22 G

TURKEY-CAULIFLOWER SKILLET

Want a dish that takes minutes to prepare but tastes like it was simmering for hours? This curry preparation is just that. Bold curry transforms basic turkey, cauliflower, and spinach to create a warm and hearty meal that nourishes inside and out. Brighten this dish with fresh cilantro. Double the recipe for gatherings and enjoy with those you love.

PREP TIME: 15 MINUTES
COOKING TIME:
20 MINUTES

MAKES 1 SERVING

1 tablespoon (14.17 g) salted butter

4 cups (430 g) chopped cauliflower

1 medium onion, chopped

1 tablespoon curry powder

2 teaspoons sea salt

1 teaspoon ground black pepper

1 teaspoon garlic powder

1 pound (455 g) ground turkey

4 cups (120 g) baby spinach

½ cup (30 g) chopped fresh cilantro (optional)

1. In a large skillet, melt the butter over medium-low heat. Add the cauliflower, onion, curry powder, sea salt, pepper, and garlic powder and cook, stirring often, until the cauliflower is soft and the onion is translucent, 8 to 10 minutes.

2. Add the ground turkey to the skillet, and mince with a wooden spoon, stirring until cooked through, about 10 minutes.

3. Stir in the spinach and allow to wilt. Drain off any excess water. Serve with cilantro, if desired.

MACRONUTRIENTS PER SERVING
CALORIES: 251
FAT: 12 G
CARBOHYDRATE: 11 G
PROTEIN: 26 G

ZAM ZAM VEGGIE STIR-FRY

Zucchini, asparagus, and mushrooms seem like nothing special, but when you stir-fry them together and add the simple combination of lemon, olive oil, butter, and garlic, this preparation becomes a satisfying meal all by itself and makes you go "Zam this is good!"

PREP TIME: 10 MINUTES
COOKING TIME:
15 MINUTES

MAKES 4 SERVINGS

- 1 tablespoon extra-virgin olive oil
- 1 tablespoon (14.17 g) salted butter
- 2 cloves garlic, minced
- 1 bunch asparagus, woody ends cut off, cut crosswise into thirds
- 2 medium zucchini (green or yellow), cut into bite-size slices
- 2 cups (140 g) cremini mushrooms, cut into thin slices

  Sea salt and ground black pepper

- 1 lemon, halved

In a large skillet, heat the olive oil and butter over medium heat. Add the garlic, asparagus, zucchini, and mushrooms. Cook, stirring frequently to avoid browning, until the asparagus is crisp-tender, about 8 minutes. Season with sea salt and pepper, and squeeze in the lemon right before serving.

MACRONUTRIENTS PER SERVING

CALORIES: 88

FAT: 7 G

CARBOHYDRATE: 6 G

PROTEIN: 3 G

LONGEVITY SUPERFOOD ORGAN MEATS

BEEF TONGUE AND GRIBICHE SAUCE

Considered offal, beef tongue is a relatively inexpensive meat that also supports the concept of nose-to-tail, sustainable eating. Beef tongue becomes tender and flavorful when cooked slowly. A beef tongue weighs between 2 and 3 pounds (about 900 g to 1.4 kg) and requires submerging in vinegar and water for 30 minutes prior to cooking. This "cleansing" time, along with the long cooking time, should be factored into your overall recipe timing. Beef tongue is typically served with gribiche sauce (page 234), a traditional French pickle-and-egg mayonnaise-style sauce. Both keto-friendly recipes were contributed by Tania Teschke, author of *The Bordeaux Kitchen*.

PREP TIME: 45 MINUTES
COOKING TIME: 4 HOURS 40 MINUTES

MAKES 7 SERVINGS

1	beef tongue (3 pounds/1.36 kg)
½	cup (118.29 ml) white wine vinegar
1	onion, peeled, halved, and pierced with 4 whole cloves
1	small leek, trimmed and halved lengthwise
1	teaspoon ground nutmeg
3	bay leaves
10	black peppercorns
	Several sprigs of fresh thyme or 1 tablespoon dried thyme
1	tablespoon coarse sea salt
	Gribiche Sauce (recipe follows), for serving

1. Place the beef tongue in a large nonreactive bowl, pour in ¼ cup of the vinegar, and add water to cover. Keep the tongue submerged for 30 minutes, then rinse it under cold water.

2. In a large Dutch oven, combine the tongue, onion, leek, nutmeg, bay leaves, peppercorns, thyme, sea salt, and the remaining ¼ cup vinegar. Add enough water to just submerge the tongue. Cover the pot and bring to a boil over high heat, then reduce the heat to medium-low or low and simmer for 4 hours 30 minutes. The long cooking time will ensure that the meat becomes tender.

3. Remove the tongue from the pot. Peel and discard the white outer layer of skin from the tongue. Slice the tongue into bite-size pieces and return to the pot.

4. Serve slices of tongue hot in bowls with a bit of the broth over the meat. Serve with a dollop of the gribiche sauce, at room temperature or chilled.

MACRONUTRIENTS PER SERVING

CALORIES:	455
FAT:	31 G
CARBOHYDRATE:	11 G
PROTEIN:	29 G

WINE TIP: With the beef tongue, Tania recommends a Syrah blend (such as a Rhône Valley red) or a Cabernet Sauvignon (such as a Left Bank Bordeaux Médoc).

GRIBICHE SAUCE

Gribiche sauce is a mayonnaise-like mixture using eggs, oil, mustard, pickled vegetables, and herbs. The French use *sauce gribiche* as a condiment for beef tongue, head cheese, and cold fish dishes, and here Tania shows us an easy, tangy recipe. Chervil or tarragon may be used in place of, or in addition to, the parsley.

MAKES ABOUT 1 CUP (250 ML)

3 hard-boiled eggs

1 tablespoon yellow mustard

2 tablespoons white wine vinegar

⅓ cup (78.86 ml) extra-virgin olive oil or avocado oil

2 pinches of fine sea salt

Pinch of ground white or black pepper

3 small dill pickles, diced

1 tablespoon capers, rinsed, squeezed in a paper towel, and minced

1 tablespoon minced fresh chives

1 tablespoon minced fresh parsley leaves

1. Separate the yolks from the whites of the eggs. Transfer the yolks to a medium bowl and discard the whites. Add the mustard and vinegar and use a fork to blend into the yolks. Adding 1 tablespoon at a time, whisk in the oil to create a mayonnaise-style emulsion.

2. Stir in the sea salt, pepper, pickles, capers, chives, and parsley.

3. The sauce can be served at room temperature or chilled. Store in an airtight glass container in the refrigerator for up to 1 week.

MACRONUTRIENTS PER SERVING
CALORIES: 151
FAT: 15 G
CARBOHYDRATE: 1 G
PROTEIN: 3 G

BRAISED VEAL HEART STEW

According to Tania Teschke, the French cook many types of meat by braising, meaning that they slow-cook the meat in water or fat after having browned it. The heart is a very strong muscle and therefore requires several hours of slow cooking, the longer the better. Tania says that generally, the butcher will cut the heart in two pieces to remove the large arteries inside, but will leave the outside rim of fat around the top of the heart. This fat may be removed or left on as desired. Like most slow-cooked meals, this one tastes best the next day, after a night in the refrigerator, allowing for the flavors to settle into the meat. This dish goes well with a side of vegetables sautéed in ghee or duck fat, such as asparagus.

PREP TIME: 15 MINUTES
COOKING TIME: AT LEAST 3 HOURS, PREFERABLY 6 OR MORE HOURS

MAKES 5 SERVINGS

3 tablespoons duck or goose fat

1 teaspoon coarse sea salt

1 veal heart (about 2 pounds/907.12 g), cut into 1-inch (2.5 cm) cubes

1 small to medium carrot, diced

2 medium onions, diced

½ stalk celery, chopped

4 cloves garlic, peeled but whole

3 tablespoons (42.52 g) salted butter

1 sprig fresh rosemary

5 sprigs fresh thyme

1 bay leaf

Pinch of ground black pepper

1 cup (236.59 ml) water

1. In a medium cast-iron pot or Dutch oven, melt the duck fat over medium-high heat. Add the sea salt and begin browning the cubes of meat in batches. Brown for 2 minutes on one side, then turn each piece over using metal tongs, and continue browning on the other side for 2 to 3 minutes. Stir the pieces around in the pot so that all sides are browned a bit before transferring them to a bowl.

2. Once all the meat has been browned and removed from the pot, stir in the carrot, onions, celery, and garlic, allowing these to caramelize and the onions to become translucent, about 15 minutes.

3. Stir in the butter until it has melted. Return the meat to the pot and add the rosemary, thyme, bay leaf, pepper, and water. Cover and bring the liquid to a boil, then reduce the heat to low or medium-low and simmer for at least 3 hours, but preferably for 6 hours or more. Remove the herb sprigs and bay leaf and discard.

4. Serve hot, garnished with the sour cream and a sprinkling of minced parsley.

recipe continues . . .

2 tablespoons sour cream, for garnish

Minced fresh parsley, for garnish

MACRONUTRIENTS PER SERVING
CALORIES: 359
FAT: 23 G
CARBOHYDRATE: 5 G
PROTEIN: 32 G

WINE TIP: Tania recommends a red Malbec blend (such as a Southwestern French Bergerac or Cahors) to go with this braised veal heart stew.

CHICKEN HEARTS WITH SHALLOTS AND SAGE

As organ meats go, heart has a milder flavor than liver. As you might imagine, heart is a very nutrient-dense organ meat, packed with mitochondria. The combination of shallots, garlic, and sage create a savory flavor similar to sour-cream-and-onion chips, making this dish very palatable.

PREP TIME: 15 MINUTES
COOKING TIME: 15 TO 20 MINUTES

MAKES 3 SERVINGS

- 1 pound (453.59 g) chicken hearts
- 2 tablespoons duck fat, olive oil, clarified butter, or ghee
- 1 teaspoon sea salt
- 2 shallots, minced
- 2 cloves garlic, minced
- 2 tablespoons minced fresh sage leaves (about 6 leaves)
- 1 teaspoon fleur de sel or coarse sea salt, for serving

MACRONUTRIENTS PER SERVING

CALORIES: 318

FAT: 23 G

CARBOHYDRATE: 4 G

PROTEIN: 24 G

1. Wash the hearts in cold water to remove the blood. Cut off the large outer vein from the end of the hearts and cut each heart in half. No need to remove the fat on the hearts, as the fat adds to the flavor.

2. In a large skillet, melt the duck fat over medium-high heat. Add the heart halves and cook, stirring frequently, for 3 minutes. Add the sea salt, shallots, and garlic and cook, stirring frequently, for 3 more minutes.

3. Reduce the heat to medium and stir in the sage. Cook, stirring occasionally, until the hearts, shallots, and garlic look cooked through, about 10 more minutes. You can ensure the chicken hearts are cooked through by slicing into one and seeing that it is a soft pink. They become tough when cooked past medium-rare, so be careful to not overcook.

4. Serve garnished with fleur de sel.

WINE TIP: For these chicken hearts, Tania recommends either a red or white wine: for red, a Pinot Noir (such as a red Burgundy) or a Syrah blend (such as a Rhône Valley red), or for white, a Pinot Blanc or a Muscat (such as those from Alsace).

CHICKEN LIVER BITES

Chicken liver—didn't that use to be part of playground teasing? Even if you aren't big on beef liver, give chicken liver a try. When you mix it into bites as in this recipe, it's delicious. A great superfood appetizer for parties, these store and reheat easily at home.

To prepare the livers and chicken meat in this recipe, chop by hand or run briefly through a food processor.

PREP TIME: 25 MINUTES

COOKING TIME: 15 TO 20 MINUTES

MAKES 6 SERVINGS

1	tablespoon olive oil
3	boneless and skinless chicken breasts or 5 chicken thighs (12 ounces/340.19 g), minced
8	ounces (226.80 g) chicken livers, finely chopped
1	tablespoon tomato paste
1	teaspoon garlic powder
½	teaspoon smoked paprika
1	teaspoon sea salt
½	teaspoon ground black pepper
2	large eggs
2	cups (192 g) almond flour

1. Preheat the oven to 400°F (200°C). Grease a large baking sheet with the olive oil.

2. In a large bowl, mix together the chicken meat, livers, tomato paste, garlic powder, smoked paprika, sea salt, and ground pepper. Form the mixture into balls 2 inches (5 cm) in diameter.

3. In a shallow bowl, whisk the eggs together. Spread the almond flour on a plate. Dip the balls into the eggs, then roll in the almond flour to coat completely.

4. Arrange the balls on the baking sheet. Bake until golden brown, 15 to 20 minutes, turning the balls over halfway through cooking.

MACRONUTRIENTS PER SERVING

CALORIES: 318

FAT: 7 G

CARBOHYDRATE: 1 G

PROTEIN: 22 G

CHICKEN LIVER MIRACLE RECIPE

Dr. Cate offers up another creative way to get your organ meat quota. This Filipino adobo-style (marinated in soy sauce) dish also works with beef liver. Even kids love this recipe.

PREP TIME: 15 MINUTES
COOKING TIME: 15 TO 20 MINUTES

MAKES 4 SERVINGS

- ¼ cup (60 ml) extra-virgin olive or peanut oil
- 2 green bell peppers, cut into 1-inch (2.5 cm) chunks
- 6 cloves garlic, minced
- 1 pound (453.59 g) chicken livers, rinsed and cut into individual lobes
- ¼–½ teaspoon ground black pepper
- 2 tablespoons soy sauce (naturally brewed, not hydrolyzed)

MACRONUTRIENTS PER SERVING

CALORIES: 302

FAT: 20 G

CARBOHYDRATE: 6 G

PROTEIN: 28 G

1. Heat a skillet over medium heat. Pour in the oil, allowing it to coat the bottom of the pan. Add the bell peppers and cook, stirring occasionally, until softened, 3 to 5 minutes. Stir in the garlic and heat it until it begins to sizzle. Stir the mixture for a few more seconds.

2. Add the livers and brown them for 2 to 3 minutes. Turn the livers over to brown the other side for another 2 to 3 minutes.

3. Working quickly, sprinkle the black pepper over the ingredients in the pan. Pour the soy sauce into the pan, being careful not to pour it over the livers (to avoid washing the pepper off). Cover the pan, turn the heat off, and leave the pan on the hot stovetop until the blood from the livers turns pale brown, 5 to 10 minutes.

4. Serve with the juices from the pan.

LAMB KIDNEYS WITH GARLIC AND BUTTER

As organ meats go, lamb kidneys are pungent, but less so than lamb liver. The ghee (clarified butter) or duck fat brings a richness to this dish to match the richness of the kidneys themselves. A nice touch to add to this and really any savory or sweet dish is fleur de sel, the "crème de la crème" of French sea salts, special because of its mild salty flavor, cubical shape, and satisfying crunch. If you can't find it, use a high-quality flakey sea salt from a natural foods store or the Internet instead. Lamb kidneys are definitely a longevity superfood!

PREP TIME: 15 MINUTES
COOKING TIME: 10 MINUTES
MAKES 1 SERVING

2 lamb kidneys

1 tablespoon ghee, clarified butter, or duck fat

1 teaspoon minced garlic

Fine sea salt

1 tablespoon minced fresh parsley, for garnish

Freshly cracked pepper, for serving

Fleur de sel or flakey sea salt, for serving

MACRONUTRIENTS PER SERVING
CALORIES: 468
FAT: 26 G
CARBOHYDRATE: 7 G
PROTEIN: 51 G

1. Rinse the kidneys in cold water, peel the outer visceral skin with the help of a sharp paring knife, and halve each kidney lengthwise. Remove the inner white tubular tissue with the paring knife.

2. In a skillet, heat the ghee over medium-high heat. Add the garlic. Salt both sides of each kidney half and place the kidneys in the skillet. Sauté until lightly browned on each side, 2 to 3 minutes. Reduce the heat by a notch to cook the kidneys through without burning, 2 to 3 more minutes.

3. Serve the kidneys with the pan juices. Garnish with the parsley and sprinkle with some pepper and fleur de sel.

WINE TIP: For these lamb kidneys, Tania recommends a medium tannic red (such as a Bordeaux Graves) or a Pinot Noir (such as a red Burgundy).

LIVER BURGER BLEND

This delicious burger blends a wide variety of ingredients with distinct tastes. You'll get a pleasant hint of liver flavor instead of the overpowering dose you get when you eat it straight.

PREP TIME: 15 MINUTES
COOKING TIME: 10 MINUTES

MAKES 8 SERVINGS

½ red or yellow onion, roughly chopped

1 cup (45 g) chopped kale

2 pounds (910 g) ground grass-fed beef

1 cup (225 g) beef or chicken liver

¼ cup (30 g) walnuts, almonds, or pecans

2 large eggs

1 tablespoon (14.17 g) salted butter

FOR SERVING (OPTIONAL)

Cheese, such as cheddar

Sliced avocado

1. In a food processor, combine the onion, kale, ground beef, liver, nuts, and eggs. Pulse to form a uniform burger mixture. It will feel softer than just ground beef. Form the mixture into 8 patties.

2. In a cast-iron skillet, melt the butter over medium-high heat. Lay the patties down carefully, cover the pan, and cook until you can slide a spatula underneath, about 5 minutes. You will likely need to cook these in two batches since they will not all fit in one pan. Flip the burgers when they feel crispy, a little or a lot based on your preference. After flipping, press down on the patty to slightly flatten. You may flip repeatedly to achieve the desired crispy exterior. If desired, before the burgers are fully done, grate cheese on top and let melt as the burgers finish cooking, and garnish with avocado when serving.

MACRONUTRIENTS PER SERVING
CALORIES: 321
FAT: 19 G
CARBOHYDRATE: 4 G
PROTEIN: 34 G

SUPERFOOD SOUP WITH SPROUTED SEED CROUTONS

Dr. Cate touts this recipe as a remedy for assorted inflammatory skin problems, thanks to the dehydrated liver and trachea in the recipe. (You can find these in capsule form from AncestralSupplements.com.) This dish is rich in B vitamins, minerals, branched chain amino acids, and glycosaminoglycans.

PREP TIME: 5 MINUTES
COOKING TIME: 1 TO 2 MINUTES

MAKES 1 SERVING

2 cups (473.18 ml) chicken bone broth, preferably organic

½ ounce (14.17 g) French Comté cheese, sliced into very thin chips (keep refrigerated before slicing)

1 tablespoon nutritional yeast (use Foods Alive brand, free from synthetic B vitamins)

1 ounce (28.35 g) sprouted pumpkin seeds or sprouted sunflower seeds

1 capsule desiccated liver (optional)

1 capsule desiccated marrow fat (optional)

1 capsule desiccated trachea (optional)

In a microwave-safe bowl, heat the bone broth until it is hot. Sprinkle the cheese, nutritional yeast, and seeds over the broth. If using the desiccated capsules, open them up and sprinkle over the broth. Serve hot.

MACRONUTRIENTS PER SERVING
CALORIES: 370
FAT: 13 G
CARBOHYDRATE: 5 G
PROTEIN: 35 G

VEAL KIDNEYS IN CREAMY MUSTARD SAUCE

Like lamb kidneys, veal kidneys are tucked inside visceral fat. The fat is usually cut and peeled away by the butcher. You can cut out the largest portion of white nerve tissue left on the inside of each kidney without cutting the kidney into pieces. You may choose to remove the thin outer membrane around the kidney lobe, but it can be left intact so that the kidney does not fall apart during the cooking process. The bits of white fat on the kidney may be used as cooking fat for the kidney.

PREP TIME:
20 MINUTES, PLUS 1 TO 4 HOURS SOAKING
COOKING TIME: 35 TO 40 MINUTES

MAKES 4 SERVINGS

- 2 veal kidneys (about 2 pounds/907.12 g total), rinsed and soaked in buttermilk for at least 1 hour and up to 4 to tenderize them and reduce the strong kidney odor
- Buttermilk, for soaking
- 2 tablespoons extra-virgin olive oil, tallow, clarified butter, or ghee
- 2 cloves garlic, minced
- 2 shallots, minced
- ¼ cup (60 ml) red wine vinegar
- 3 tablespoons sour cream
- 3 tablespoons Dijon mustard
- 2 pinches of fine sea salt
- Pinch of ground black pepper
- Fleur de sel or flakey sea salt, for garnish

1. Drain and pat dry the veal kidneys. Slice the kidneys into 1-inch (2.5 cm) thick slices.

2. Heat a cast-iron skillet over medium-high heat. Add 1 tablespoon of the oil to the pan. Sauté the kidney slices for 1 minute on each side and set aside in a bowl.

3. Add the remaining 1 tablespoon oil to the pan over medium to medium-high heat. Add the garlic and shallots and sauté until the shallots turn translucent, about 5 minutes.

4. Reduce the heat to medium or medium-low, and stir in the vinegar, sour cream, mustard, fine sea salt, and pepper, mixing well. Return the kidneys to the pan, making sure they are covered in sauce. Reduce the heat to medium-low or low, cover, and simmer, stirring a couple of times during cooking, until the kidneys are firm, 25 to 30 minutes.

5. Serve garnished with fleur de sel or flakey salt.

WINE TIP: Tania recommends either red or white wine for this kidney recipe: for red, a Syrah blend (such as a Rhône Valley red), or for white, a Sauvignon Blanc (such as a white Bordeaux).

MACRONUTRIENTS PER SERVING
CALORIES: 212
FAT: 9 G
CARBOHYDRATE: 2 G
PROTEIN: 29 G

VEAL LIVER IN SHALLOT CREAM SAUCE

Liver and onions used to be a staple in American restaurants in the eighteenth and nineteenth centuries. Let's bring its popularity back! Grass-fed veal liver needs to be properly stripped of the membrane and ventricle tissues on it to make it less chewy. You can do this yourself with a paring knife or ask the butcher to prepare the liver for you. Tania recommends using a cast-iron pan for this recipe, as it will retain heat when you make the sauce.

PREP TIME: 5 MINUTES

COOKING TIME: 5 TO 8 MINUTES

MAKES 1 SERVING

- 1 tablespoon coconut oil or duck fat

  Fine sea salt

- One 4-ounce (113.40 g) piece veal liver

- 1 tablespoon minced shallot

- 2 tablespoons sour cream

  Fleur de sel or flakey sea salt, for garnish

MACRONUTRIENTS PER SERVING
CALORIES: 359
FAT: 22 G
CARBOHYDRATE: 3 G
PROTEIN: 33 G

1. In a cast-iron skillet, melt the coconut oil over medium-high heat. Sprinkle a pinch of sea salt on each side of the liver and place in the pan. Cook on each side until browned, 2 to 3 minutes per side (longer if the liver is thick). Turn the liver over a few more times if necessary to cook evenly through. Remove the liver and place on a warmed plate.

2. Reduce the heat to low and add the shallot to the pan. Stir in the sour cream and turn off the heat. The pan will retain enough heat to gently cook the sauce. Once the shallot and cream are fully mixed together, drizzle this sauce over the liver. Garnish with fleur de sel or flakey sea salt.

WINE TIP: For this creamy veal liver recipe, Tania recommends either white or red wine: for white, a Sauvignon Blanc (such as a white Bordeaux), or for red, a Merlot blend (such as a Right Bank red Bordeaux).

INTERNATIONAL KETO FAVORITES

BRETON BUTTER SCALLOPS WITH GARLIC AND BACON

Like other shellfish, scallops are a good source of DHA, iodine, magnesium, potassium, and vitamin B12, among other nutrients. This dish is so simple to make and can be served as a starter or a main course. Tania Teschke explains that France's northwestern region of Brittany is famous for its salted Breton butter, which is used liberally on everything. For this dish, the combination of garlic, bacon, and salted butter helps bring out the richness of the scallops.

In the United States, scallops are usually sold as just the white muscle of the scallop. Sometimes, though, you can find scallops sold with the orange organ (a gonad) attached to the muscle; it can be eaten as well and cooked in the same browning manner as the muscle of the scallop. Try to find scallops that are "MSC approved" (Marine Stewardship Council) to be assured that you are consuming sustainably harvested scallops. Scallops do not reproduce until about the age of four years and need protection from premature harvesting so they have time to grow.

PREP TIME: 5 MINUTES
COOKING TIME: 15 TO 20 MINUTES
MAKES 1 SERVING

2 slices bacon

2 tablespoons (28.35 g) salted butter

2 cloves garlic, minced

Fine sea salt

12 sea scallops, rinsed and patted dry

MACRONUTRIENTS PER SERVING
CALORIES: 443
FAT: 32 G
CARBOHYDRATE: 8 G
PROTEIN: 34 G

1. Cook the bacon in a skillet over medium heat until crispy, about 10 minutes. Crumble and set aside the bacon to use as a garnish for later. Wipe the skillet clean.

2. In the same skillet (just large enough to hold the scallops in one layer, but with space around them), melt the butter over medium-high heat until the butter is bubbling and darkening slightly. Add the garlic to the pan. Sauté the garlic until it begins to brown, about 2 minutes.

3. Sprinkle a pinch of sea salt over the scallops. Place the scallops in the pan and sprinkle them with another pinch of salt. Brown the scallops in the pan for about 3 minutes on each side. Turn the scallops again if they need to be cooked through.

4. Sprinkle the bacon bits over the scallops in the pan and serve immediately, drizzling some of the buttery, garlicky sauce over the scallops.

WINE TIP: Tania recommends a white wine to go with these buttery scallops, either a Sauvignon Blanc (such as a white Bordeaux) or a Chardonnay (such as a white Burgundy) or a dry Champagne or sparkling wine.

CHINESE DUMPLING SOUP

This is a really fun hands-on recipe with a variety of distinct tastes and textures. These are meat-only dumplings and not coated in heavy carbs so you will feel great after eating them.

PREP TIME: 15 MINUTES

COOKING TIME: 20 TO 25 MINUTES

MAKES 2 SERVINGS

FOR THE "DUMPLINGS"

- ½ pound (250 g) ground pork
- ½-inch (1.25 cm) piece fresh ginger, peeled and grated
- 1 teaspoon tamari or soy sauce (optional)
- 1 teaspoon toasted sesame oil
- 1 scallion, sliced

FOR THE SOUP

- 3½ cups (828 ml) chicken stock
- 1-inch (2.5 cm) piece fresh ginger, peeled and grated
- 1 clove garlic, minced
- 2 scallions, chopped
- ¼ pound (113.40 g) napa cabbage, sliced

  Handful of fresh cilantro, chopped
- 1 tablespoon tamari or soy sauce (optional)

1. Make the "dumplings": In a bowl, combine the pork, ginger, tamari (if using), sesame oil, and scallion and mix thoroughly using your hands. Form the pork mixture into "dumplings" the size of golf balls.

2. Make the soup: In a saucepan, warm the chicken stock over medium-high heat. Add the ginger and garlic and simmer for 10 minutes.

3. Using a slotted spoon, add the dumplings one by one. Stir in the scallions, napa cabbage, cilantro, and tamari (if using). Bring to a boil, then reduce the heat and simmer until the dumplings are cooked through, 8 to 10 minutes. Serve hot.

MACRONUTRIENTS PER SERVING
CALORIES: 468
FAT: 39 G
CARBOHYDRATE: 7 G
PROTEIN: 37 G

FRENCH BISTRO LAYERED SALMON AND AVOCADO TARTARE

The French enjoy eating raw foods, including fish. Tania Teschke says salmon tartare is often served as an appetizer in France, but this recipe can be used either as an appetizer for two people or a meal for one. The citrus and sour cream lend a nice acidic flair to this refreshing dish. Smoked salmon may be used instead, but leave out the salt, as smoked salmon tends to be salted already. For a bit of crunch, Tania suggests garnishing with a few lightly toasted pine nuts. Pregnant women may want to avoid eating raw fish.

PREP TIME: 10 MINUTES

MAKES 1 SERVING

---

6 ounces (170.10 g) sushi-grade salmon fillet, diced

Fine sea salt

½ avocado

1 tablespoon sour cream

1 tablespoon olive oil or avocado oil

½ small shallot, minced

1 tablespoon minced fresh cilantro

Grated zest and juice of ½ lime

Freshly cracked black pepper

1 tablespoon pine nuts (optional), lightly toasted, for garnish

1. In a small bowl, season the salmon with a pinch of fine sea salt. Transfer to a clear dish (so the layers will show).

2. Scoop the avocado into a medium bowl and mash lightly with a fork. Mix in the sour cream, oil, shallot, cilantro, lime zest, lime juice, and 2 pinches of sea salt. Spread the avocado mixture in a layer on top of the salmon. Garnish with black pepper and toasted pine nuts (if using).

WINE TIP: For this salmon tartare, Tania recommends white wine, either a Sauvignon Blanc (such as a white Bordeaux) or a dry Champagne or sparkling wine.

MACRONUTRIENTS PER SERVING
CALORIES: 458
FAT: 33 G
CARBOHYDRATE: 5 G
PROTEIN: 36 G

QUICK ITALIAN CHICKEN WITH BASIL AND AVOCADO DRESSING

Even with the minimal ingredients and quick prep time, this turns out like a gourmet meal.

PREP TIME: 10 MINUTES
COOKING TIME:
20 MINUTES

MAKES 2 SERVINGS

FOR THE CHICKEN

- 1 tablespoon olive oil
- 1 pound (453.59 g) boneless and skinless chicken breasts or thighs, cut into 2-inch pieces
- 1 teaspoon garlic powder
- 1 teaspoon onion powder
- 1 teaspoon Italian seasoning

FOR THE DRESSING

- ½ avocado
- 1 large egg yolk
- Juice of ½ lime
- Generous 3 tablespoons unsweetened almond milk
- ½ teaspoon garlic powder (optional)
- 7 fresh basil leaves
- Sea salt

1. Prepare the chicken: In a large saucepan, heat the olive oil over medium heat. Add the chicken and sprinkle in the garlic powder, onion powder, and Italian herbs. Toss to coat the chicken and cook until the chicken is cooked through, 10 to 15 minutes.

2. Make the dressing: In a blender, combine the avocado, egg yolk, lime juice, almond milk, garlic powder (if using), and basil. Blend to a thick, creamy dressing. Add sea salt to taste.

3. Serve the dressing alongside the chicken.

MACRONUTRIENTS PER SERVING
CALORIES: 338
FAT: 19 G
CARBOHYDRATE: 8 G
PROTEIN: 35 G

THAI MINCED PORK SALAD

Thai food combines food and flavors wonderfully. This dish mimics traditional Thai cooking by combining cleansing radish and cilantro with cooling mint and warming almonds. This dish is colorful and tasty. Try serving it over colorful radicchio or vibrant arugula.

PREP TIME: 15 MINUTES
COOKING TIME: 8 TO 10 MINUTES
MAKES 2 SERVINGS

- 6 ounces (170.10 g) ground pork
- ½ teaspoon garlic powder
- ½ teaspoon sea salt
- ⅛ teaspoon ground black pepper
- 4 cups (400 g) shredded cabbage
- ½ cup (58 g) sliced radishes
- ¼ cup (15 g) chopped cilantro
- 10 fresh mint leaves, minced
- ⅓ cup (50 g) almonds, chopped

1. In a large skillet, combine the pork, garlic powder, sea salt, and pepper and cook over medium heat, mincing the meat with a wooden spoon, until the meat is cooked through, 8 to 10 minutes.

2. Drain off the grease and transfer the pork to a large bowl. Add the cabbage, radishes, cilantro, mint, and chopped almonds and toss to combine. Serve on a plate.

MACRONUTRIENTS PER SERVING
CALORIES: 481
FAT: 36 G
CARBOHYDRATE: 18 G
PROTEIN: 24 G

THAI OMEGA BALLS

A delight to the taste buds when you pair salmon, anchovies, coconut, lime, and red pepper flakes! It's a perfect combo to serve in ball form, and makes a very interesting appetizer. Your dish will be the talk of the potluck party for sure.

PREP TIME: 15 MINUTES
COOKING TIME:
20 MINUTES

MAKES 4 SERVINGS

2 cans (7.5 ounces/212 g each) wild red salmon, drained

Juice of 1 lime

3 tablespoons unsweetened shredded coconut

5 oil-packed anchovy fillets, finely chopped

2–3 teaspoons red pepper flakes, to taste

1 large egg

Handful of fresh cilantro, chopped

¼ cup (58 g) mayonnaise made with avocado oil, for serving

1. Preheat the oven to 350°F (180°C). Line an 8 x 12-inch baking pan with parchment paper.

2. Place the salmon in a large bowl. Add the lime juice, coconut, anchovies, pepper flakes, egg, and cilantro. Combine all the ingredients thoroughly. Taste the mixture at this stage and amend as desired (more lime, more pepper flakes, etc.).

3. Take one handful of the mixture at a time and squeeze carefully, shaping it into balls the size of golf balls.

4. Arrange the balls on the baking pan. Bake until they begin to brown, about 20 minutes.

5. Serve with the mayonnaise.

MACRONUTRIENTS PER SERVING
CALORIES: 341
FAT: 27 G
CARBOHYDRATE: 2 G
PROTEIN: 25 G

THAI PRAWN SCOTCH EGGS

Scotch eggs are a popular breakfast option in the United Kingdom, and variations abound. But can you get any more creative than this one? Try it out and you'll become an immediate devotee of Scotch eggs, and British culture in general.

PREP TIME: 15 MINUTES
COOKING TIME: 20 TO 25 MINUTES

MAKES 4 SCOTCH EGGS

---

4   eggs

14 ounces (396.89 g) peeled and deveined jumbo shrimp

1   teaspoon garlic powder

1   teaspoon red pepper flakes

½   teaspoon ground ginger

    Grated zest and juice of 1 lime

    Sea salt

2   tablespoons almond flour

2   teaspoons sesame seeds

MACRONUTRIENTS PER SCOTCH EGG
CALORIES: 157
FAT: 8 G
CARBOHYDRATE: 3 G
PROTEIN: 19 G

1. Preheat the oven to 350°F (180°C). Line a baking sheet with parchment paper.

2. Bring a saucepan of water to a boil. Place the eggs into the boiling water, return to a boil, and set the timer for 4 minutes. Drain and immediately transfer to cold water to stop them from cooking any further.

3. Meanwhile, in a food processor, combine the shrimp, garlic powder, pepper flakes, ground ginger, lime zest, and lime juice. Blend thoroughly into a paste, then season with a pinch of sea salt.

4. Peel the eggs. Scatter the almond flour and sesame seeds on a plate with a little more sea salt.

5. Shape the shrimp mixture around each egg (being careful not to layer it too thick) and roll the covered egg in the almond mixture.

6. Place the Scotch eggs on the lined baking sheet and bake until golden and cooked through, 20 to 25 minutes.

SHAKSHUKA

This egg and vegetable dish popular in the Middle East and North Africa can be served any time of day. It's definitely a crowd-pleaser!

PREP TIME: 10 MINUTES
COOKING TIME:
25 MINUTES

MAKES 4 SERVINGS

1 tablespoon coconut oil, avocado oil, or butter

2 fresh chicken sausages, sliced into small bits

1 onion, sliced

1 bell pepper (red, orange, or yellow), cored and diced

3–5 cloves garlic, chopped

Pinch each of sweet paprika, ground cumin, cayenne pepper, ground black pepper, and sea salt

2 cans (14.5 ounces/411 g each) diced tomatoes

4 large eggs

1 tablespoon feta cheese

1 tablespoon fresh cilantro leaves, chopped

1. In a large skillet, heat the oil over medium heat. Cook the sausage, stirring frequently—don't overcook. Scoop the sausages out of the pan.

2. Return the pan to medium heat. Add the onion and bell pepper and cook until they are softened, about 5 minutes.

3. Return the sausages to the pan, then add the garlic, paprika, cumin, cayenne, black pepper, sea salt, and finally the tomatoes. Cook everything on low for a couple more minutes to allow the flavors to blend.

4. Make 4 small holes in the mixture and crack an egg into each hole. Sprinkle the feta cheese and cilantro across the pan, cover, and cook until the eggs are cooked as desired, 3 to 6 more minutes.

MACRONUTRIENTS PER SERVING
CALORIES: 481
FAT: 26 G
CARBOHYDRATE: 18 G
PROTEIN: 31 G

KETO
SIDE DISHES

BAKED CAULIFLOWER

Cauliflower has long been the darling of paleo eating, for its versatility in replacing things like pizza crust or mashed potatoes. It's easy to forget how delicious it is when you keep it in familiar floret form and cook it up!

PREP TIME: 15 MINUTES
COOKING TIME: 25 TO 30 MINUTES

MAKES 4 SERVINGS

1 large head cauliflower, cut into florets

1 onion, sliced

Juice of 1 lemon

3 tablespoons olive oil

1½ teaspoons curry powder

2 teaspoons garlic powder

½ teaspoon ground cinnamon

1. Preheat the oven to 350°F (180°C).

2. Arrange the cauliflower florets and onion slices in a 9 x 13-inch baking pan.

3. In a small bowl, combine the lemon juice, olive oil, curry powder, garlic powder, and cinnamon. Pour the oil mixture over the onion and cauliflower and toss to coat the vegetables.

4. Bake until soft and golden brown on top, 25 to 30 minutes, tossing once halfway through cooking.

MACRONUTRIENTS PER SERVING
CALORIES: 164
FAT: 11 G
CARBOHYDRATE: 15 G
PROTEIN: 5 G

BROCCOLI-BACON SOUP

Everyone needs to be able to whip up a go-to broccoli soup, and this recipe delivers the winning formula. A pinch of nutmeg enhances flavor while aiding in digestion and helping with sleep. Be sure to keep some around for when you need it. This soup is wonderful to serve as a side dish, or amp it up with a bit more bacon to serve as a main meal.

PREP TIME: 10 MINUTES
COOKING TIME: 20 MINUTES

MAKES 6 CUPS

3	slices bacon
1	tablespoon ghee or butter
1	medium onion, diced
3	cloves garlic, minced
1	pound (453.59 g) broccoli, chopped
4	cups (946.35 ml) chicken stock
1	cup (236.59 ml) full-fat coconut milk
1	teaspoon sea salt
½	teaspoon ground black pepper
⅛	teaspoon ground nutmeg

1. In a 3-quart (3-liter) soup pot, cook the bacon over medium heat until it is crispy, about 10 minutes. Set the bacon aside on a plate, reserving the bacon grease in the soup pot.

2. Add the ghee, onion, and garlic to the pot and cook on medium heat until soft, about 5 minutes. Add the broccoli, chicken stock, coconut milk, sea salt, pepper, and nutmeg. Bring to a simmer, cover, and cook until all the ingredients are soft, about 20 minutes.

3. Transfer to a blender and pulse until creamy. Serve in bowls and garnish with the crumbled bacon.

MACRONUTRIENTS PER SERVING

CALORIES: 304

FAT: 25 G

CARBOHYDRATE: 14 G

PROTEIN: 12 G

CHEESY GARLIC BREAD

Who knew you could bring cheesy garlic bread back into the picture and still be keto? What's more, this preparation is so much better than the real namesake that you'll make a keto convert of anyone you serve it to.

PREP TIME: 15 MINUTES
COOKING TIME: 40 TO 45 MINUTES

MAKES 8 SERVINGS

5 large eggs

1 tablespoon garlic powder

1 teaspoon onion powder

1 teaspoon sea salt

1 tablespoon dried rosemary

1 teaspoon baking powder

2 small zucchini, grated and squeezed in a kitchen towel to remove excess moisture

3 ounces (85.05 g) Parmesan cheese, grated

7½ tablespoons (52.50 g) coconut flour

1. Preheat the oven to 350°F (180°C). Line a 9 x 5-inch loaf pan with parchment paper (you may need a couple pieces of parchment paper to do this).

2. In a blender, combine the eggs, garlic powder, onion powder, and sea salt, and puree. Pour the mixture into a bowl and stir in the rosemary, baking powder, zucchini, Parmesan, and coconut flour. Pour the batter into the prepared loaf pan.

3. Bake until golden and cooked through, 40 to 45 minutes. Allow to cool on a cooling rack before removing from the pan to slice and serve.

MACRONUTRIENTS PER SERVING
CALORIES: 76
FAT: 5 G
CARBOHYDRATE: 3 G
PROTEIN: 6 G

CURRIED CREAMED SPINACH

This is one of those dishes that you can prepare when you are low on groceries, as long as you have staples like frozen spinach, mayo, and curry powder on hand. The mayonnaise really brings this dish together with its high-quality fat working to emulsify with each ingredient.

PREP TIME: 10 MINUTES
COOKING TIME:
15 MINUTES

MAKES 4 SERVINGS

1 can (13.66 fluid ounces/403 ml) coconut cream

1 scallion, minced

3 cloves garlic, minced

1 tablespoon curry powder

1 teaspoon sea salt

½ teaspoon ground black pepper

1 tablespoon (14.17 g) salted butter

1 bag (10 ounces/283 g) frozen spinach, thawed, excess water squeezed out and drained

2 tablespoons mayonnaise made with avocado oil

1. In a large bowl, whisk together the coconut cream, scallion, garlic, curry powder, sea salt, and pepper.

2. In a skillet, melt the butter over medium-low heat. Pour the coconut cream mixture into the skillet, add the spinach, and increase the heat to medium-high. Stir until the liquid from the spinach is mostly evaporated, about 10 minutes.

3. Remove from the heat and stir in the mayonnaise. Serve hot.

MACRONUTRIENTS PER SERVING
CALORIES: 338
FAT: 30 G
CARBOHYDRATE: 10 G
PROTEIN: 6 G

EASY GREEN KALE SALAD

A lot of people claim that they don't like kale, but after having it massaged, they often really enjoy it. To make the marinade even creamier, add a tablespoon or two of creamy raw almond butter.

PREP TIME: 10 MINUTES

MAKES 4 SERVINGS

- 2 tablespoons extra-virgin olive oil
- 1 tablespoon toasted sesame oil
- 1 tablespoon coconut aminos
- 1 scallion, minced
- ½ teaspoon garlic powder
- ½ teaspoon red pepper flakes
- 1 teaspoon sea salt
- ½ teaspoon ground black pepper
- 4 cups (168 g) chopped curly or lacinato (Tuscan) kale
- 1 avocado, diced

1. In a large bowl, whisk together the olive oil, sesame oil, coconut aminos, scallion, garlic powder, pepper flakes, sea salt, and black pepper.

2. Add the kale to the bowl and, with your hands, massage the kale in the oil mixture until the kale leaves are broken down and soft. Toss in the avocado and serve immediately.

MACRONUTRIENTS PER SERVING
CALORIES: 184
FAT: 15 G
CARBOHYDRATE: 4 G
PROTEIN: 1 G

FENNEL CRUNCH SALAD

Fennel is delicious served raw or cooked, so feel free to use either in this recipe, though raw will give you the greatest crunch to excite your taste buds. This salad is an excellent nourisher, as fennel and celery work their detoxifying powers and walnuts promote brain health.

PREP TIME: 20 MINUTES

MAKES 4 SERVINGS

2	cups (175 g) sliced fennel
½	cup (50.50 g) chopped celery
½	cup (30 g) chopped fresh parsley
1	scallion, minced
2	tablespoons chopped walnuts
¼	cup (55 g) mayonnaise made with avocado oil
1	teaspoon sea salt
½	teaspoon ground black pepper

In a large bowl, toss together all the ingredients until well combined.

MACRONUTRIENTS PER SERVING

CALORIES: 142

FAT: 14 G

CARBOHYDRATE: 5 G

PROTEIN: 1 G

PECAN CABBAGE SALAD

Chinese cabbage salads are often full of processed noodles and higher-carb nuts, but not this version. Crunchy radish aids in healthy hormone balance, and pecans finish this salad as the perfect low-carb garnish.

PREP TIME: 20 MINUTES

MAKES 4 SERVINGS

¼ cup (60 ml) toasted sesame oil

1 teaspoon minced fresh ginger

1 tablespoon apple cider vinegar

½ teaspoon garlic powder

1 teaspoon salt

½ teaspoon ground black pepper

1 scallion, minced

¼ cup (15 g) chopped fresh cilantro

4 cups (305 g) shredded napa cabbage

¼ cup (30 g) chopped pecans

½ cup (58 g) sliced radishes

1. In a large bowl, whisk together the sesame oil, ginger, apple cider vinegar, garlic powder, sea salt, and pepper. Gently toss in the remaining ingredients until everything is evenly coated.

2. This salad can be served right away or made up to 2 days in advance.

MACRONUTRIENTS PER SERVING

CALORIES: 194

FAT: 19 G

CARBOHYDRATE: 6 G

PROTEIN: 2 G

SPICED BRAISED CABBAGE

Braising cabbage in warming spices such as rosemary, cinnamon, and cloves transforms it into a dish you may want to serve up each winter, maybe even at your next holiday gathering. You can leave the bacon out to keep this vegan, but it's wonderful with it.

PREP TIME: 15 MINUTES
COOKING TIME: 55 MINUTES

MAKES 4 SERVINGS

4	slices bacon, chopped
1	medium onion, diced
6	cups (600 g) shredded red cabbage
1	teaspoon dried rosemary
1	teaspoon ground cinnamon
¼	teaspoon ground cloves
1	teaspoon sea salt
¼	teaspoon ground black pepper
¼	cup (60 ml) red wine vinegar
3	bay leaves

1. In a large soup pot, cook the bacon over medium heat, covered, tossing with a spatula once every minute until done, about 10 minutes.

2. Leave the bacon grease in the pot. Add the onion and cabbage and toss well with the cooked bacon. Add the rosemary, cinnamon, cloves, sea salt, pepper, vinegar, and bay leaves. Reduce the heat to low, cover, and cook until the cabbage is very soft and has soaked up all of the flavors from the spices, about 45 minutes.

3. Remove the bay leaves and serve, or store in the refrigerator for up to 5 days.

MACRONUTRIENTS PER SERVING

CALORIES: 171

FAT: 11 G

CARBOHYDRATE: 13 G

PROTEIN: 6 G

SWEET AND SAVORY CURLY KALE WITH EASY BALSAMIC REDUCTION

According to Dr. Cate, this restaurant-worthy recipe will turn die-hard kale haters into kale-ophiles.

PREP TIME: 15 MINUTES
COOKING TIME: 10 TO 15 MINUTES

MAKES 4 SERVINGS

4 slices thick-cut bacon

8 cups (336 g) chopped curly kale

1–2 tablespoons raisins

2–4 ounces (55 to 115 g) walnuts, chopped

2 tablespoons balsamic vinegar

MACRONUTRIENTS PER SERVING (WITH 1.5 TABLESPOONS RAISINS AND 3 OUNCES WALNUTS)

CALORIES: 414

FAT: 31 G

CARBOHYDRATE: 29 G

PROTEIN: 13 G

1. In a large saucepan, cook the bacon over medium heat until crispy, about 10 minutes. Remove from the pan and chop the bacon into bits, leaving the bacon fat in the pan.

2. Meanwhile, in a steamer, cook the kale until darkened in color, soft, and fragrant, about 5 minutes

3. Add the steamed kale to the pan with the bacon fat. Stir over medium heat to distribute the bacon fat around the kale. Stir in the bacon bits, raisins, and walnuts and remove from the heat.

4. Heat the balsamic vinegar for 30 seconds at a time in the microwave, stirring occasionally, until it reduces and thickens.

5. Pour the reduced vinegar over the kale and serve.

KETO CONDIMENTS, SAUCES, AND VINAIGRETTES

COCONUT ALFREDO SAUCE

Coconut cream can make a mean Alfredo sauce, but the secret here is a pinch of nutmeg. Try it—you'll see how these flavors combined is magic! Serve it over poultry, fish, or vegetables.

PREP TIME: 5 MINUTES
COOKING TIME:
15 MINUTES

MAKES 8 SERVINGS

- 2 tablespoons (28.35 g) salted butter
- 1 teaspoon garlic powder
- 1 teaspoon sea salt
- ¼ teaspoon finely ground pepper
  Juice of ½ lemon
- 1 can (13.66 fluid ounces/403 ml) coconut cream
- 1 tablespoon arrowroot powder
- ½ cup (30 g) minced fresh parsley

1. In a small saucepan, melt the butter over medium-low heat. Whisk in the garlic powder, sea salt, pepper, lemon juice, and coconut cream and combine well. Heat until the mixture begins to simmer.

2. Add the arrowroot powder and whisk well so that it is completely absorbed into the sauce. Stir the parsley into the sauce.

3. If not using right away, store in a glass jar in the refrigerator for up to 1 week.

MACRONUTRIENTS PER SERVING
CALORIES: 147
FAT: 13 G
CARBOHYDRATE: 6 G
PROTEIN: 2 G

CREAMY RED PEPPER SAUCE

The extra few minutes it takes to char red bell peppers are definitely worth it! A cast-iron skillet is ideal to use, but a baking sheet works just as well. Add a little extra depth to this sauce by tossing in a handful of walnuts before pulsing in the food processor. Serve the sauce with meats, fish, and vegetables.

PREP TIME: 15 MINUTES
COOKING TIME: 10 MINUTES

MAKES 6 SERVINGS

- 1 cup (150 g) chopped red bell peppers
- 1 cup (226 g) mayonnaise made with avocado oil
- 1 tablespoon smoked paprika
- 2 teaspoons sea salt
- 1 teaspoon garlic powder
- ½ teaspoon ground black pepper
- ½ teaspoon cayenne pepper
- ½ cup (30 g) fresh basil leaves

1. Preheat the broiler.

2. Place the bell peppers in a cast-iron skillet or on a baking sheet and broil until they blister, about 10 minutes.

3. Allow the peppers to cool for a few minutes and then transfer to a food processor. Add the mayonnaise, smoked paprika, sea salt, garlic powder, black pepper, cayenne, and basil and pulse until very creamy.

4. If not using right away, store in a glass container in the refrigerator for up to 1 week.

MACRONUTRIENTS PER SERVING
CALORIES: 278
FAT: 32 G
CARBOHYDRATE: 2 G
PROTEIN: 0 G

HERBED BUTTER

Fancy up your butter by smashing in salt, pepper, garlic, and fresh herbs. You can use it throughout the week in place of plain butter to cook meat and veggies or to toss steamed veggies in. Before starting this recipe, set the butter out for 20 to 30 minutes to soften to room temperature.

PREP TIME: 35 MINUTES

MAKES 16 SERVINGS

1   pound (453.59 g) grass-fed salted butter

½   cup (30 g) fresh basil leaves, minced

½   cup (30 g) fresh parsley leaves, minced

1   scallion, minced

1   teaspoon garlic powder

1   teaspoon sea salt

¼   teaspoon ground black pepper

    Juice of ½ lemon

1. Allow the butter to soften to room temperature by setting it on a plate on the counter for 20 to 30 minutes.

2. While the butter is softening, in a bowl, combine the basil, parsley, scallion, garlic powder, sea salt, and pepper.

3. Place the butter in the bowl along with the lemon juice and smash well with a potato masher until the herbs and seasonings are completely combined in the butter (a very fast alternative to this step is pulsing all the ingredients in a food processor).

4. If not using right away, store in a glass container for about 1 week.

MACRONUTRIENTS PER SERVING
CALORIES: 205
FAT: 23 G
CARBOHYDRATE: 0 G
PROTEIN: 0 G

LEMON-TURMERIC VINAIGRETTE

Vinaigrettes are often used on salads, but this mixture is great on meats, fish, seafood, and to pour over steamed veggies. This recipe using turmeric and lemon is both warm and bright, and it's perfect to use as a year-round staple.

PREP TIME: 10 MINUTES

MAKES 8 SERVINGS

- 1 cup (236.59 ml) extra-virgin olive oil
- ¼ cup (60 ml) lemon juice
- 2 tablespoons ground turmeric
- 2 teaspoons sea salt
- 1 teaspoon garlic powder
- ½ teaspoon ground black pepper

In a jar with a screw-top, combine all the ingredients. Secure with a lid and shake vigorously. (Another option is to blend all the ingredients in a blender.) If not using right away, store in the jar in the refrigerator for up to 1 week.

MACRONUTRIENTS PER SERVING

CALORIES: 248

FAT: 27 G

CARBOHYDRATE: 2 G

PROTEIN: 0 G

OLIVE-ALMOND SAUCE

This sauce is perfect atop meats and veggies, to add to a scramble, or for a salad. Keep canned olives and almonds on hand and making this will be a breeze. No cilantro? Try using fresh parsley or basil.

½   cup (118.29 ml) extra-virgin olive oil

7   ounces (200 g) canned or jarred pitted green olives (about 1⅓ cups)

½   cup (50 g) almonds

½   cup (30 g) fresh cilantro leaves

1   tablespoon smoked paprika

1   teaspoon garlic powder

2   teaspoons sea salt

½   teaspoon ground black pepper

In a food processor, pulse all the ingredients until creamy. If not using right away, store in a glass container in the refrigerator for up to 1 week.

MACRONUTRIENTS PER SERVING
CALORIES: 392
FAT: 38 G
CARBOHYDRATE: 9 G
PROTEIN: 8 G

SMOKY MARINADE

Implement a winning kitchen strategy by making a big batch of the dry ingredients for this marinade. Then, when it's time to marinate meat, add the appropriate amount of olive oil and you'll have a fresh marinade every time.

PREP TIME: 5 MINUTES

MAKES 8 SERVINGS

½   cup (118.29 ml) extra-virgin olive oil

1   tablespoon ground cumin

1   tablespoon dried oregano

1   tablespoon mustard powder

1   tablespoon smoked paprika

2   teaspoons sea salt

1   teaspoon garlic powder

½   teaspoon ground black pepper

½   teaspoon red pepper flakes

In a screw-top jar, combine all the ingredients. Secure with the lid and shake vigorously. (Another option is to blend all the ingredients in a blender.)

MACRONUTRIENTS PER SERVING

CALORIES: 129

FAT: 14 G

CARBOHYDRATE: 1 G

PROTEIN: 0 G

LONGEVITY BEVERAGES

These nutrient-dense concoctions have unique ingredients that are hard to find in routine daily meals. Keto enthusiasts who are worried about missing important dietary elements such as fiber or prebiotics can implement a smoothie strategy to ensure they cover all their bases. This is especially important for athletic types striving to recover quickly from long or intense workouts.

CHOCOLATE MINT CRÈME SMOOTHIE

What's more rewarding on a hot day than anything chocolate mint? Add protein powder if you are elderly and/or have a high workout caloric expenditure.

½ cup (118.29 ml) half-and-half

2 cups (60 g) baby spinach

2 scoops (20 g) collagen powder

Pinch of sea salt

1 tablespoon unsweetened cocoa powder

10 fresh mint leaves

4 ice cubes

¼ teaspoon vanilla powder (optional)

In a blender, combine all the ingredients and blend until very creamy, scraping down the sides with a spatula as needed. Pour into a tall glass and serve immediately.

MACRONUTRIENTS PER SERVING

CALORIES: 248

FAT: 13 G

CARBOHYDRATE: 11 G

PROTEIN: 24 G

GINGER-TURMERIC-VANILLA COFFEE

This buttery bomb of a coffee is packed with intense flavor. It's an anti-inflammatory superstar with grated fresh ginger, turmeric root, and black pepper (to improve turmeric absorption). You can add any number of popular extras to this mixture, like açai powder, matcha tea powder, ginkgo biloba powder, chaga mushroom powder, MCT oil, collagen peptides, or gelatin powder.

Prepare for an intense ginger flavor, and back off to 1 teaspoon ginger if you're overwhelmed. For a nondairy option, you can use canned coconut cream (or separate the cream from the liquid in full-fat coconut milk).

PREP TIME: 5 MINUTES, PLUS COFFEE BREWING

MAKES 1 SERVING

- 1 cup (236.59 ml) brewed coffee
- 1 tablespoon (14.17 g) grass-fed unsalted butter, cream from coconut milk, or canned coconut cream
- 1 tablespoon grated fresh ginger
- 1 tablespoon grated fresh turmeric root

  Sweetener (such as monkfruit, erythritol, or stevia), to taste

  Pinch of vanilla powder

  Pinch of fine sea salt

  Pinch of ground black pepper

1. Brew your coffee as usual. Warm a blender jar and your cup by pouring very hot water into them.

2. Add the coffee, butter, ginger, turmeric, sweetener, vanilla powder, sea salt, and pepper to the blender jar. Blend on low for 10 to 15 seconds.

3. Pour into your preheated cup, take a deep breath through your nose over the cup to experience all the aromas of your deluxe coffee, and relax.

MACRONUTRIENTS PER SERVING

CALORIES: 159

FAT: 15 G

CARBOHYDRATE: 4 G

PROTEIN: 1 G

HOMEMADE GINGER KOMBUCHA

If you are a big enthusiast of store-bought kombucha, you may want to consider brewing your own at home. You'll appreciate the budget savings, as spending three to four dollars every time you consume a small bottle can add up. Furthermore, many store-bought bottles have been strongly flavored to the point that the carbohydrate count rivals that of a fruit juice or sports drink! In contrast, an authentic home brew ferments out around 70 percent of the original sugar in 14 days, even more after 21 days. This leaves you with a drink of 4 to 6 grams of sugar per pint, and low-glycemic sugar at that. In contrast, a typical 16-ounce (473 ml) bottle in the store can contain as much as 20 grams of sugar.

While there are some steps and logistics to respect, and supplies to acquire, it's much easier than it looks to get into the kombucha business. This can quickly become a fun hobby, where you are nurturing a living, breathing organism that can do wonders for your gut health, especially when doing the second fermentation with ginger. Brad claims that an intensive regimen of slamming more than a gallon per week of homemade kombucha helped cure gut dysfunction resulting from high-dose antibiotics for a string of surgeries.

All you really need to get started is a friend who can provide the beloved SCOBY—Symbiotic Culture of Bacteria and Yeast. These are easy to come by, because every batch of kombucha yields a baby SCOBY. Ask around among healthy eating types or even put an ad in Craigslist. The SCOBY's job is to consume the sugar and caffeine from the black tea and convert it into kombucha after a typical fermentation period of 11 to 21 days.

PREP TIME: 11 TO 21 DAYS

MAKES 1 GALLON

1   SCOBY in 2 cups (473.18 ml) of its own liquid (kombucha)

Two   1-gallon (3.78 l) glass jars and assorted smaller quart and/or pint jars

1. Place the SCOBY and the 2 cups of kombucha in which it came into a 1-gallon (3.78 liters) jar. Fill a large pitcher or loose-leaf tea dispenser with boiling water and brew the tea for the recommended brewing time. Add the sugar and stir well. Let cool, then squeeze every drop out of the tea bags for maximum potency, and then discard the bags or empty the loose leaf container.

8 bags regular black tea, or 3 tablespoons of loose black tea

1 cup (195 g) organic raw sugar

MACRONUTRIENTS PER 12 OZ
CALORIES: 30
FAT: 0 G
CARBOHYDRATE: 7 G
PROTEIN: 0 G

2. Pour the cooled tea into the gallon container with the SCOBY. Add water to create 1 gallon of liquid. Cover the top of the jar with cheesecloth (or other breathable mesh or gauze-like cloth) and place a rubber band around the mouth of the jar to secure the cloth. You want the SCOBY to breathe while keeping out bugs and debris.

3. Mark the date on the glass with a sticky note and store in a warm dry place away from direct sunlight (75° to 85°F/24° to 29°C is the ideal temperature for fermenting). Brew for at least 11 days and up to 21. A shorter fermentation time yields a sweeter drink, while a longer fermentation time yields a more acidic drink.

4. Pour the kombucha into four 1-quart (950 ml) or eight 1-pint (475 ml) bottles with sealable lids. Preserve the SCOBY and 2 cups of liquid in the original gallon jar (you can temporarily park them in a pitcher or bowl, wash the gallon jar, then return the SCOBY and kombucha back to home base). A baby SCOBY will be generated from the fermentation of each batch. You can give it to a friend to get them started in kombucha adventures, get an additional gallon jar to make a double batch next time, or simply discard it.

5. With the kombucha that you placed into individual quart or pint jars, you can store it in the refrigerator and drink it now or perform a second fermentation to create some distinct flavors. For example, you can slice several strips of fresh ginger or jalapeño peppers, drop them into the fermented liquid, and seal the jar. You can also add freshly squeezed lemon or lime, herbal tea bags, or drop in some fresh or dried fruit. Yes, drop the fruit into the jar and seal the lid. Allow 3 days to ferment, remove the flavorings, and then put the kombucha in the fridge to enjoy a lifespan of a couple months. It's a pretty strong drink, especially with a second fermentation, so consider serving with half sparkling water and half kombucha, or even two-thirds sparkling water. You'll get a nice fizzy soft drink–like experience while nourishing your gut microbiome with potent probiotics.

MORNING LONGEVITY SMOOTHIE

This preparation is inspired by longevity expert Dr. Rhonda Patrick's viral YouTube video of her dumping massive servings of assorted nutrient-dense fruits and vegetables into the ultrapowerful Blendtec machine and ending up with a salad bar in a glass.

High-performance blenders like Blendtec or Vitamix will make things easy for you when making this kind of smoothie. Using a traditional blender, you will have to strategically blend the drink in segments. Blender instructions typically suggest you start with liquids and softer ingredients first, then powders, then produce, and finally the hard ingredients such as frozen bananas or nuts. The Blendtec Classic is much less expensive than a Vitamix and does a fantastic job with its one-touch smoothie button. It will vary speeds and cycles over the course of a minute and blend up pretty much everything you dare to throw in there.

Adaptations have been made to this recipe to keep the macronutrient content keto-friendly, and include some longevity-boosting supplements. Collagen protein is great for joint health, gut-lining support, and overall longevity benefits. Creatine and glutamine, the darlings of the bodybuilding community for their proven muscle-building benefits, are also effective for older athletes trying to perform and recover like the youngsters. Resistant starch is tough to incorporate into the diet when eating keto, so raw potato starch and green bananas are good smoothie options. Get the greenest bananas you can find, cut them in half, then peel them—much easier than battling an intact banana! Cut bananas into small pieces and freeze them—they'll act like ice cubes in your smoothie. To prepare the prefrozen produce: Wash and chop up kale, spinach, chard, beets, cucumber, celery, and anything else. Keep the entire plant instead of discarding chard stems or beet leaves. Stuff your bounty into sturdy zippered plastic bags and freeze.

If the following ingredient list looks too intimidating, get the basics down (use a nut milk as the base, lots of frozen produce, and a bit of protein powder) and consider everything else optional.

PREP TIME: 15 MINUTES, PLUS VEGETABLE FREEZING TIME

MAKES 2 SERVINGS

recipe continues...

2	cups (473.18 ml) liquid (a mix of unsweetened full-fat coconut or almond milk and water)
3	tablespoons plain, whole-milk yogurt
3	handfuls frozen leafy greens (chard, kale, spinach)
½	cup of other chopped frozen produce such as beets, cucumber, celery, avocado
½	green banana, frozen
	Several frozen berries
	Juice of ½ lemon
1–2	scoops (20 to 40 g) collagen protein
1	teaspoon sea salt, Himalayan pink salt, or mineral Real Salt
2	tablespoons unsweetened shredded or flaked coconut
¼	cup (1 ounce/30 g) walnuts
1	tablespoon cacao nibs (added after blending, for nutty texture)

OPTIONAL PERFORMANCE/COGNITIVE/LONGEVITY INGREDIENTS

1	tablespoon raw potato starch (great as a resistant starch, especially if you have no green banana)
2	tablespoons MCT oil (assists with internal ketone production and fat metabolism)
	Desiccated liver powder or Ancestral Supplements capsules
5	capsules vitamin D (2,000 IU per capsule)

In a blender, combine the liquid, yogurt, frozen vegetables and fruits, and lemon juice and blend. Then add the collagen, salt, coconut, walnuts, and any of the optional ingredients and continue blending. (If you hear the blender suddenly make a louder noise, it's possible that cavitation has occurred. This is caused by frozen ingredients forming a pocket of air around the blade. Stop the blender, stir the ingredients, and possibly add more liquid.) After blending, stir in the cacao nibs.

MACRONUTRIENTS PER SERVING (WHEN USING ½ CUP CELERY AND ½ OF AN AVOCADO)

CALORIES: 325

FAT: 21 G

CARBOHYDRATE: 24 G

PROTEIN: 13 G

KETO SNACKS AND TREATS

Remember, fasting and eating in a compressed time window is the centerpiece of a winning keto strategy. Furthermore, with metabolic flexibility, snacking between meals should not be necessary and is not recommended. This is especially true if you are trying to drop excess body fat. If you are going to snack, let it be in place of a proper meal instead of between meals. If you are going to enjoy life and have an occasional dietary indulgence, let it be a very well-chosen and deeply appreciated treat. The savory offerings in this section are fun and easy to make, incredibly satisfying, and packed with good nutrition, including longevity superfoods.

ALMOND-CACAO ENERGY BALLS

If you are trying to escape carbohydrate dependency and still enjoy a treat once in a while, this creation satisfies, is extremely low in carbohydrates, and is packed with energy and good nutrition. For the chocolate in this recipe, search for the "bean-to-bar" and "Fair Trade" designations on the label. Alter Eco is a popular brand available on Amazon. If you don't have coconut butter, you can also puree shredded or flaked coconut until it becomes buttery, adding dabs of coconut oil as needed.

PREP TIME: 15 MINUTES, PLUS REFRIGERATION TIME

MAKES 12 SERVINGS

- ½ cup (74.5 g) macadamia nuts
- 1 bar (3.5 ounces/100 g) very dark chocolate (80 to 90% cacao), broken into very small bits
- 1¾ cups (16 ounces/453.59 g) almond butter, peanut butter, or other nut butter (with only nuts and no added oils and sugars in its ingredients)
- ¼ cup (25 g) unsweetened shredded coconut
- ¼ cup (55 g) coconut butter
- ¼ cup (24 g) almond flour
- ¼ cup (30 g) cacao nibs

1. In a small food processor, blend the macadamia nuts until they resemble a crumbly flour. Transfer to a large bowl and add the chocolate bits, nut butter, shredded coconut, coconut butter, almond flour, and cacao nibs and stir until you have achieved a paste-like consistency. Mold into 12 balls, each about the size of a golf ball, and arrange them in a glass baking dish.

2. Refrigerate or freeze for several hours to firm up the balls. Serve them cool, consume immediately, and store in the refrigerator.

MACRONUTRIENTS PER SERVING
CALORIES: 421
FAT: 39 G
CARBOHYDRATE: 14 G
PROTEIN: 12 G

BACON-WRAPPED CHICKEN TENDERS

Recommended for a tasty party snack, but great with any meal. Try them for an egg-free breakfast or chop them up and add to a salad. Try sprinkling on some fresh herbs, such as parsley.

PREP TIME: 20 MINUTES
COOKING TIME: 20 MINUTES

MAKES 12 APPETIZER SERVINGS

- 36 asparagus spears, woody ends cut off
- 12 chicken tenders, patted dry
- 12 slices bacon
- ½ teaspoon ground black pepper

MACRONUTRIENTS PER SERVING

CALORIES: 154

FAT: 11 G

CARBOHYDRATE: 2 G

PROTEIN: 11 G

1. Preheat the oven to 425°F (220°C).

2. Secure 3 asparagus spears to each chicken tender by wrapping firmly with a slice of bacon. Season with the pepper.

3. Arrange on a baking sheet and bake until the chicken is cooked through and the bacon is crispy, about 20 minutes, turning them over after the first 10 minutes.

4. Serve hot on a platter.

KETO CHOCOLATE MOUSSE À LA JORGE MUCHO

Incredibly simple, with three ingredients and only minutes of prep time. Nutritious enough to eat for breakfast, and extremely low in carbs and sugar for full-on gold star keto. This recipe is celebrated from the streets of Paris to the shores of Lake Tahoe thanks to chocolate mousse legend Jorge Mucho of Tahizzle Culinary Academy.

PREP TIME: 15 MINUTES, PLUS REFRIGERATION TIME

COOKING TIME: 5 MINUTES

MAKES 6 SERVINGS

- 10 ounces (283.50 g) dark chocolate (80% cacao or higher), broken into chunks
- 8 tablespoons (113.40 g) unsalted butter
- 6 large eggs, separated

MACRONUTRIENTS PER SERVING
CALORIES: 539
FAT: 47 G
CARBOHYDRATE: 10 G
PROTEIN: 18 G

1. In a double boiler or a heatproof bowl set over a pan of simmering water, melt the chocolate and butter. (Or microwave in a glass bowl in bursts of 10 seconds, stirring after each.)

2. Lightly whisk the egg yolks together and stir into the hot chocolate and butter, blending thoroughly. This will cook the raw yolks if you are averse to eating raw egg.

3. In a bowl, with an electric mixer, whip the egg whites until very fluffy.

4. Carefully fold the chocolate mixture into the whites, mixing gently. Pour the mixture into an 8-inch round or 9 x 5-inch rectangular glass baking dish. Refrigerate for 2 hours, then serve.

CINNAMON TAHINI BUTTER AND CELERY

Tahini spiced with cinnamon and sea salt is a cinch to prepare, and adds some flair to your nut butter experience. You may never go back to plain ol' peanut and almond. Tahini, high in magnesium and phosphorous, is made from ground sesame seeds, so it's a wonderful nut-free option for anyone with nut allergies. Look for it where your market sells nut butters, or find it in the international aisle.

PREP TIME: 5 MINUTES

MAKES 1 SERVING

2   tablespoons tahini

½   teaspoon sea salt

½   teaspoon ground cinnamon

Celery sticks, for serving

MACRONUTRIENTS PER SERVING
CALORIES: 101
FAT: 8 G
CARBOHYDRATE: 5 G
PROTEIN: 2 G

In a bowl, blend together the tahini, sea salt, and cinnamon. Serve with celery sticks.

CREAMY GUACAMOLE

There are so many ways to prepare guacamole, but have you tried it with mayonnaise? It's a winning combination and goes perfectly with crunchy veggie crudités, added to a scramble, or served over some tender slow-cooked meat.

PREP TIME: 10 MINUTES

MAKES 4 SERVINGS

1 avocado, halved and pitted

¼ cup (58 g) mayonnaise made with avocado oil

 Juice of ½ lime

½ cup (30 g) fresh cilantro leaves, chopped

1 scallion, minced

½ teaspoon sea salt

Scoop the avocado into a bowl and mash with a fork. Add the mayo, lime juice, cilantro, scallion, and sea salt and gently toss. Serve immediately.

MACRONUTRIENTS PER SERVING
CALORIES: 162
FAT: 18 G
CARBOHYDRATE: 4 G
PROTEIN: 1 G

DARK CHOCOLATE AND SEA SALT SQUARES

The keto movement still fields complaints from folks who claim to be unable to get rid of their sweet tooth. Well, they haven't tried this recipe. Put creations like this, the Almond-Cacao Energy Balls (page 280), and the Keto Chocolate Mousse à la Jorge Mucho (page 282) into the mix for when you crave an occasional indulgent treat, and you will habituate your taste buds to rich and satiating high-fat desserts. When you taste one of your old-time sugary favorites, it will suddenly seem way too sweet—seriously!

PREP TIME: 10 MINUTES, PLUS 30 MINUTES REFRIGERATION
COOKING TIME: 10 MINUTES

MAKES 16 SQUARES

10½ ounces (297.67 g) dark chocolate (85 to 100% cacao), cut into chunks

3 tablespoons cacao nibs

3½ ounces (99.22 g) almond butter

1 teaspoon vanilla extract

2 tablespoons chopped pecans

Generous sprinkling of sea salt

OPTIONAL ADD-INS

1–2 tablespoons collagen powder

Toasted nuts or seeds

2–3 tablespoons coconut cream or unsweetened shredded coconut

MACRONUTRIENTS PER SQUARE
CALORIES: 156
FAT: 13 G
CARBOHYDRATE: 6 G
PROTEIN: 3 G

1. Line a 9 x 9-inch square baking pan with parchment paper. You may need a couple of pieces of parchment paper to cover the pan.

2. In a double boiler or a heatproof bowl set over a pan of simmering water, melt the chocolate. Remove the bowl of melted chocolate from the heat and allow to cool a little.

3. Add the cacao nibs, almond butter, vanilla, pecans, sea salt, and any of the optional add-ins to the melted chocolate and combine well. Pour the chocolate mixture into the baking pan and place in the freezer for 20 to 30 minutes to set. Once set, cut into 16 squares and serve.

EASY EGG SALAD

The combination of eggs, cottage cheese, and green olives is perhaps unexpected, but if you toss in some sea salt, black pepper, and crunchy celery, you'll wonder where it's been all your life! Make this even fancier with baby spinach leaves or spice it up with smoked paprika. Enjoy the salad as a fast snack or small meal.

PREP TIME: 10 MINUTES

MAKES 1 SERVING

½ cup (113.50 g) low-fat cottage cheese

¼ cup (25 g) diced celery

¼ cup (50 g) pitted green olives, chopped

1 teaspoon (5 g) natural mineral or sea salt

⅛ teaspoon ground black pepper

2 hard-boiled eggs, peeled and chopped

In a bowl, stir together the cottage cheese, celery, olives, sea salt, and pepper. Gently toss in the eggs.

MACRONUTRIENTS PER SERVING
CALORIES: 286
FAT: 15 G
CARBOHYDRATE: 7 G
PROTEIN: 28 G

HOMEMADE PROTEIN BARS

There are more and more keto-friendly energy bars and snacks on the store shelves these days, but it's hard to top the freshness and rich texture of a homemade batch. You can double or triple the portions and freeze them to always have a steady supply around.

PREP TIME: 15 MINUTES, PLUS 60 TO 90 MINUTES FREEZING TIME
COOKING TIME: 10 MINUTES

MAKES 4 BARS

2 ounces (56.70 g) whey protein (vanilla or unflavored)

¾ cup plus 2 tablespoons (90 g) almond flour

3 tablespoons coconut flour or ¼ cup (25 g) unsweetened shredded coconut

1½ teaspoons orange extract

5–7 tablespoons (80 to 100 ml) almond milk

2 ounces (56.70 g) dark chocolate (85 to 100% cacao), broken into pieces

Several drops of stevia (optional)

MACRONUTRIENTS PER BAR

CALORIES: 143

FAT: 7 G

CARBOHYDRATE: 8 G

PROTEIN: 13 G

1. In a large bowl, mix together the whey protein, almond flour, and coconut flour. Add the orange extract, then *slowly* add the almond milk, tablespoon by tablespoon. To keep the mixture from getting too soggy, add only about 3 tablespoons of the milk at first, mixing it with your hands. Carefully add a little more until the mixture turns into a doughy paste that you can shape into bars without it sticking to your hands. (If it gets too soggy, add some more almond flour; if the mixture isn't sticking together, add a little more almond milk.)

2. Shape into 4 bars and place on a parchment paper–lined plate. Put in the freezer to firm up a little.

3. Meanwhile, in a double boiler or a heatproof bowl set over a pan of simmering water, melt the chocolate.

4. Remove the bars from the freezer and dip each bar into the melted chocolate, coating it thoroughly. The chocolate should set quickly on the cold bars. Place the coated bars on the parchment paper again and refrigerate for 30 to 60 minutes to harden completely. Store leftover bar mixture in the freezer.

KETO CHEESECAKE

If you're a cheesecake fan, you will quickly habituate to this less sweet but just as rich offering. Keto cheesecake is all the rage, having been designated by *Food and Wine* magazine as one of the "The Five Foods the Internet Was Most Obsessed With in 2018." Be sure to use quality ingredients: Make sure that the label on your vanilla extract says "pure," and use organic cream cheese in order to steer clear of hormones and antibiotics in conventional dairy. If you are tightly restricting carbs, use stevia, otherwise use honey. If you are using an Instant Pot, skip the crust, as you will cook the cheesecake in a glass bowl or springform pan.

PREP TIME:
40 MINUTES, PLUS
REFRIGERATION TIME
COOKING TIME: 1 HOUR

MAKES 8 SERVINGS

FOR THE FILLING

- 16   ounces (453.59 g) organic cream cheese, at room temperature
- 2   tablespoons pure vanilla extract
- 2   teaspoons fresh lemon juice
- 1   teaspoon sea salt
- 2   large eggs
- ¼   cup powdered stevia or 1 to 2 tablespoons honey

FOR THE CRUST
(OVEN METHOD ONLY)

- 1   cup (96 g) almond flour or 1 cup (128 g) coconut flour
- 4   tablespoons (56.7 g) butter, at room temperature
- 1–2   tablespoons powdered stevia
- 1   tablespoon pure vanilla extract

1. Make the filling: In a large bowl, combine the cream cheese, vanilla, lemon juice, sea salt, eggs, and sweetener. Mix thoroughly with an electric mixer on low speed.

2. Choose between the Instant Pot method and Oven method and proceed as directed.

3. *Instant Pot Method:* Pour the filling into a round glass bowl or springform pan that can fit inside the Instant Pot. Cover the bowl carefully with foil. Pour 2 cups water into the Instant Pot. Place the cheesecake on the handled steam rack (or in a steamer basket accessory if you have one), and lower the cheesecake into the pot. Cook on High pressure for 25 minutes. When the Instant Pot beeps, allow the pressure to release naturally, about 15 minutes, then lift out the cheesecake.

4. *Oven Method:* Preheat the oven to 350°F (180°C).

5. Make the crust: In a bowl, combine the almond flour, butter, stevia, and vanilla until well blended. Press the mixture into the bottom of an 8-inch springform pan or round glass or ceramic baking dish.

FOR THE CHOCOLATE CRUNCH TOPPING

- ¼ cup (34 g) macadamia nuts or assorted nuts
- 1 bar (3.5 ounces/100 g) dark chocolate (85% cacao or greater), broken into pieces
- 1 tablespoon coconut oil
- 2–3 tablespoons fine coconut flakes

6. Bake until the crust darkens slightly, about 10 minutes. Allow to cool for 10 minutes (leave the oven on). Pour the cheesecake filling mixture into the pan and smooth out the top with your hand (just kidding, use a spatula).

7. Bake until the middle is almost firm, but not quite, about 50 minutes. Allow to cool for 10 minutes.

8. While the cheesecake is cooling, make the chocolate crunch topping (use for either version): In a small food processor, blend the macadamia nuts until they resemble a crumbly flour. In a double boiler or a heatproof bowl set over a pan of simmering water, melt the chocolate and coconut oil. Mix the nuts and coconut flakes into the melted chocolate.

9. Drizzle the topping carefully across the top of the cooked and cooled cheesecake. Refrigerate the cheesecake until the crust feels hard, 30 minutes to 1 hour. Slice and serve.

MACRONUTRIENTS PER SERVING (INSTANT POT METHOD)
CALORIES: 323
FAT: 29 G
CARBOHYDRATE: 8 G
PROTEIN: 7 G

MACRONUTRIENTS PER SERVING (OVEN METHOD)
CALORIES: 459
FAT: 42 G
CARBOHYDRATE: 12 G
PROTEIN: 10 G

QUICK SNACK MEATBALLS

Most meatball recipes require breadcrumbs and eggs, but this recipe proves you can make a tasty batch without, and serve to people with gluten or egg allergies. Try dipping them in mayonnaise or pesto sauce.

PREP TIME: 10 MINUTES
COOKING TIME:
25 MINUTES

MAKES 16 MEATBALLS

1 pound (453.59 g) ground turkey

1 tablespoon coconut aminos

1 teaspoon garlic powder

1 teaspoon red pepper flakes

1 teaspoon sea salt

¼ teaspoon ground black pepper

1 scallion, minced

MACRONUTRIENTS PER MEATBALL
CALORIES: 44
FAT: 2 G
CARBOHYDRATE: 0 G
PROTEIN: 6 G

1. Preheat the oven to 350°F (180°C). Line a baking sheet with parchment paper.

2. In a large bowl, gently mix all the ingredients together. Form into 16 small meatballs and arrange on the lined baking sheet.

3. Bake until golden brown, about 25 minutes, turning them over after the first 15 minutes.

PARTY BITES

Strive to find an assortment of interesting salami, being sure to choose uncured and minimally processed only.

PREP TIME: 10 MINUTES

MAKES 24 BITES

24 slices of extra-sharp cheddar cheese

24 pre-sliced pieces of salami

24 pitted green or black olives

Place a slice of cheese on a slice of salami. Place an olive on the slice of cheese and roll up the salami, securing it with a toothpick. Arrange on a platter to serve.

MACRONUTRIENTS PER BITE

CALORIES: 85

FAT: 7 G

CARBOHYDRATE: 0 G

PROTEIN: 4 G

SMOKED TROUT DIP

Smoked trout often gets forgotten compared with the more popular salmon, but that might change after making this recipe. It takes only a few minutes to prepare, including cleanup, and is perfect for veggie crudités, added to a scramble, or as a salad topping.

PREP TIME: 10 MINUTES

MAKES 8 SERVINGS

- 1 package (8 ounces/227 g) smoked trout, broken into pieces
- ½ cup (113 g) mayonnaise made with avocado oil
- ½ cup (30 g) fresh parsley leaves
- 2 tablespoons extra-virgin olive oil

  Juice of ½ lemon
- 1 teaspoon sea salt
- ½ teaspoon ground black pepper

In a food processor, pulse together all the ingredients until well combined and creamy.

MACRONUTRIENTS PER SERVING
CALORIES: 127
FAT: 12 G
CARBOHYDRATE: 0 G
PROTEIN: 6 G

SMOKY SAUSAGE SNACKS

Who can turn down the bucket-list item of making your own sausage? Once you try it, you may become a true aficionado, as you can imagine the many flavor variations from this foundation. Go for it, and cook enough to store some in the fridge for a convenient snack.

PREP TIME: 15 MINUTES
COOKING TIME:
20 MINUTES

MAKES 4 SERVINGS

1   pound (453.59 g) ground pork

3–4   cloves garlic, finely chopped

Handful of fresh parsley, chopped

1   tablespoon smoked paprika

1   teaspoon ground cumin

1   teaspoon dried thyme

Sea salt and ground black pepper

MACRONUTRIENTS PER SERVING

CALORIES: 348

FAT: 24 G

CARBOHYDRATE: 2 G

PROTEIN: 30 G

1. Preheat the oven to 350°F (180°C).

2. In a bowl, combine the pork, garlic, parsley, smoked paprika, cumin, thyme, and sea salt and pepper to taste. Shape into 16 to 20 mini sausages.

3. Arrange on a baking sheet and bake until golden and cooked through, 15 to 20 minutes.

TURKEY ROLL-UPS

These turkey roll-ups are perfect for your next get-together and don't require any cooking or special tools to make. They'll likely be eaten all up once served, but if you have leftovers, cut a couple up with a pair of kitchen scissors and toss in a skillet with some eggs, and a quick keto meal is served!

PREP TIME: 10 MINUTES

MAKES 12 ROLL-UPS

2   avocados, halved and pitted

2   tablespoons mayonnaise made with avocado oil

¼   cup (50 g) pitted chopped green olives

1   scallion, minced

½   teaspoon garlic powder

½   teaspoon sea salt

⅛   teaspoon ground black pepper

12   slices deli turkey

1. Scoop the avocados into a large bowl and mash with a fork. Add the mayonnaise, chopped olives, scallion, garlic powder, sea salt, and pepper and gently toss everything together.

2. Lay the turkey slices flat on a large cutting board. Scoop 12 equal amounts of the avocado mixture and place 1 scoop onto each turkey slice. Roll up each turkey slice so that it holds the avocado mix and can be grabbed easily for a snack or appetizer.

MACRONUTRIENTS PER SERVING
CALORIES: 90
FAT: 6 G
CARBOHYDRATE: 3 G
PROTEIN: 6 G

ACKNOWLEDGMENTS

With the digital world enveloping us and hyperconnectivity permeating our environment and our beings in every way imaginable, it's a great pleasure to connect with you via a good old-fashioned book! Unlike a random Facebook diatribe or a selfie YouTube video filmed at the kitchen table, this book is a prolonged and complex effort from a high-powered group of professionals devoted to delivering an exceptional final product into your hands.

We are particularly honored to work with two dream teams! At Harmony Books, we appreciate the interest and support from editor-in-chief Diana Baroni and the excellent guidance provided by Michele Eniclerico, Christina Foxley, and the entire Harmony team. At the awesome new Park & Fine Literary and Media, Celeste Fine, John Maas, and Anna Petkovich are trusted companions every step of the way.

Thank you Jennifer May Photography for the great recipe photos, and to recipe contributors Tania Teschke (author of *The Bordeaux Kitchen*), Sarah Steffens (SavorandFancy.com), Matt Whitmore and Keris Marsden (authors of *The Paleo Primer*), Dr. Catherine Shanahan (author of *Deep Nutrition*), William Shewfelt (co-author of *Carnivore Cooking for Cool Dudes*), and Elle Russ (author of *The Paleo Thyroid Solution*).

The original project that has now become four publications with Harmony Books (*The Keto Reset Diet*, *The Keto Reset Instant Pot Cookbook*, *The Keto Reset Diet Cookbook*, and *Keto for Life*) never would have happened without the inspiration of Mia Moore on C Street.

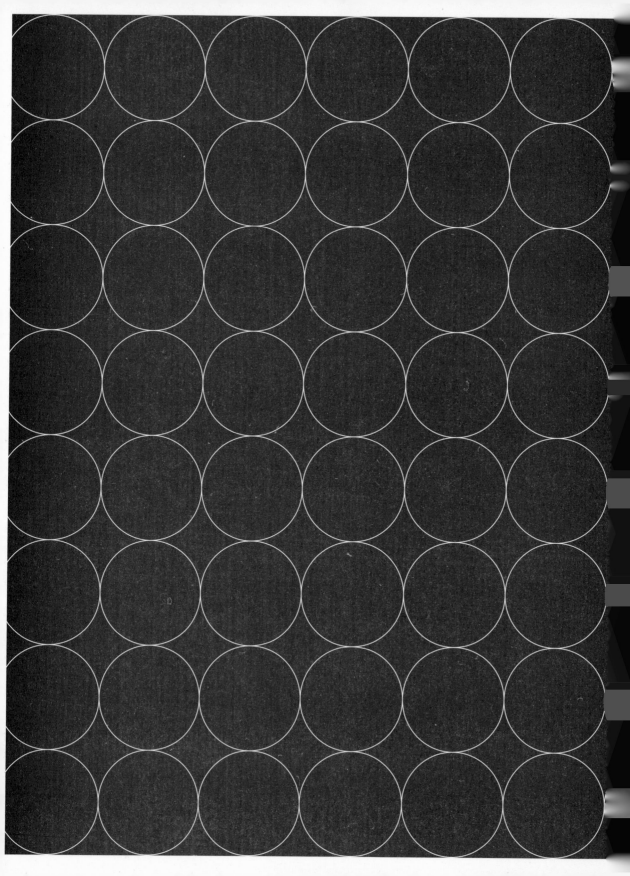

INDEX

MARK SISSON is the bestselling author of *The Keto Reset Diet, The Keto Reset Diet Cookbook,* and *The Keto Reset Instant Pot Cookbook,* and a former 2:18 marathoner and fourth-place Hawaii Ironman triathlete. He presides over a wide-ranging Primal enterprise, featuring the Primal Kitchen line of healthy condiments, the Primal Health Coach Institute, a line of premium performance and nutritional supplements, and numerous books and online educational courses. He publishes daily tips and inspiration at MarksDailyApple.com, which has been the top-ranked blog in its category for more than a decade.

BRAD KEARNS is the coauthor of *Primal Endurance* and *The Keto Reset Diet,* and has worked closely with Mark Sisson for a decade promoting the Primal lifestyle. He is a Guinness World Record–setting speed golfer, host of the award-winning *Get Over Yourself* podcast, and former number three world-ranked professional triathlete.

"Mark Sisson reveals that there's so much more to the story than just choosing a ketogenic way of eating. By incorporating the pillars of metabolic flexibility—movement and exercise, mental flexibility, and rest and recovery—we can amplify the benefits of mere ketosis and attain an even higher level of health and disease resistance."

—DAVID PERLMUTTER, MD, #1 *New York Times* bestselling author of *Grain Brain* and *Brain Wash*

"Mark Sisson has cracked the code for vitality, strength, and self-confidence at any age. With *Keto for Life,* you can move, eat, sleep, and play your way to optimal health and fitness in every season of life."

—MELISSA HARTWIG URBAN, coauthor of the *New York Times* bestseller *The Whole30*

"Leave it to one of the grandfathers of the keto movement to show readers how to achieve exceptional physical and mental health. Packed with great recipes, dietary advice, physical fitness, and activity instructions, this book is a must-read for achieving your longevity goals."

—STEVEN R. GUNDRY, MD, *New York Times* bestselling author of *The Plant Paradox* and *The Longevity Paradox*